D1480826

The Elvis Atlas

A Journey Through Elvis Presley's America

Michael Gray and Roger Osborne

A Henry Holt Reference Book
Henry Holt and Company
New York

A Henry Holt Reference Book
Henry Holt and Company, Inc.
Publishers since 1866
115 West 18th Street
New York, New York 10011

Henry Holt ® is a registered
trademark of Henry Holt and Company, Inc.

First published in the United States in 1996 by
Henry Holt and Company, Inc.
Published in Canada by Fitzhenry & Whiteside Ltd.,
195 Allstate Parkway, Markham, Ontario L3R 4T8.
Published in the United Kingdom in 1996 by
Swanston Publishing Limited under the title *Elvis's America*.

Library of Congress Cataloging-in-Publication Data
Gray, Michael.
The Elvis atlas: a journey through Elvis Presley's America/
Michael Gray and Roger Osborne
p.   cm.
Includes bibliographical references and index.
1. Presley, Elvis, 1935–1977—Homes and haunts—Guidebooks.
2. United States—Description and travel   I. Osborne, Roger.
ML420.P96G72   1996   96–13313
782.42166'092—dc20   CIP
[B]   MN

ISBN 0-8050-4159-1

First American Edition—1996

Printed in Great Britain
All first editions are printed on acid-free paper. ∞

10   9   8   7   6   5   4   3   2   1

Preface

In the mid fifties Elvis Presley hit America and the world like a creature from another planet. Exotic, untamed and emitting strange sounds — where on earth could he have come from? The answer of course was the South, that part of the country most caricatured and reviled by everyone else. The backward, segregated, uncultured South, populated by corrupt politicians, downtrodden blacks and poor white trash. Outside of New Orleans what cultural interest could the place possibly have? Elvis's achievement was to turn American music upside down by showing that its greatest glories lay in exactly that which was most despised.

Our aim in writing and compiling *The Elvis Atlas* is to follow Elvis on his journey from Tupelo and Memphis to the world, and to show how he carried with him the musical culture that changed that world. Elvis himself was changed by his fame, but unlike any other comparable figure he remained true to his roots. It is the collision of worldwide fame with the instincts of a deeply rooted mind that makes the geography of Elvis's life so fascinating. *The Elvis Atlas* is our attempt to understand how these opposing forces affected his life and his music.

Elvis's career took off when he worked up such a fever down South that in the end the national music industry couldn't ignore him. Elvis was drenched in the culture of the South, but he was pulled by the TV stations of New York, the film studios of Hollywood, the showrooms of Las Vegas and the millions who wanted to see him. He visited them all, but in the end he came back to Memphis.

The Elvis Atlas tells the story of his life, but it is not a conventional biography. The book is arranged in double-page spreads, which can each be read as a self-contained topic, though the book can also be sensibly read from start to finish. Each section carries a short introduction and a chronology of events. In the chronologies we have given dates for all Elvis records released in his lifetime, but we have not included budget-priced compilations.

In the course of writing this book we have conducted original research, while also leaning on that of others. In particular the work of Lee Cotten, Peter Guralnick and Andreas Schroer has been invaluable. Theirs and other works are listed in the Bibliography at the end of the book. In addition we would like to thank the following people for information and encouragement: Judy Peiser at the Center For Southern Folklore in Memphis, Michael Conway at Sun Studios, Marvin Bensman at the University of Memphis, Robert Dye, the staff of Memphis Public Library, Ronnie Pugh at the Country Music Foundation in Nashville, Trevor Cajiao, Charles White, Wolfram Altenhövel, Alan Balfour, Sarah Banbury, Sarah Beattie, Tony Charles, Sue Clements, Roger Ersson, Nigel Hinton, Johannes Lenz, Tyler Lott, William Neill, Tony Russell, Roger Semon, Bruce H. Siemon, Chris Smith and Nicola Wilson. We have used our own judgement in updating information and in resolving inconsistencies that have come to light. We take responsibility for any errors in our work.

Michael Gray, Roger Osborne, 1996

Contents

Part One: THE BACKDROP – AMERICAN MUSIC BEFORE ELVIS

"Negro entered into white man as pro-
foundly as white man entered into negro
— subtly influencing every gesture, every
word, every emotion and idea, every
attitude."
W.J. Cash, *The Mind of the South*, 1940

"That name 'hillbilly' — we fought it
teeth and toenails, and took every insult
ever slurred, that you could possibly send
towards anybody, and fought the pioneer
trail for it, to make somethin' out of it."
Clayton McMichen, ex-Skillet Lickers
fiddler

"(James Baldwin was asked) how he
could explain to unsympathetic whites
that Black people had earned the right to
equal treatment through the history of
their presence in America. Baldwin
mused, 'Ask them how America would
sound without us. How would the language sound?' Everyone laughed. It was
just so obvious..."
Val Wilmer, *Mama Said There Would Be
Days Like This*, 1989

"*My name is Sam, I was raised in the
sand
I'd rather be a nigger than a poor white
man.*"
Traditional black American song

"Looks like I'll have to quit makin'
moonshine and start makin' records."
Fiddlin' John Carson, first hillbilly field-
recorded

"... I pick up the guitar — the guitar's
mostly for blues — and I get started singin' some old blues. It's just according to
how a man feels, to what he's got on his
mind when he takes a notion to play
one... I don't care if it suits anybody else
or not: just so's as its done me good."
Hillbilly musician Roscoe Holcomb, 1962

"I put in the music what I wanted to have
in it. You'll have to find Scots bagpipes in
it and Methodist holiness singing in it."
Bill Monroe, King of Bluegrass

"You've got to have smelled a lot of mule
manure before you can sing like a
hillbilly."
Hank Williams

Introduction

When you're young, and Elvis is too, first hearing him obliterates everything else. His uniqueness is obvious and thrilling. You don't want to hear that he stands in a tradition occupied by wrinkly old guys in hairy clothes on the absurdly-named Grand Ole Opry, or by shaky old black men on records too crackly to comprehend. They're all sexless and far too grown-up. These country bumpkins with scrawny granddad necks, these old gents ... like the dreaded oily crooners, they can't be the same species as Elvis Presley.

They were, of course, and it was true: Elvis did create himself out of this rich musical inheritance. Ballads, cowboy songs, southern poor white music, spirituals, medicine-shows, jazz, Tin Pan Alley and blues. All this yielded the music on radio and record when Elvis was a child.

Radio WSB Atlanta was playing hillbilly music by 1923, Chicago's National Barn Dance in 1924. "Hillbilly music" on record begins with Fiddlin' John Carson, 'field-recorded' in Atlanta in 1921; then Vernon Dalhart, flagging opera singer, made a hillbilly record in 1924 — and sold six million. Important early stars include Frank Hutchinson, Charlie Poole, Bradley Kincaid, the Skillet Lickers, Cliff Carlisle, Kelly Harrell and Narmour & Smith. Ralph Peer discovered the all-important Carter Family and Jimmie Rodgers in Virginia in 1927. (The Carter's repertoire included 'Are You Lonesome Tonight').

The Grand Ole Opry started on WSM Nashville, its earliest stars Uncle Dave Macon, the Delmore Brothers and Roy Acuff. In the 1930s hillbilly music continued but also evolved into bluegrass, via the Monroe Brothers and then Bill's Blue Grass Boys. Western Swing arrived too, with Bob Wills. Honky-tonk, in the 1940s, was crying, drinking music, as by Ernest Tubb and Hank Williams, the first modern mega-star. (There were also singing cowboy movie-stars: Gene Autry, Roy Rogers, Tex Ritter). In the 1950s acts like the Louvin Brothers kept mountain sounds alive — and Gladys Presley bought their records.

Meanwhile Memphis had long been the home of the blues. WDIA blasted out Howlin' Wolf and B.B.King — but it ignored a previous generation of Memphis greats, people who'd made seminal records of the 1920s-30s. Furry Lewis, Frank Stokes, Memphis Minnie and Garfield Akers, whose only four recorded tracks include the transcendant 'Cottonfield Blues', made inside the Peabody Hotel, Memphis in 1929 yet bursting with the inspired madness of rock and roll: all these were still living in poverty in Memphis in the 1950s. Sleepy Joe Estes, from nearby Brownsville, even recorded for Sun in 1952. Gus Cannon had lived and worked in Memphis since 1916, and outlived Elvis, dying aged 96 in 1979.

These communities, these people helped define country music and the blues. They helped define the essential Elvis: Elvis the musician, the artist.

The European Tradition

White settlement and immigrant folksong

American Indians' Asian ancestors crossed to North America by a land bridge during the last Ice Age, in 60,000–35,000 BC. Europeans probably arrived in 600 AD, when an Irish saint seems to have settled on the coast. When the Vikings arrived 400 years later, savage white people attacked them on the shore. The Vikings settled Greenland from 986 AD, then went west into Canada and 'Vinland'(maybe Newfoundland/Nova Scotia, or maybe Massachusetts/ Virginia). In 1408 they abandoned Greenland, but not, perhaps, all North America. Later Europeans who followed had mixed success. Columbus never knew where he was, nor set foot on the mainland. Other Spaniards and Portuguese perished. Not until the early 1500s were British and Spanish ships busily traversing the Atlantic.

Spain claimed Florida in 1513, and settled it in 1565. Francis Drake landed in Virginia, naming it New Albion. In 1587, the founders of the 'lost colony' of Roanoke landed in North Carolina. The first permanent English settlement was at Jamestown, Virginia, in 1607. Its colonists brought in the first black Africans in 1619. These arrived before the first New Englanders. The French settled Nova Scotia, 'Arcadie', in 1604. Another short–lived English colony began in Newfoundland in 1610. The Dutch settled Manhattan in 1611.

The Pilgrims landed at Plymouth, in an area long since mapped, to found the colony of Massachusetts in 1620, and later Connecticut. English Catholics founded Maryland in 1634 and English Quakers Pennsylvania in 1682. Until the English won the French and Indian War 1756–63 (the Seven Years War) the French were pushing from the Lakes to the Gulf. De la Salle sailed right down the Mississippi and claimed Louisiana for France in 1682. (It was sold to the USA in 1803 with Missouri, Arkansas, Iowa, Nebraska, the Dakotas and Oklahoma in a deal between Napoleon and Jefferson.)

So there were four main waves of English–speaking colonization. Puritans came from England to New England in 1620–1640. Ruling–class politico–adventurers and their servants (including Africans) came to Virginia in 1642–1675. English Midlanders and the Welsh reached the Delaware Valley by 1675. And huge numbers from Northern Ireland and Scotland, including the first Pressley, came to the Appalachians between 1718 and 1775: the year the thirteen colonies rose against British government. Cherokee lived in the Southern

Appalachians too, and taught the arrivistes to grow corn, squash and tobacco, and to play the mouth–bow. In return, the whites drove the Cherokee west into Oklahoma.

From about 1790–1860 came white expansion west and south, kick-started by the 1803 Louisiana Purchase. Yet by the 1820s Kentucky and Georgia's foothills were still 'the West' — Atlanta was called Terminus until 1847 — though families had reached Mississippi by the 1820s. The 1840s Mexican

The Pilgrim Fathers who landed at Plymouth, Massachusetts in 1620 didn't set foot on Plymouth Rock, didn't call themselves Pilgrims, or Puritans, and didn't preserve the Mayflower, which was dismantled within three years of its historic arrival. They were also hopelessly ill-equipped for survival. One hundred and two of them arrived in December; by April only 54 were still alive.
But the British kept a-coming, and they brought their sea-shanties, hymns, worksongs and ballads with them. In 1775 the thirteen long-established colonies revolted against British rule. They declared independence in 1776, the constitution was created in 1789 and Washington was elected first President.

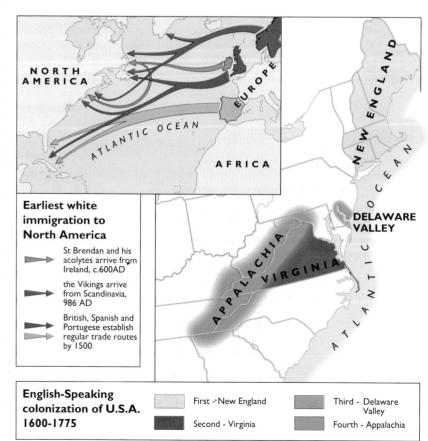

Earliest white immigration to North America

➤ St Brendan and his acolytes arrive from Ireland, c.600AD

➤ the Vikings arrive from Scandinavia, 986 AD

➤ British, Spanish and Portugese establish regular trade routes by 1500

English-Speaking colonization of U.S.A. 1600-1775

☐ First - New England

■ Second - Virginia

☐ Third - Delaware Valley

☐ Fourth - Appalachia

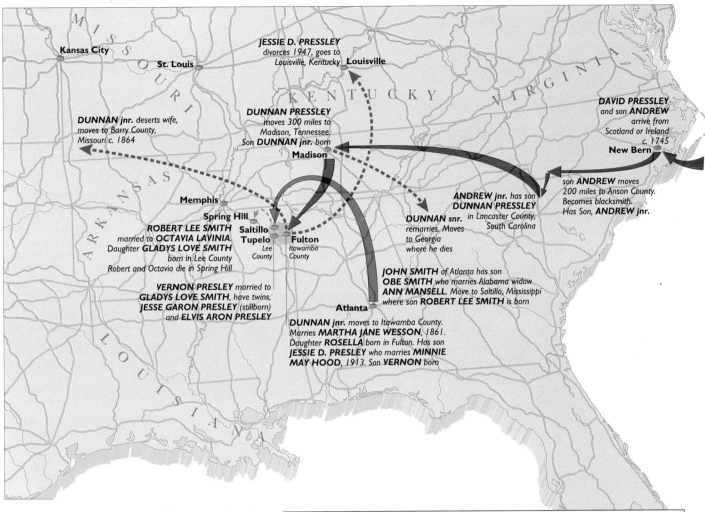

Kansas City

St. Louis

JESSIE D. PRESSLEY *divorces 1947, goes to Louisville, Kentucky* Louisville

DAVID PRESSLEY *and son* **ANDREW** *arrive from Scotland or Ireland c. 1745* New Bern

K E N T U C K Y

V I R G I N I A

M I S S O U R I

DUNNAN jnr. *deserts wife, moves to Barry County, Missouri c. 1864*

DUNNAN PRESSLEY *moves 300 miles to Madison, Tennessee. Son* **DUNNAN jnr.** *born*

Madison

son **ANDREW** *moves 200 miles to Anson County. Becomes blacksmith. Has Son,* **ANDREW jnr.**

Memphis

ANDREW jnr. *has son* **DUNNAN PRESSLEY** *in Lancaster County, South Carolina*

Spring Hill

ROBERT LEE SMITH *married to* **OCTAVIA LAVINIA.** *Daughter* **GLADYS LOVE SMITH** *born in Lee County. Robert and Octavia die in Spring Hill*

Saltillo Tupelo

Fulton *Itawamba County*

Lee County

DUNNAN snr. *remarries. Moves to Georgia where he dies*

A R K A N S A S

VERNON PRESLEY *married to* **GLADYS LOVE SMITH,** *have twins,* **JESSE GARON PRESLEY** *(stillborn) and* **ELVIS ARON PRESLEY**

JOHN SMITH *of Atlanta has son* **OBE SMITH** *who marries Alabama widow* **ANN MANSELL.** *Move to Saltillo, Mississippi where son* **ROBERT LEE SMITH** *is born*

Atlanta

DUNNAN jnr. *moves to Itawamba County. Marries* **MARTHA JANE WESSON,** *1861. Daughter* **ROSELLA** *born in Fulton. Has son* **JESSIE D. PRESLEY** *who marries* **MINNIE MAY HOOD,** *1913. Son* **VERNON** *born*

L O U I S I A N A

War secured Arizona, California, Nevada, Utah, New Mexico, Texas and more. Meanwhile a new wave of immigrants arrived from Ireland after the 1845 famine. (A German wave came after 1848, and then massive immigration from the Slavonic countries and southern Europe.)

The Appalachians, stretching 1500 miles from Quebec to Alabama, include the Allegheny, Catskill and Blue Ridge mountains. The banjo arrived when they were the south–west frontier. Those who settled also brought the dulcimer and fiddle, and, as folklorist Alan Lomax says, "they brought with them, as their invisible baggage, the great ballads of the past." Here was "seventy thousand square miles of tangled green hills where British balladry could re–form itself while it was being cut to pieces by the Industrial Revolution back in England". These mountains nurtured a white folk-music: the hillbilly music that the Pressley/Presley family lived and breathed, that would contribute so much to twentieth century popular music, and would prove as important as the blues to the birth of rock and roll.

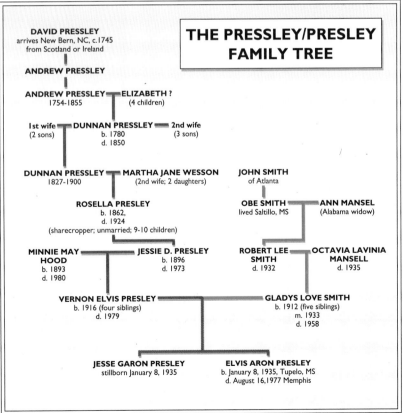

THE PRESSLEY/PRESLEY FAMILY TREE

DAVID PRESSLEY arrives New Bern, NC, c.1745 from Scotland or Ireland

ANDREW PRESSLEY

ANDREW PRESSLEY 1754-1855 — **ELIZABETH ?** (4 children)

1st wife (2 sons) — **DUNNAN PRESSLEY** b. 1780 d. 1850 — 2nd wife (3 sons)

DUNNAN PRESSLEY 1827-1900 — **MARTHA JANE WESSON** (2nd wife; 2 daughters)

JOHN SMITH of Atlanta

ROSELLA PRESLEY b. 1862, d. 1924 (sharecropper; unmarried; 9-10 children)

OBE SMITH lived Saltillo, MS — **ANN MANSEL** (Alabama widow)

MINNIE MAY HOOD b. 1893 d. 1980 — **JESSIE D. PRESLEY** b. 1896 d. 1973

ROBERT LEE SMITH d. 1932 — **OCTAVIA LAVINIA MANSELL** d. 1935

VERNON ELVIS PRESLEY b. 1916 (four siblings) d. 1979 — **GLADYS LOVE SMITH** b. 1912 (five siblings) m. 1933 d. 1958

JESSE GARON PRESLEY stillborn January 8, 1935

ELVIS ARON PRESLEY b. January 8, 1935, Tupelo, MS d. August 16, 1977 Memphis

The African Tradition

Black Americans and their music

Europeans brought their musical traditions with them across the Atlantic. They transported their instruments, their sheet music and their memories. Africans had only their memories. Torn from their homes in the interior, and marched hundreds of miles to the coast, they were transported in the millions to the Caribbean, to South America, and to the coast of North America. In the two centuries of the slave trade the banjo was the only African instrument that made the journey to America. When they arrived Africans were forbidden to speak or sing in their own language, the only songs allowed being English hymns or work-songs. Given this degree of cultural repression what, if anything, of the African musical tradition survived in America?

In the years before the Civil War, Africans became Americans. Stripped of their language and culture they were forced to take on the culture of their masters — white Europeans and their descendants. Though now forced to speak only English, some of the spirit of Africa lived on in the slaves' work songs. The call-and-response pattern of the songs is similar to songs heard in the present day Sahel region of Africa, as is the five-note scale in which they were sung.

After the Civil War blacks were supposed to benefit from the Federal-funded Reconstruction of the South, and to be made full participatory citizens in the newly-enlarged United States. Within a few years, though, Reconstruction failed through corruption, mismanagement and the lack of political will to give blacks equal rights. Blacks were routinely discriminated against. But then some local and State legislatures began to put segregation into law. In the latter decades of the last century, more States followed suit and segregation was codified throughout the South.

Integration was an impossibility, so black society turned in on itself. Whites could no longer control the entertainment that blacks provided for themselves. Black musicians wrote ballads about their own people and their own situations. They adapted tunes they heard from travelling bands, or they worked up the old field songs that had survived in penitentiaries and railroad work gangs. These musicians were a law unto themselves, travelling on the ever-spreading railroads, working for handouts, always moving on. They were heroic figures to blacks, and their travels were exposing them to the work of other musicians — black and white.

In their own churches blacks developed their own ways of singing the hymns they had been reciting for generations. Unrestrained by white views of what religious worship should sound like, black congregations brought passion, and energy to church singing. Gospel music was born.

Appalachian mountain music is often thought to be the product of isolated white communities. But railroads crossed the Appalachians early in the 1850s (see maps), bringing black workers, and therefore authentic black work song — the prime source of what would become the blues — to the ears of white mountain-folk. This was a far more powerful, affecting form of black music than the travelling minstrel shows. White mountain music was changed forever by the assimilation of black musical techniques, styles and repertoire.

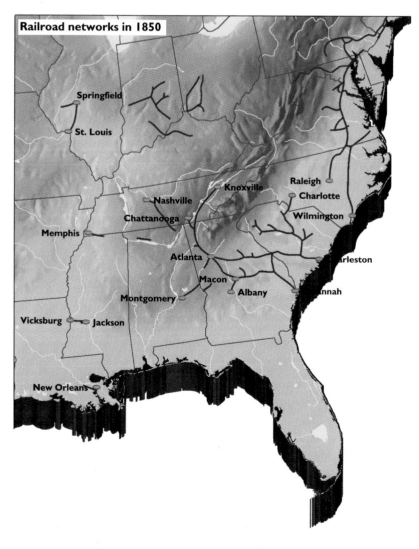

Railroad networks in 1850

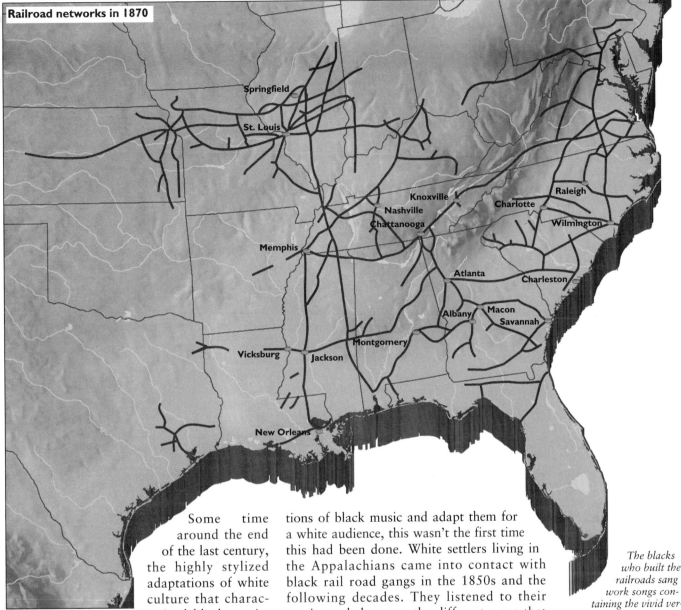

Railroad networks in 1870

Some time around the end of the last century, the highly stylized adaptations of white culture that characterized black music, became a recognizable musical form, created by blacks and speaking only to them. The blues carries echoes of the call-and-response of the work songs. It also adapts the five note scale of the African tradition to the eight-note European system by the use of sliding or 'blue' notes. The blues, with its characteristic twelve-bar chord progression, has been so influential, that it was assumed to be an old musical form. But it is a turn-of-the century invention, emerging from the collective identity of a community and its musicians. Jazz and ragtime were born out of this same communal identity. But whereas they became commercially successful, and were taken on by whites as well as blacks, the blues remained a black music.

Although in the mid fifties a young man called Elvis Presley was to take the blues tradi-

tions of black music and adapt them for a white audience, this wasn't the first time this had been done. White settlers living in the Appalachians came into contact with black rail road gangs in the 1850s and the following decades. They listened to their music, and they saw the different ways that blacks used instruments like banjos. Ironically black musicians threw away their banjos and fiddles as soon as they could afford to buy the new mass-produced guitars and pianos.

Elvis is supposed to have fused black rhythm and blues with elements of country music, an exclusively white form. But country music itself was born out of a fusion of western 'cowboy' songs with the direct unmannered vocal style of blues singers. Jimmie Rodgers, the founding father of country music, sang songs with titles like 'Train Whistle Blues'. In his first recording phase, Elvis created a revolution by singing country songs as if they were rhythm and blues. He was labelled a country or hillbilly singer because he was white, and a white rhythm and blues singer simply could not exist.

The blacks who built the railroads sang work songs containing the vivid vernacular of African traditions and those formed by slavery, and the white mountain men listened. Black songs became white ballads. 'John Henry', 'Lost John', 'Casey Jones', 'Stackalee' and countless others were joint property. Hillbilly and country music, supposedly the unique expressive form of the white rural south, is actually of bi-racial origin. Black influences on Appalachian music making were also indelible. The banjo was the one instrument African slaves had brought with them, though whites gave it a fifth string and its high, whining note. Blacks first put banjo and fiddle together, and first used the fiddle as a rhythm instrument.

Blacks On The Move

The migration to the cities

If the railroads brought black music to whites, they brought it also to other blacks. It was at a railway station in tiny Tutwiler, Mississippi, in 1903, in the middle of the night, that W.C. Handy first heard a blues holler with slide guitar; and the line he heard was about the railroads: *"I'm goin' where the Southern cross the Dog..."* The railroads brought everything: sharecropping, goods, people and music. But mostly, they aided migration. If oppression created the blues, migration passed its message.

Black Americans had always moved north. Escaped slaves ran north. In the Civil War of 1861–65, 200,000 blacks fought in the Union Army. In the Reconstruction, 1865–1877, emancipated slaves found work, shelter and lost relatives – but many remained landless labourers. Segregation was legalized in 1896, and outlawed, in theory, only in 1954.

The twentieth century's first great north-ward migration began around 1915, when Northern business, enjoying wartime boom, needed black workers, while in the south cotton production had been decimated by the boll weevil and by floods. In Mississippi the railroads had transformed the importance of cotton, and the Delta had been forced into intensive farming. The annual flooding of the Mississippi, as of the Nile, had kept the land replenished. But with the wilderness cleared, and plantations pushing to the river edge, the floods became disasters. In the great flood of 1927, the Mississippi overran an area the size of the state of Ohio.

Migration next peaked after 1941, when war boosted the North's economy. In 1949 a black wage in Chicago was $1900 a year; in Mississippi it was $439. Mississippi lost a quarter of its blacks in the 1940s. (Whites left their home states in equally large numbers, but without segregation's extra burden against them.)

Migration followed a pattern. If you lived in Delaware, Maryland, the Virginias, Carolinas, Georgia or Florida, you moved due north to New York, New Jersey or Pennsylvania; if you lived in Alabama, Mississippi, Tennessee or Kentucky, you moved to Illinois, Michigan, Ohio, Wisconsin or Indiana; after the 1930s from Louisiana, Arkansas, Oklahoma or Texas, you probably moved west to California, Washington or Oregon.

Chicago pulled hardest. Rail-routes led there. It was the home of the mail-order catalogues known to every rural community, and of *The Defender*, the crusading black newspaper.

Almost as many Mississippi-born migrants

(Below right) Born in Mississippi, 1915, Muddy Waters' journey was archetypal. First recorded in his Stovall's Plantation shack in 1941 (for the Library of Congress) he migrated to Chicago in 1943, went electric in 1944, made unsuccessful Columbia sides in 1946 and then made the ground-breaking 'I Can't Be Satisfied' for Chess, 1948. A prime shaper of post-war blues, he died in Chicago in 1983.

Little Junior Parker (right). Born in West Memphis in 1927, he was Memphis-based for many years. After recording for Modern, he made successful sides for Sun in 1953 (including 'Mystery Train') but moved west to Houston in 1954 to record for Duke. He died in Chicago in 1971.
Arthur 'Big Boy' Crudup (second right), born Forest, Mississippi in 1905, migrated to Chicago in 1939. He went electric in 1942, recorded, got ripped off by his manager, returned to Mississippi and began bootlegging, while continuing to record until 1962. He was "rediscovered" and re-recorded in 1967-70. He died in 1974.

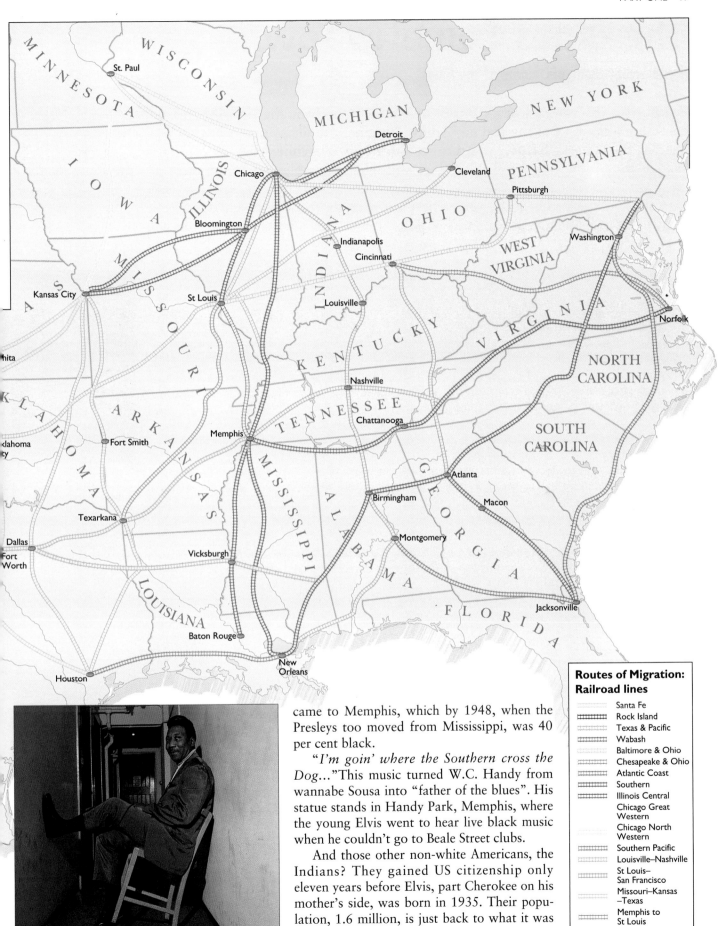

came to Memphis, which by 1948, when the Presleys too moved from Mississippi, was 40 per cent black.

"I'm goin' where the Southern cross the Dog..." This music turned W.C. Handy from wannabe Sousa into "father of the blues". His statue stands in Handy Park, Memphis, where the young Elvis went to hear live black music when he couldn't go to Beale Street clubs.

And those other non-white Americans, the Indians? They gained US citizenship only eleven years before Elvis, part Cherokee on his mother's side, was born in 1935. Their population, 1.6 million, is just back to what it was when Columbus arrived.

**Routes of Migration:
Railroad lines**

	Santa Fe
	Rock Island
	Texas & Pacific
	Wabash
	Baltimore & Ohio
	Chesapeake & Ohio
	Atlantic Coast
	Southern
	Illinois Central
	Chicago Great Western
	Chicago North Western
	Southern Pacific
	Louisville–Nashville
	St Louis– San Francisco
	Missouri–Kansas –Texas
	Memphis to St Louis

The Blues Come To Town

Beale Street Memphis, Home of the Blues

For nearly one hundred years Beale Street, Memphis was Main Street for the black population of the entire mid-South. Originally built as prosperous white district, Beale has a history as a magnet for blacks stretching back to the Civil War. Black people came to Beale to buy and sell, to gamble and drink, to meet up and to be entertained. So Beale became a magnet for black musicians too. Jazz orchestras heard country blues singers, jug bands heard gospel. Beale Street wasn't just the home of the blues, it was the nursery for a huge variety of black music styles.

"If whisky was flowing ankle deep in Memphis you couldn't get drunk quicker than you can on Beale Street."

By the 1940s Beale Street in Memphis had been the social and commercial center for blacks in the city and throughout the South for eighty years. Union troops had been stationed here during the Civil War and provided protection for the black freedmen that increasingly settled in the area. In 1878 a yellow fever epidemic caused half the population of the city to flee, leaving mostly poor blacks and some Irish residents. Blacks came to see the area south of downtown as their own.

Over the next few decades, as Memphis began to prosper again Beale Street came into its heyday. From the river end goods and people came in from St Louis and the north and from New Orleans. People came by train, wagon or by foot from all over the South. The stores were packed with things you just could not get anywhere else, and the saloons and hotels were full of drinkers and travellers. Farmers brought their produce to the markets, or sold them straight off their wagons. And at night the reputed 592 saloons and jook joints and theaters would be jumping to the sounds of musicians, bands and orchestras from all over the South, and all over America. The place was alive for 24 hours a day.

During the 1920s, 30s and 40s hundreds of black musicians had gone north in search of work and money. Those that made it were often reluctant to come back to the South. Segregation meant that they were forced into bad hotels and treated with contempt by the same whites that wanted to hear their music. On Beale Street it was different. The hotels were pretty good, and there was a big audience of fellow blacks, with money. Itinerant musicians from the South mingled with the northerners, learning from each other, trying new things.

There had always been a white audience for black music in America. But this tended to focus on the sophisticated musicianship of jazz orchestras and the harmonized singing of minstrel groups. The music on Beale Street was by blacks and for blacks. Over the decades from 1920 to 1950 the songs moved from the blues singers' eerie recitation of the rural black man's plight, to the confident, witty and sexy sounds of the new urban black population. Joe Turner's 'Shake, Rattle & Roll' is a million miles from Robert Johnson's 'At The Crossroads'. These new 'rhythm and blues' and 'race' records were broadcast by new black radio stations, and whites tuned in in increasing numbers. Dewey Phillips came to Beale Street in the fifties to buy records to sell in the store where he worked and to broadcast on his own radio show. Sam Phillips came too and started to record some of the musicians he heard. But at the moment when Beale Street was about to have its biggest influence on white America, it was within fifteen years of being destroyed by the city of Memphis.

Visitors to Memphis can be forgiven for being perplexed by Beale Street. The present day double row of store fronts surrounded by derelict land, just doesn't fit with the image of the bustling heart of the black South. Beale Street was pulled down in large part because it was a self–possessed, self contained black community. Though economically on hard times, Beale was still doing OK in the 1960s. But the city fathers wanted a Bourbon Street–style district where white folks could go and hear the blues in comfort and safety. So the blacks were moved out and the buildings pulled down. Only 65 buildings remain out of the 625 that were there in 1968.

The whole of Beale Street would have been bulldozed in the late sixties and early seventies, if a small section hadn't been placed on a national register of historic places. What is left is a theme park of gift shops and blues clubs standing like a movie set in the middle of a desert.

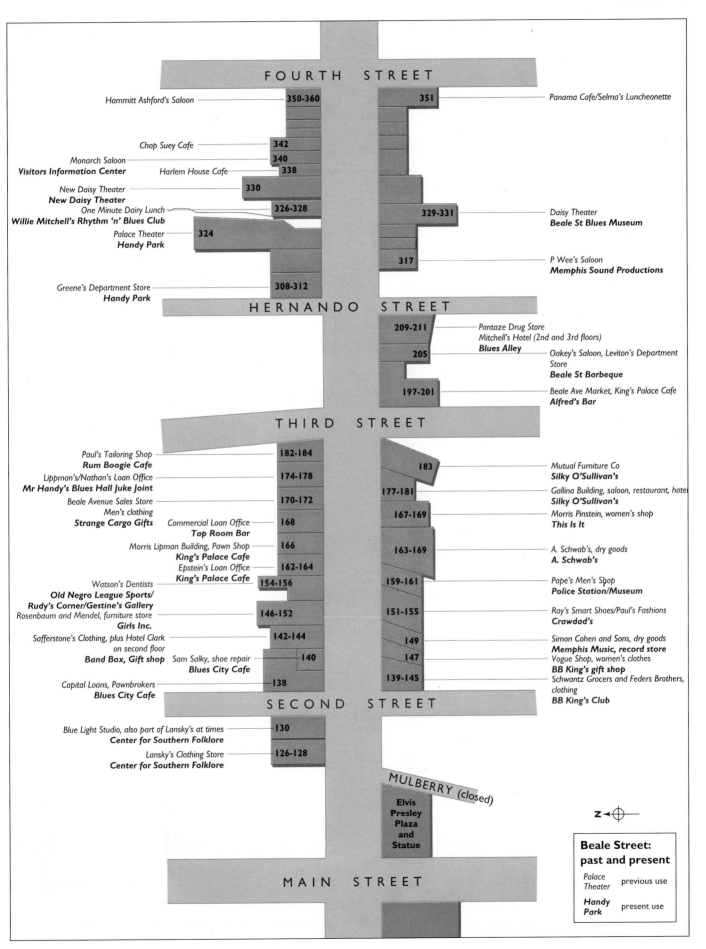

FOURTH STREET

Hammitt Ashford's Saloon — 350-360

351 — Panama Cafe/Selma's Luncheonette

Chop Suey Cafe — 342

Monarch Saloon — 340
Visitors Information Center
Harlem House Cafe — 338

New Daisy Theater — 330
New Daisy Theater
One Minute Dairy Lunch — 326-328
Willie Mitchell's Rhythm 'n' Blues Club

329-331 — Daisy Theater
Beale St Blues Museum

Palace Theater — 324
Handy Park

317 — P Wee's Saloon
Memphis Sound Productions

Greene's Department Store — 308-312
Handy Park

HERNANDO STREET

209-211 — Pantaze Drug Store
Mitchell's Hotel (2nd and 3rd floors)
Blues Alley

205 — Oakey's Saloon, Leviton's Department
Store
Beale St Barbeque

197-201 — Beale Ave Market, King's Palace Cafe
Alfred's Bar

THIRD STREET

Paul's Tailoring Shop — 182-184
Rum Boogie Cafe

183 — Mutual Furniture Co
Silky O'Sullivan's

Lippman's/Nathan's Loan Office — 174-178
Mr Handy's Blues Hall Juke Joint

177-181 — Gallina Building, saloon, restaurant, hotel
Silky O'Sullivan's

Beale Avenue Sales Store — 170-172
Men's clothing
Strange Cargo Gifts

167-169 — Morris Pinstein, women's shop
This Is It

Commercial Loan Office — 168
Tap Room Bar

Morris Lipman Building, Pawn Shop — 166
King's Palace Cafe

163-169 — A. Schwab's, dry goods
A. Schwab's

Epstein's Loan Office — 162-164
King's Palace Cafe

Watson's Dentists — 154-156
**Old Negro League Sports/
Rudy's Corner/Gestine's Gallery**

159-161 — Pape's Men's Shop
Police Station/Museum

Rosenbaum and Mendel, furniture store — 146-152
Girls Inc.

151-155 — Ray's Smart Shoes/Paul's Fashions
Crawdad's

Safferstone's Clothing, plus Hotel Clark — 142-144
on second floor
Band Box, Gift shop
Sam Salky, shoe repair — 140
Blues City Cafe

149 — Simon Cohen and Sons, dry goods
Memphis Music, record store
147 — Vogue Shop, women's clothes
BB King's gift shop

Capital Loans, Pawnbrokers — 138
Blues City Cafe

139-145 — Schwantz Grocers and Feders Brothers,
clothing
BB King's Club

SECOND STREET

Blue Light Studio, also part of Lansky's at times — 130
Center for Southern Folklore

Lansky's Clothing Store — 126-128
Center for Southern Folklore

MULBERRY (closed)

Elvis
Presley
Plaza
and
Statue

MAIN STREET

Z

**Beale Street:
past and present**

*Palace
Theater*   previous use

**Handy
Park**   present use

Recording Pioneers

The independent labels and the musical revolution

Blues records began to sell in the booming 1920s, faltered in the Depression and picked up again as the 1930s ended. After World War II, everything changed: the music, public taste, the media and the record companies. Yet the pre–war blues had defined, and captured the fresh excitement of a musical form which began anonymously as the low–life voice of an oppressed minority... and became a key part of the American popular music which has conquered the world. Elvis Presley was one of the relay–sprinters who brought the blues into this international arena. But behind him were generations of black Americans who, some working locally and communally, some via enormous individual fame and influence, created the blues music Elvis loved and which was a crucial part of his art.

The raucous electric city blues coming out of Chicago in the late 1940s and early 1950s was also utterly saturated in the pre–war blues music of town and countryside alike. So there would have been no 'That's All Right' or 'My Baby Left Me' or 'So Glad You're Mine' without Arthur Big Boy Crudup, but there would have been no Arthur Crudup without the great and mysterious Blind Lemon Jefferson. Similarly, there would have been no Howlin' Wolf, no Muddy Waters were it not for the rich pre–war Mississippi blues world which yielded giants of the idiom like Charley Patton, Tommy Johnson and Son House. But there were also hundreds of artists who went unrecorded, and/or enjoyed but local fame, or became lonely hobos, or died young — all of whom built up this astonishingly rich, expressive music: a music whose quirks, signatures, sounds and phrases are now second–nature all around the western world.

Annual sales of American records first reached 100 million in 1921, which also saw the début of 'race records': records made specially for the black market. Big sales continued all through the 1920s, with all the major record–companies competing in the 'race' market, each issuing its own series of blues and gospel records. These companies were: Victor, taken over by Radio Corporation of America (RCA) in 1929, and its subsidiary from 1933 onwards, Bluebird; Columbia and OKeh, which merged in 1926, retaining both label names; the sister companies Brunswick and Vocalion; the American Record Company (ARC), which was formed by the merger of many labels and continued to trade under them; Gennett and its cheap subsidiary Champion; Paramount and its all–black sub-

sidiary Black Swan; and, as from 1934, Decca, an offshoot of the English company. Further fusions and takeovers between all these continued through the 1930s.

These companies recorded some of their blues (and gospel) sessions in their own studios, but they also recorded widely on annual 'field–trips' to other locations, using either portable equipment or local radio station facilities.

There were other, non–commercial outfits undertaking 'field–recordings' of blues and gospel, notably the Library of Congress Archive of (American) Folk Song, which first recorded black songsters on portable cylinders in North Carolina and Georgia in 1925–1928. Next came extensive field–trips by the eminent folklorists John A. Lomax, his son Alan and others, using cylinder and disc equipment, every year from 1933 until the early 1940s. A few Library of Congress recordings were issued, on 78s, but these trips yielded many more riches, and their influence was huge, especially on later collectors and musicians. The only pre–war session by one of Elvis Presley's favorites, Ivory Joe Hunter (writer of 'I Need You So', 'I Will Be True' and other Elvis tracks), was a Library of Congress field–recording in 1933. After the war, it was Alan Lomax for the Library of Congress who first recorded Muddy Waters.

On the post–war blues scene (Billboard dropped 'race' in favour of 'rhythm and blues' in 1949) the commercial labels fell into two groups: the nationally–distributed majors — ABC–Paramount, Decca/Brunswick/Coral, Capitol, Columbia/OKeh, Mercury, MGM and RCA Victor — and the plethora of new, locally–based, small independent labels which

Blues recording locations

recording location

OKeh — company

△ pre-war record company field-recording location

▢ pre-war record company studio

△ post-war major record company studio

▢ post-war independent record-label base

● location of significant blues/rhythm'n'blues recordings by this label

△ **ABC-Paramount Capitol MGM**

▢ **Aladdin Imperial Keen Kent Liberty Modern/RPM/Flair Specialty**

Los Angeles/ Hollywood

CALIFORNIA

Fort Worth

San Antonio

Indie labels launched most of the biggest artists in post-war blues, R&B and rock and roll. Modern and King found John Lee Hooker; Aladdin, Imperial and Gold Star launched Lightnin' Hopkins; Ray Charles found his sound on Atlantic, Little Richard his on Specialty; Muddy Waters did nothing on Columbia but thrived on Chess, as did Chuck Berry and Howlin' Wolf. Sun found Elvis and Jerry Lee Lewis

in so many cases knew their own markets and catered to them far more accurately and keenly than the majors, and were crucial in discovering and recording big new talents. Prominent among these 'indies' were: Aladdin, Atlantic, Chess, Excello, Gold Star, Imperial, King, Modern, Peacock/Duke, Savoy, Specialty, Sun and Vee Jay.

Arthur Crudup's 'That's All Right' was cut for RCA Victor but many of the other black records Elvis Presley picked out were inevitably from the indies: Roy Brown's 'Good Rockin' Tonight', cut in New Orleans for De Luxe; Chuck Berry's 'Maybellene', cut in Chicago for Chess; Lowell Fulson's

'Reconsider Baby', cut in Dallas for Checker; Little Junior Parker's 'Mystery Train', cut in Memphis for Sun; Lonnie Johnson's 'Tomorrow Night', cut in Cincinnati for King; Ray Charles' 'I Got A Woman' in Atlanta for Atlantic; Little Richard's 'Tutti Frutti' in New Orleans for Specialty; and Arthur Gunter's 'Baby Let's Play House' in Nashville for Excello.

Many of the indies also recorded country acts, and in the same year that Elvis recorded 'That's All Right' and 'Blue Moon Of Kentucky' for Sun (1954), they began offering rock and roll records to an eager, mixed audience of young blacks and whites.

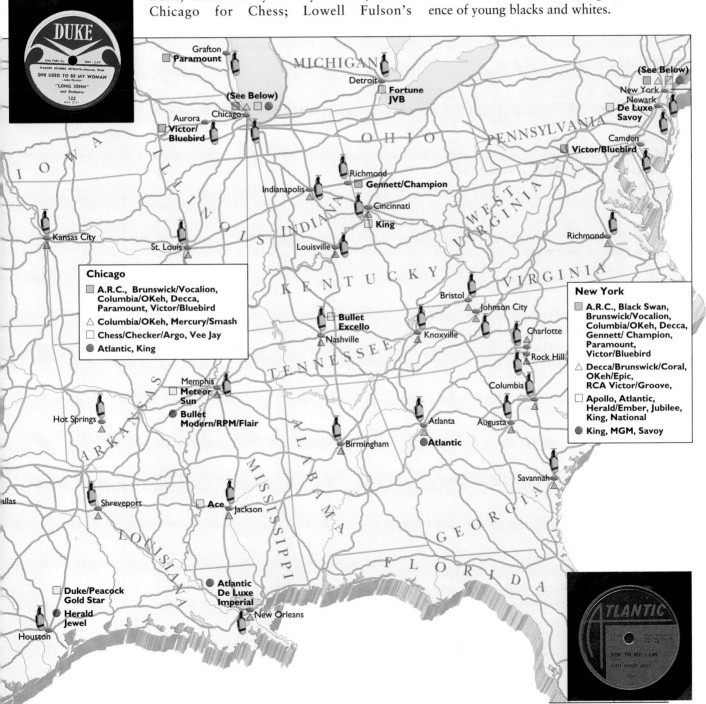

The World From Elvis's Window

The musical figures that looked into Presley's early life

When Elvis listened out from Tupelo and then Memphis, what did he hear? The general answer, already elaborated, is that he heard a great welter of different things that could all be called country music, another great mystery-bag of blues and rhythm'n'blues, and everything down Tin Pan Alley. All kinds of voices, instruments and rhythms were on the radio. How do you quantify what influences you, what lodges somewhere in your heart or in your head? Many a forgotten fiddle-player, banjoist, vocal group, gospel quartet, cowboy-movie B-side must have passed across and under the young Elvis's consciousness: heeded and unheeded stuff of every age and every level of sophistication. Local dance and church music too. And when you're a child you don't make judgments. It's all music. Judgments come later.

"I had records by Mario Lanza when I was seventeen, eighteen years old. I would listen to the Metropolitan Opera. I just loved music. Music period."
Elvis Presley

For Elvis himself, judgment came healthily late. In the end, though, however eclectic his personal taste, certain individual peaks could be distinguished, rising up out of this great musical landscape. Elvis looked out and saw particular stars of country music, blues, gospel, R&B, and certain particular crooners — the people who at one time or another, if not for life, influenced him most. Even a couple of movie-stars who didn't make music at all, James Dean and Marlon Brando, can be seen to have had an impact on Elvis's stance in the world, and so on his musical style.

Some of these artists are here on the map. There are the nationally broadcast figures beamed out of New York City: stars from Bing Crosby to the Ink Spots, and other, less homogeneous figures like gospel supremos the Golden Gate Quartet and R&B outfit Billy Ward and the Dominoes, whose vocalist in 1953, when Elvis loved their 'Rags To Riches', was Jackie Wilson. (He heard Wilson again, singing 'Don't Be Cruel' in Las Vegas in 1956, and thought it better than his own recording. A highlight of the "Million Dollar Quartet" session is Elvis imitating Jackie Wilson imitating Elvis on 'Don't Be Cruel'. They would meet, finally, back in Las Vegas in August 1974).

In California there was the exquisite pop of the Platters (whose vocalist, Tony Williams, Elvis much admired), the Hollywood smoothness of Dean Martin and the biting Texas/West Coast-style blues of Lowell Fulson, whose 1954 classic 'Reconsider Baby' so haunted Elvis that he recorded it in the 1950s and 60s, and performed it live in the 1970s.

Then there were the regional peaks, including Memphis itself. From south of Tupelo, in Mississippi ("the land where the blues began") came music men as disparate as Arthur Big Boy Crudup and the great pre-war blues yodeller Jimmy Rogers who influenced everyone, whether they knew it or not.

There was Nashville, too. We've shown some of the key figures, but others should be in there too, not least Jake Hess and the Statesmen, whose gospel style was a crucial influence on Elvis's own.

Down from the Appalachian hills came

Dean Martin   Mario Lanza
Hollywood

Marlon Brando   James Dean

Texas and the West Coast
The Platters   Lowell Fulson
Ivory Joe Hunter

giants of the pre-war hillbilly scene, from the Carter Family to Bill Monroe. From the northern industrial cities of Chicago and Cincinatti came music from figures of all sorts. Mahalia Jackson singing 'The Lord's Prayer' shows her influence on Elvis; Lonnie Johnson singing 'Tomorrow Night' shows his; without Georgia Tom turning himself into gospel composer and publisher Thomas A. Dorsey, the boundaries of the gospel music Elvis loved would not have been the same; and without the Chicago blues scene — well, the *world* would have been different... just as it would have been without Elvis himself.

Jackie Wilson

The Golden Gate Quartet

Bing Crosby

The Inkspots

New York

Mahalia Jackson

Georgia Tom

Lonnie Johnson

Chicago and Cincinnati

Little Junior Parker

B.B. King

Memphis

Blackwood Brothers

Carter Family

Bill Monroe

Appalachians

Hank Williams

Hank Snow

Eddy Arnold

Nashville

Mississippi and New Orleans

Little Richard

Fats Domino

Arthur 'Big Boy' Crudup

Jimmie Rodgers

New York

Chicago

Cincinnati

Nashville

Memphis

New Orleans

New Orleans

In 1955 Little Richard's 'Tutti Frutti' roared out of New Orleans, but most famously it was the great post-war R&B king Fats Domino whose astonishing run of massive hits came pounding out of the city. His unmistakeable voice, churning piano and fabulous band, led by the great Dave Bartholomew, defined the "New Orleans sound".

Part two: BEFORE THE STORM – FROM EAST TUPELO TO SUN RECORDS

"The colored folks been singin' it and playin' it for more years than I know. They played it like that in the shanties and in their juke joints, and nobody paid it no mind til I goosed it up. I got it from them. Down in Tupelo Mississippi I used to hear old Arthur Crudup bang his box the way I do now, and I said if I ever got to the place where I could feel all old Arthur felt, I'd be a music man like nobody ever saw."

"I was raised in a pretty decent home and everything. My folks always made me behave whether I wanted to or not. I guess they're just like myself. We always had a kind of common life, we never had any luxuries but we were never real hungry."

"We were a religious family, going round together to sing at camp meetings and revivals. Since I was two years old, all I knew was gospel music. That music became such a part of my life it was as natural as dancing. A way to escape from the problems. And my way of release."

"My daddy knew a lot of guitar players and most of them didn't work, so he said 'You should make your mind up to either be a guitar player or an electrician, but I never saw a guitar player that was worth a damn'."

"I sang some with my folks in the Assembly of God Church choir. It was a small church so you couldn't sing too loud. Getting a guitar was Mama's idea. I beat on it a year or two and never did learn much about it. I still know only a few major chords. I don't read music but I know what I like."

"From the time I was a kid I knew something was going to happen to me. I didn't know exactly what, but it was a feeling that the future looked kind of bright."

"I wanted to be a singer, because I didn't want to sweat. I had a job driving a truck when I got out of high school. After that I got a job at a dollar an hour in a defense plant. Then, when I first started singing, I figured it was for me."

"During the singing the preachers would cut up all over the place, jumping on the piano, moving every which way. The audience liked them and I guess I learned a lot from them."

"I took the guitar and I watched people and I learned to play a little bit. But I would never sing in public. I was very shy about it."

"We were broke and we left Tupelo overnight. Dad packed all our belongings in boxes and put them on the top and in the trunk of a 1939 Plymouth."

"The first time I sang in public was at an amateur program at a fair. I wasn't doing this type of song that I do now. Nobody knew what rock and roll was back in those days."

Introduction

The small family of Gladys, Vernon and Elvis Presley lived out a version of the American Dream. Coming from poor beginnings — the shotgun shack in East Tupelo — after years of struggle they eventually found themselves in the mansion on the hill. Part of the fascination of Elvis's story is that, far from being an oddity, the Presleys were a typical Mississippi family.

Like thousands before them the Presleys and the Smiths (Gladys's family) fetched up in a small southern town after generations of drifting westwards. In the early decades of this century, the old South was changing from a rural to an industrial economy. Mechanization was taking people off the land and into the towns and cities, where with luck they would find work in factories. Elvis was born in the middle of the 1930s Depression, during which Vernon worked at odd jobs including time as a carpenter on the Federal-funded WPA. But after his imprisonment for a minor forgery, Vernon never did get well paying work in Tupelo. During World War II he worked at a munitions plant in Memphis and, not many years after, he took the family up there with him. The same move to the city was experienced by hundreds of thousands of American families, particularly those in the South. Ask around in Memphis today and you'll find a good number of people have grandparents or great grandparents who came to the city from the small towns and the farms of Mississippi, Arkansas and Alabama.

Elvis had shown a keen interest in music in Tupelo. He heard gospel music all the time, and saw the antics of the preachers. He heard blues and country on the radio and he saw outdoor shows at the fairgrounds and elsewhere. He had even learned a few chords on the guitar. But when he arrived in Memphis in 1948 at the age of 13, his appetite for music found a sumptuous feast. In later years Sam Phillips said that he was amazed by Elvis's encyclopedic musical knowledge. He certainly had a remarkable facility for memorizing songs and he seemed to know every song that Phillips had ever heard. He himself said that he knew almost every religious song that had ever been written. At this time the crossover between black music and a white audience was just beginning to happen. Radio played a big part in this. White teenagers couldn't walk into black jook joints, but no-one could stop them listening to the increasing flow of black music coming over the airwaves. Some black artists, like Fats Domino, were beginning to realize that there was a big white audience and out there and were tailoring their music for it. Others like Lloyd Price and Little Richard just kept on doing what they were doing, and found the audience anyway. It was a great time for music, particularly in Memphis and the South, with the boundaries between musical cultures being pushed back all the time. Elvis growing up in Memphis must have sensed this, though he didn't know that he was going to be the one who blew all the boundaries away.

Small Town America

Life in East Tupelo, Mississippi, 1935 to 1948

Elvis Aron Presley was born at around 4:30 a.m. on January 8, 1935, in a shot-gun shack at 306 Old Saltillo Road, East Tupelo, Mississippi. As the world now knows, Elvis Aron was the younger of twin brothers — the older twin, Jesse Garon, was still-born. The younger brother grew up in a community of poor sharecroppers and factory workers. Both Gladys and Vernon Presley were supported by their families, but life in East Tupelo was unrelentingly hard. Eventually poverty forced the Presleys and their 13-year-old son to quit the small town and head for the promised land of Memphis.

East Tupelo is physically little changed since the 1940s. A small collection of streets with modest timber houses is tucked behind the row of stores on Main Street. Back then it was the poor relation to the main town of Tupelo, separated by a couple of creeks and the main Kansas City Southern Railway line.

Vernon and Gladys Presley had both moved to East Tupelo with their parents. They eloped to get married in Verona, Mississippi, in 1933. Vernon worked at a host of jobs, including that of carpentry foreman for the Works Progress Administration (WPA) and as milkman on a dairy farm. In 1934 the farm's owner, Orville Bean, advanced Vernon $180 to build a house for the family he was planning. Vernon, together with his brother Vester and his father Jesse, built the tiny house in the grounds of his father's home at 306 Old Saltillo Road.

The hardware store on Main Street (below) is where Gladys bought Elvis his first guitar. The shack where Elvis was born (opposite top right) is shown now restored and repainted, but is worth seeing because of its size. The picture below shows a young Elvis.

Although East Tupelo was the poor relation of the bigger town, the Presleys were better off there, than when they moved into poor districts of Tupelo itself. After a few years there they decided that Tupelo held no future for them, so they headed out for Memphis.

The small settlement of East Tupelo was home for the Presleys until 1948. They lived in houses on Berry Street and Adams Street as well as Old Saltillo Road. Social life centred around the Assembly of God church on Adams Street. Elvis attended Lawhon Elementary School on the other side of Main Street, then Milam Junior High School in Tupelo itself. The Presleys lodged in poor parts of Tupelo towards the end of their time there. Vernon's last job was in the Leake and Goodlett lumberyard, which still stands alongside the railway track.

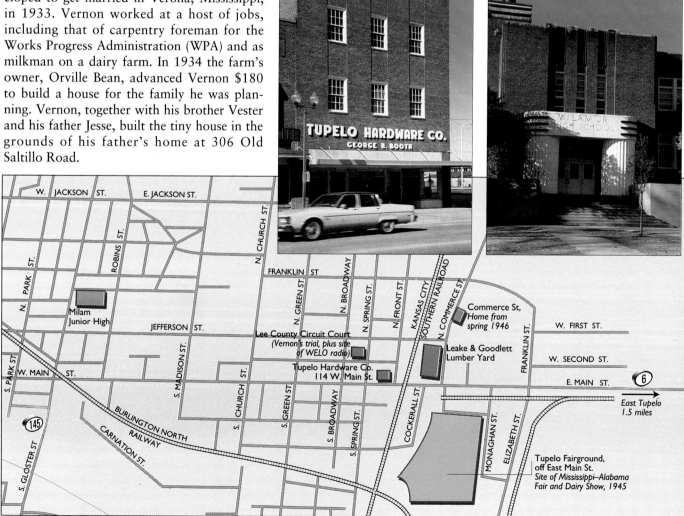

The community of East Tupelo revolved around church — in this case the Assembly of God Church on Adams Street. Church singing was undoubtedly the first music that Elvis heard, with music provided not by a piano or organ, but a guitar. The musical influences on the young Elvis are hard to assess. By the time he was 19 he had accumulated an astonishingly wide musical knowledge — a process that must have started in Tupelo. He certainly listened to WELO, the local radio station, and attended some live broadcasts from their studio in the county courthouse building. When the Presleys fell on hard times, they had to find lodging in Tupelo, on the edge of the colored district. It would have been hard for Elvis, with his passion for all things musical, to miss the sounds emanating from the churches, the juke joints and the open air concerts. In a later interview Elvis talked about the Tupelo gospel music: "During the singing the preachers would cut up all over the place,

jumping on the piano moving every which way. I guess I learned something from that."

Three crucial events symbolize Elvis's time in Tupelo. It's hard to judge their effect on him at the time, though on reflection they help to make sense of his extraordinary life. On November 17, 1937, Vernon was indicted for forging a check. The offence seemed minor — the check, from his employer Orville Bean, was altered and cashed for the gain of a few dollars. It was plainly an inept crime, being so easily detectable. In May 1938 he was sentenced, together with Gladys's brother and one other man, to three years in the state penitentiary. Bean also called in the loan on the Presley's home, and Gladys and Elvis were forced out. For 30 months of his early life Elvis's only contact with his father was a weekly visit to the prison at Parchman. As well as giving Elvis a determination to find his way out of the poverty that had brought his father to petty crime, Vernon's imprisonment virtually made Gladys and Elvis into an independent family. They were to remain extraordinarily close for the next 20 years.

The second symbolic event was Elvis's first public appearance, made as a 10 year old, in a talent contest at the annual Mississippi–Alabama Fair and Dairy Show. On October 3, 1945, Gladys took her son to the Tupelo Fairgrounds, where he stood on a chair and sang 'Old Shep'. Elvis won second prize and five dollars.

The following summer Elvis asked Gladys for a bicycle. She was able to persuade him to settle for a guitar costing one third the price. Some time in August 1946 Elvis and Gladys went to George Booth's Tupelo Hardware store on Main Street and bought a guitar. This was, perhaps, the real beginning.

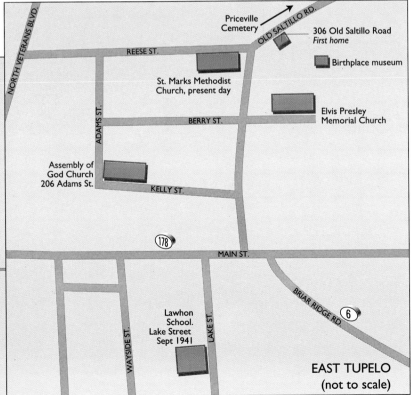

EAST TUPELO
(not to scale)

Living in the City

Memphis 1948 to 1954

Like thousands of poor southerners before them, Vernon, Gladys and Elvis Presley came to Memphis not out of choice but out of necessity. After fighting losing battles against poverty and lack of opportunity in the small towns and farmlands of the region, blacks and whites came to the city. In a time-honored pattern, the Presleys already had a family toehold in Memphis. Two of Gladys's brothers were employed in a tool factory that was hiring new workers. There were old friends from Tupelo who could get them a place to live.

Once Elvis got a car his world grew. Among the places he hung out were Overton Park, where bands performed in the summer (lower right). The photos show Humes High School (below) and the outside of Lauderdale Courts (lower left).

For the teenage Elvis Presley, life in Memphis revolved around the area just north of downtown. The family rented one room on Poplar Avenue on their arrival in Memphis in November 1948. Vernon applied for public housing in June 1949, and in September they were given an apartment in Lauderdale Courts, near to Vernon's work at United Paint. From there Elvis could walk to school at Humes on North Manassas Street, and Gladys was within reach of occasional work in clothing factories, and then at St Joseph's Hospital.

Lauderdale Courts was a bustling self-contained village of around 300 dwellings, full of people just like the Presleys — factory workers from out of town. They were the first decent housing most had ever had. The Presleys went from living in one room to having a two-bedroom apartment with kitchen, living-room and bathroom. All the families had moved up in the world when they came there. There was a sense of purpose about the place and the people. There were lots of kids around and it wasn't just easy to make friends, it was impossible not to. And it was right in the heart of Memphis — within walking distance of the grandest stores, the liveliest clubs, the swankiest hotels, the biggest churches and the lowest dives in the South.

The Presleys stayed in the courts for three and a half years. Elvis was fourteen and a half when they moved in, and 18 when they moved out — crucial years in the life of any teenager. They moved because Vernon and Gladys's combined income exceeded the upper limit for residents. Their prosperity was fragile but real. Within two months Vernon was able to stump up 35 dollars to buy Elvis a 1942 Lincoln Zephyr and within six months Elvis was out of school and working full time at Parker Machinists. The young Elvis was out in the world.

In the summer of 1953 Elvis Presley graduated from Humes High School and immediately started to earn his living. After short periods with Parker Machinists and Precision Tool, in November 1953, Elvis joined the Crown Electric Company at 353 Poplar Avenue, the firm he was to stay with until he turned professional singer. At first he was a stock clerk, but later got to drive the Dodge delivery truck while studying to be an electrician.

Having a car and some money in his pocket opened up Memphis to the young Elvis. The parks, the drive-ins, the drugstores, the midtown movie houses, the record stores, the fairgrounds, the roller rinks — all the

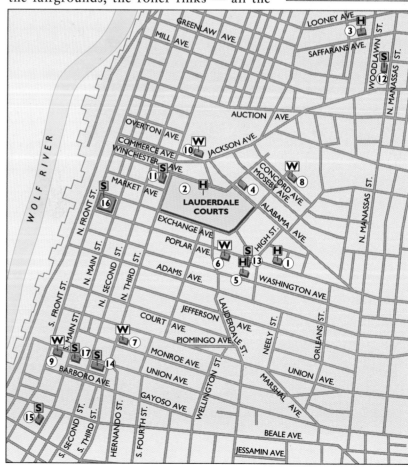

Memphis — home, work and play

1. **572 Poplar Avenue**, September 12, 1948 to September 20, 1949 (now demolished).

2. **Lauderdale Courts**, Apartment 328, 185 Winchester St, September 20, 1949 to January 7, 1953. $35 per month. Public housing. Presleys were moved out with 90 days notice on November 11, 1952.

3. **698 Saffarans Avenue**, January 7 to April 1953. $52 per month. 7 room house, four families. Presleys had two rooms.

4. **462 Alabama Avenue**, April 1953 to late 1954. Large ground floor apartment. Rent $50 per month.

5. **370 Washington Avenue**. Home for a few weeks in 1948.

6. **Crown Electric Company**, 353 Poplar Avenue. Elvis started work November 1953. $1 per hour, 35 hours a week. Stock clerk, then Dodge delivery truck driver. Studied to be electrician in evening.

7. **Fashion Curtains**, 284 Monroe Avenue. Gladys was machine operator.

8. **United Paint Co**. 446 Concord Avenue. Vernon started February 1949. $1 per hour.

9. **Britlings**. Downtown Cafeteria. Gladys started work fall 1952.

10. **St Josephs Hospital**. Gladys nurses aide from November 1952.

11. **Christine school**, Elvis's school for a few weeks in 1948.

12. **L.C. Humes High School**, 659 North Manassas Street.

13. **Poplar St. Mission**, 383 Poplar Avenue.

14. **Peabody Hotel**, Humes Senior Prom held here.

15. **Loew's State Theater**, 152 South Main. School job on week nights.

16. **Ellis Auditorium**. Humes High School graduation.

17. **Tennessee Employment Security Office**, 122 Union Avenue. Career assessment, June 1953.

18. **MARL Metal Manufacturing Co.**, 208 Georgia Avenue. Elvis worked evening shift after school. September to November 1952.

19. **Upholsteries Specialities Co.** 210 W Georgia Avenue.

20. **MB Parker Machinists Shop**, 1449 Thomas Street. Elvis started work June 4, 1953.

21. **Precision Tool**, 1132 Kansas Street. (Gladys's brothers worked there in 1948, Vernon joined them for a short while). Elvis started September 1953. $1.65 per hour 7.00 a.m. to 3.30 p.m.

22. **East Trigg Baptist Church**, 1189 East Trigg Avenue.

23. **Assembly of God**, 1085 McLemore Avenue Elvis attended with Dixie Locke.

24. **Rainbow Rollerdome**, out of town on Lamar.

25. **South Side High School**, Dixie's Prom 1955.

26. **Leonard's Barbeque**, McLemore Avenue

27. **Teen Canteen**, overlooking McKellar Lake, Riverside Park.

28. **K's Drive-In**, 166 Crump Boulevard.

29. **Gaston Park**.

30. **Guthrie Park**, the Triangle.

31. **Mud Island**.

32. **Overton Park**, Bandstand.

33. **Handy Theater**, Park and Airways, 2353 Park Avenue.

H Home   **C** Church   **L** Leisure   **S** School   **W** Work

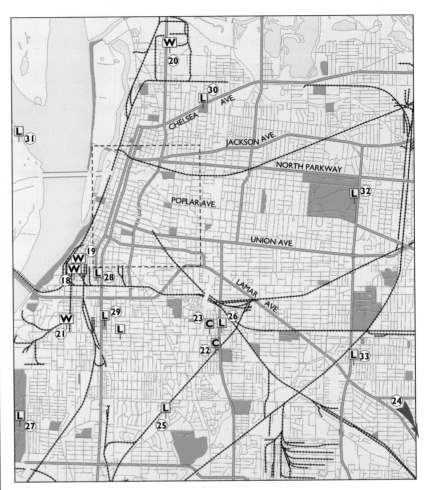

teenagers' hangouts were within reach. Friends from the time speak of Elvis as a quiet, almost shy young man. Paradoxically, he was an eccentric dresser. He often wore a bolero jacket, ruffled shirt and pegged pants, sometimes with a pink stripe down the outside leg. And, at a time when crew-cuts were stan- dard, Elvis had long blond hair, laden with vaseline and immaculately sculpted, together with long sideburns.

Dixie Locke, his first long-term girlfriend, later made an acute observation. 'He was just so different' she said, 'all the other guys were like replicas of their dads.'

Sounds of the City

Musical Memphis, 1948 to 1954

If ever there was a right place and a right time for an aspiring young singer with a passion for music, Memphis, Tennessee in mid–century was surely it. Rhythm and blues singers were packing the clubs on Beale Street, gospel music was pouring out of every church door, country singers lamented their lost loves and western swing bands played the parks and school halls. And all of this was relayed to an eager audience over a host of radio stations, and through well-stocked record stores. White people tuned in to black stations and vice versa, and for just about the first time there was the beginning of a real cross-over — of listeners and musicians. For one young white teenager it didn't much matter who was singing what. He loved what he heard and he soaked it all up like a sponge.

The relative commercial independence of black Memphis had allowed a flourishing music scene to develop over many decades. Country blues singers, jazz orchestras and rhythm and blues 'shouters' all came to Beale Street to play to the large black audience. The cross-fertilization kept giving the musicians new avenues to explore, new styles to try. The music was always developing.

A new radio station opened in Memphis in 1948 (the year Elvis arrived) catering solely to the black population. WDIA had only black DJs and played only black musicians, but whites started to tune in too. Pretty soon the other stations in Memphis saw that a good portion of their listeners wanted to hear what WDIA was playing. Radio WBHQ realized this and hired the only white guy in town who seemed to know about black music. His name was Dewey Phillips and he hosted a show called *Red Hot and Blue* every Saturday night. Dewey and his show are rightly celebrated as milestones in American music, and not just because he was the first DJ to play an Elvis Presley record. Dewey played black music to white kids and convinced them that this was the hottest thing they were ever gonna hear — and it was! The effects on the young Elvis were only too apparent. Listening to Howlin' Wolf, Joe Turner, Junior Parker or Arthur Crudup became as natural as listening to Hank Williams, Slim Whitman or Bob Wills.

The other radio stations were playing pop, gospel, country — anything and everything, but all of it with a flavour peculiar to Memphis. The city standing at the musical crossroads of the south, was for a few years the musical center of the world.

Despite rumours to the contrary, it is extremely unlikely that a white teenager like Elvis would have been able to go to any of the clubs on Beale Street. His knowledge of black music must have come mainly from radio and from records. But that didn't mean he could have picked this up anywhere. The regional nature of record companies and of the distribution business meant that many records were available only in Memphis and a few surrounding cities. When he had any money, Elvis was an avid record buyer with a small collection of 'race' and country records.

The other dominant strain of Memphis musical life was gospel. Memphis produced its own gospel stars. The Blackwood Brothers were a quartet that attended the local church, and had a national hit in 1951 with 'The Man Upstairs'. And the Statesmen brought an electrifying showmanship to their work that thrilled the young Presley. Gospel, R 'n' B, country — it was all there in Memphis.

Radio WDIA was America's first station aimed solely at blacks. Its pitch to advertisers emphasised the number of negroes in Memphis and their spending power. The station now plays gospel music from its studio on Union Avenue (below).

Poplar Tunes is still at 308 Poplar Avenue (below). Like the handful of other downtown record stores in the fifties it stocked a cross–section of country, pop, rhythm and blues and gospel records. Many of these would have been produced locally, or at any rate in the South, and wouldn't be available in the rest of the country.

The Ellis Auditorium (left) became an important place in Elvis's life. He lived just a few minutes walk away from the biggest music venue in Memphis. As well as all–night gospel sings Elvis also attended the funeral service for R W Blackwood and Bill Lyles of the Blackwood Quartet, a major event in Memphis. Elvis played here several times in his later career, once playing both halls at the same time.

1. **Hotel Chisca**, 272 South Main Street: Studio of WHBQ Radio was situated on the Mezzanine floor. Dewey Phillips presented his *Red, Hot and Blue* show on Saturday nights live from the Chisca.
2. **Peabody Hotel**, Union and Second Street: WREC Radio broadcast from here. Sam Phillips was a presenter of big band concerts broadcast live from the Peabody Skyway ballroom on the top floor.
3. **WMPS Radio**, 112 S Main St.: Pop and country radio station. Bob Neal, Elvis's manager from August 1954 to November 1955, was a celebrity DJ on WMPS.
4. **Suzore No.2 Theater**, 279 North Main Street: The nearest movie house to the Presleys. Elvis's idolization of figures like James Dean and Marlon Brando began here. Charlies Record Store: Next door to the Suzore and a popular haunt for young music fans.
5. **Ellis Auditorium**, Poplar and Main Streets: Now part of the Memphis Auditorium, this was the principal musical venue in Memphis. Elvis regularly attended all-night gospel sings here with the Blackwood Brothers and Stamps quartets featuring.
6. **WT Grant's Department Store**, 113 South Main Street: Dewey Phillips ran the record department. He was hired from here by WHBQ radio.
7. **OK Houck Piano Store**, 121 Union Ave: Music instruments shop. Elvis bought a Martin guitar here once he started to earn enough money from his concerts.
8. **Poplar Tunes**, 308 Poplar Ave: Best known record shop in Memphis, within a few minutes walk of Lauderdale Courts. Vies with Charlies Records for the distinction of selling the first copy of an Elvis Presley record.
9. **Beale Street**, between Second and Fourth Streets: Beale Street was the main thoroughfare for the black population of Memphis. The music played on Beale was reaching the ears of white youngsters just as Elvis was growing up.
10. **Memphis Recording Service**, 706 Union Ave: Sam Phillips advertised himself as a recording service rather than a record company. The word about Phillips and Sun Records spread far enough in the early 1950s to bring black and white musicians to Memphis in the hope of recording.
11. **Home of the Blues**, 107 Beale Street: Record store. Dewey Phillips and Sam Phillips were regular customers at this record shop that carried a vast selection of blues songs for its predominantly black clientele. Dewey played them on his radio show, which had a white and black audience.
12. **Loew's State Theater**, 152 South Main: Principal movie house in Memphis.
13. **WDIA**, 112 Union Ave: Now located at this address in down town Memphis, WDIA was at 2074 Union Ave in the 1950s. The first radio station in America to use only black presenters, its success was a sign of the increasing economic importance of urban blacks.
14. **KWEM**, West Memphis: Radio station broadcasting blues and country music. DJs were often blues artists themselves. Featured Sonny Boy Williamson, Howlin' Wolf and BB King as well as 'hillbilly' artists.

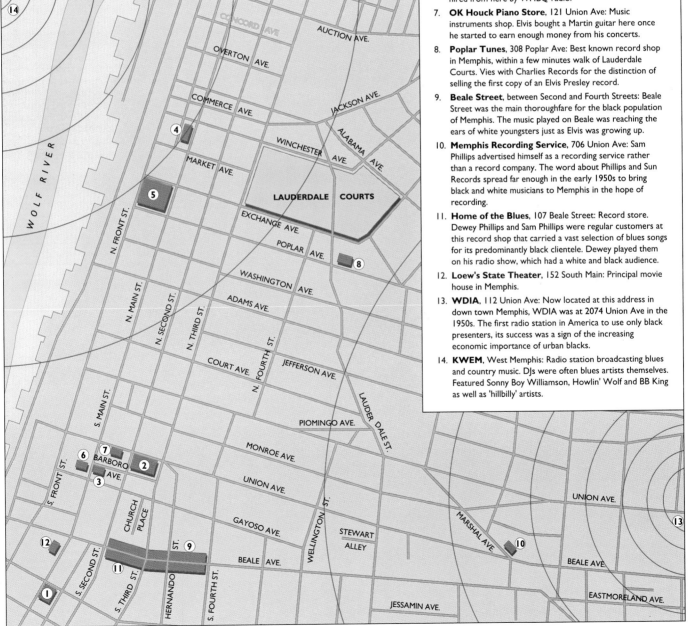

First Steps From Listening to Singing

Elvis's amateur concerts

The legend holds that Elvis Presley walked into the Memphis Recording Service sometime in July 1953 to record a take-home disk for his mother. His first attempt to sing moved Marion Keisker to tape part of the song and keep his name on file. Twelve months later, after a few botched attempts, the young Presley recorded two of the most sublime takes in popular music history, and a young man who had never tried out his voice suddenly found something he never knew he had. But we know now that this legend doesn't quite check out. Elvis always knew that he could sing, and although he never sang for money until he made his first record, he had played in front of an audience enough times to give him confidence in his own talent.

The search for evidence of Presley performances that pre-date his Sun recordings have brought forth a spectacular number of eye-witness reports that don't check out. Naturally enough, memories get confused over forty years. Let's just say that anyone lucky enough to see Elvis in his early days is surely right to treasure the memory.

We know for certain that Elvis got up in front of an audience at the tender age of ten years. The occasion was Children's Day at the annual Mississippi–Alabama Fair and Dairy Show, held at the fairgrounds in Tupelo on October 3, 1945. The following year Elvis's mother bought him a guitar, which he spent the next few years learning to play. Friends remember the shy youngster plunking away at his guitar in Lauderdale Courts in Memphis, singing quietly as if he didn't want anyone else to hear.

Some kind of transformation seems to have taken place during the winter of 1952 to 1953. Photos of Elvis show him with more obvious confidence, including the confidence to be different. There are various unconfirmed reports of Elvis performing at this time — a performance with a friend called Ronnie Smith at the South Side High School annual amateur show on November 15, 1952 for instance. This doesn't tie in too well with other events however and it might have been confused with an appearance at the same show the following year. Ronnie Smith was getting work as a musician though, and through him Elvis was pulled into the fringes of the music scene. Various clubs in Memphis held amateur nights and open-mike sessions. Elvis is thought to have got up on stage at the Silver Stallion on Union Avenue and at the Palms Club on Summer Avenue in late 1952

and early 1953. The Silver Stallion was later to get a mention in Elvis's high school prophecy.

Elvis Presley's first adult performance with a written record was at the Humes High School 'Annual Minstrel Show', held in the school auditorium on the evening of April 9, 1953. He was 16th on a bill of 22 acts, billed as 'Guitarist, Elvis Prestly.' Elvis is reported to have sung 'Cold Icy Fingers' and 'Til I Waltz Again'. He said later that no-one knew him at school before the concert, but that afterwards 'I didn't have too much trouble'. It takes a certain kind of courage for an 18-year-old to get up and sing in front of his school. The fact that Elvis managed it successfully must have increased the quality that he seemed to be acquiring in abundance — self belief.

Elvis is rumoured to have sung at basement parties held in the Chisca Hotel (above) before he became a recording artist. Like the rest of these 'performances' there is no written record, and memories can play strange tricks.

Elvis's most important amateur performance was undoubtedly at the Memphis Recording Service (left). One Saturday in July 1953 he went in to make a record, supposedly 'to surprise my mother'. But as Peter Guralnick has pointed out, he could have done that at a number of record stores, where they would cut you a disk for a few dollars. Elvis chose to sing where a professional record producer would hear him. Marion Keisker was looking after things that day and switched on the tape recorder while Elvis sang 'My Happiness' and 'That's When Your Heartaches Begin'. Nothing happened for 12 months after that, but the four dollars Elvis paid turned out to be a good investment.

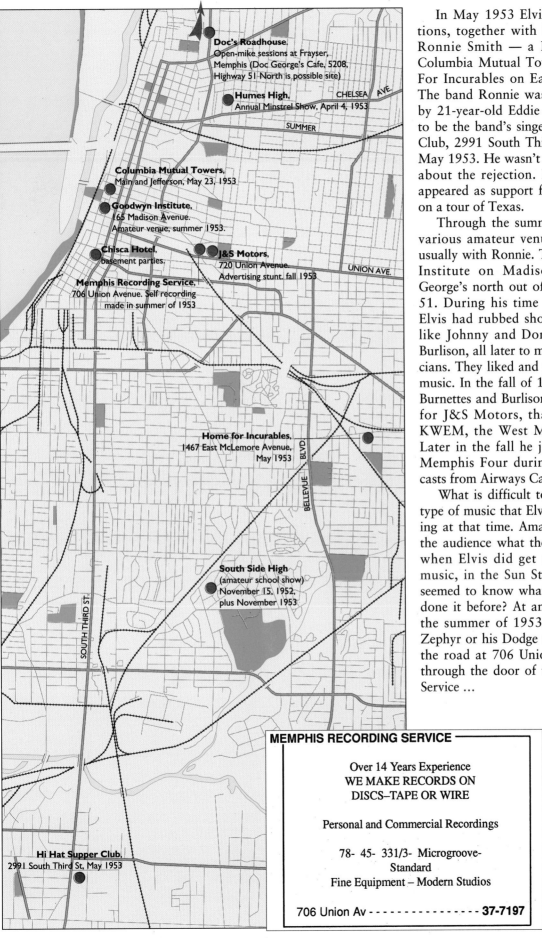

Doc's Roadhouse,
Open-mike sessions at Frayser,
Memphis (Doc George's Cafe, 5208,
Highway 51 North is possible site)

Humes High,
Annual Minstrel Show, April 4, 1953

CHELSEA AVE.

SUMMER

Columbia Mutual Towers,
Main and Jefferson, May 23, 1953

Goodwyn Institute,
165 Madison Avenue.
Amateur venue, summer 1953.

Chisca Hotel,
basement parties.

J&S Motors,
720 Union Avenue.
Advertising stunt. fall 1953

UNION AVE.

Memphis Recording Service,
706 Union Avenue. Self recording
made in summer of 1953

Home for Incurables,
1467 East McLemore Avenue,
May 1953

BELLEVUE BLVD.

South Side High
(amateur school show)
November 15, 1952,
plus November 1953

SOUTH THIRD ST.

Hi Hat Supper Club,
2991 South Third St, May 1953

In May 1953 Elvis sang at private functions, together with bands put together by Ronnie Smith — a Lodge Banquet at the Columbia Mutual Towers, and at the Home For Incurables on East McLemore Avenue. The band Ronnie was working for was lead by 21-year-old Eddie Bond. Elvis auditioned to be the band's singer at the Hi Hat Supper Club, 2991 South Third Street, some time in May 1953. He wasn't taken on, and felt bitter about the rejection. Ironically, Eddie Bond appeared as support for Elvis two years later on a tour of Texas.

Through the summer Elvis showed up at various amateur venues and private parties usually with Ronnie. There was the Goodwyn Institute on Madison Avenue, and Doc George's north out of Memphis on Highway 51. During his time in Lauderdale Courts, Elvis had rubbed shoulders with youngsters like Johnny and Dorsey Burnette and Paul Burlison, all later to make their living as musicians. They liked and played the same kind of music. In the fall of 1953 Elvis sang with the Burnettes and Burlison at an advertising stunt for J&S Motors, that was broadcast over KWEM, the West Memphis radio station. Later in the fall he joined Burlison and the Memphis Four during their KWEM broadcasts from Airways Cars.

What is difficult to discover is exactly the type of music that Elvis was singing and playing at that time. Amateur bands tend to give the audience what they think they want. But when Elvis did get to sing a new kind of music, in the Sun Studios in July 1954, he seemed to know what he was doing. Had he done it before? At any rate sometime during the summer of 1953, he pulled his Lincoln Zephyr or his Dodge truck over to the side of the road at 706 Union Avenue, and walked through the door of the Memphis Recording Service ...

This is how the entry for the Memphis Recording Service appeared in the yellow pages section of the 1953 Memphis phone directory. Sam Phillips never advertized as a record company, just as a service. Elvis would have seen the ad and driven past the small unassuming building a hundred times before he went in to make a record one day in the summer of 1953.

Chronology

1933–June 1954

1933
June 17 — Vernon Presley and Gladys Smith are married in Verona, Mississippi.

1934
Early 1934 — Vernon gets steady work on a dairy farm owned by Orville Bean, borrows money off his employer to build a house.
Dec. — Vernon and Gladys move into new home at 306 Old Saltillo Road, Tupelo.

1935
Jan. 8 — Elvis Aron Presley born at 4:30 a.m. Twin brother Jesse Garon is still-born.
Jan. 9 — Jesse Garon Presley is buried at an unmarked grave in Priceville Cemetry, East Tupelo.

1937
Nov. 17 — Vernon Presley and two other men indicted for forgery, and placed under bonds.

1938
May 25 — Vernon is sentenced to three years' imprisonment at Parchman Farm.
June — Gladys and Elvis Presley are moved out of their home on Old Saltillo Road.

1941
Jan. 4 — Vernon is released from prison five months short of his full sentence.
Sept. — Elvis enrolls at the Lawhon Elementary School, East Tupelo.
1941–42 — Vernon works at a munitions factory in Memphis, commuting home at weekends.

1942
Dispute between ASCAP and radio stations breaks the stranglehold of main stream Tin Pan Alley pop on radio; allows in country, hillbilly, and later rhythm and blues.

1945
Oct. 3 — Elvis sings 'Old Shep' at the Mississippi-Alabama Fair and Dairy Show, held at the Tupelo Fairgrounds.
Sam Phillips joins WREC radio in Memphis as a DJ some time in 1945.

1946
Summer — Gladys and Vernon buy Elvis a guitar from the Tupelo Hardware Store.
Sept. — Elvis starts at Milam Junior High School in Tupelo.
Sept. 4 — 'That's All Right' recorded by Arthur Crudup in Chicago.

1948
Feb. — 'Good Rockin' Tonight' by Winonie Harris And His All Stars released.
Sept. 12 — Vernon, Gladys and Elvis leave Tupelo to go and live in Memphis, initially at 572 Poplar Avenue.
Sept. 13 — Elvis enrolls at L.C. Humes High School, Manassas Street, Memphis.
In 1948 Memphis radio station WDIA relaunches itself as an all-black station.
Dewey Phillips starts broadcasting rhythm and blues music on Radio WHBQ in Memphis.

1949
Mar. — 'That's All Right' by Arthur Crudup re-released by RCA on new 45 rpm format – the first record by a black artist on a seven- inch 45.
May 1 — Vernon, Gladys and Elvis Presley move into Lauderdale Courts public housing project.
Nov. — Elvis works evenings (5 to 10 p.m.) as an usher at Loew's State Theater.

1950
Jan. — Sam Phillips opens a record-

	ing studio at 706 Union Avenue.
Feb.	'The Fat Man', Fats Domino's first single, released on Imperial Records.
Summer	Sam and Dewey Phillips start the Philliips record label which lasts only a couple of months. BB King records at the Memphis Recording Service.

1951

| Mar. 5 | 'Rocket 88' by Jackie Brenston with His Delta Cats recorded at Memphis Recording Service. Produced by Sam Phillips, released April 1951 by Chess Records. |
| June 1951 | 'Rocket 88' hits Number One on the national Rhythm And Blues chart. Sam Phillips resigns from WREC radio to be a full-time independent producer. |

1952

Mar. 27	First Sun record, 'Drivin' Slow' an instrumental by Johnny London, pressed. Released in April.
Apr.	'Lawdy Miss Clawdy' by Lloyd Price released on Specialty Records.
Sept.	Elvis works evenings at MARL Metal Company.
Nov.	Gladys starts work at St Joseph's Hospital.

1953

Jan. 7	Presleys move to 698 Saffarans Street, near Humes High School.
Jan. 30	'Your Cheating Heart' by Hank Williams released. Flip side is 'Kaw-Liga', a rockabilly-style country song.
Feb.	'Hound Dog' by Willie Mae "Big Mama" Thornton, written by Leiber and Stoller, released.
Mar.	Elvis gets his first car, a 1942 Lincoln Zephyr.
Mar. 8	'Bear Cat' by Rufus Thomas, an answer-record to Big Mama Thornton's 'Hound Dog' recorded at Sun studios. Sun's biggest pre Presley hit, despite legal problems over copying the melody from 'Hound Dog'.
Apr.	The Presleys move to 462 Alabama Street.
April 9	Elvis's first documented performance as an adult, at the Humes Annual Minstrel Show.
June 3	Elvis takes a General Aptitude Test at the Tennessee Employment Security Office. Graduation ceremony at Ellis Auditorium South Hall.
June 4	The day after leaving school Elvis starts full-time work at MB Parker Machinists Shop.
July	Calls in at Memphis Recording Service to record a take-home disk.
Sept.	Elvis starts work at Precision Tool, munitions factory.
Sept.	'Money Honey' by Clyde McPhatter and the Drifters released.
Nov.	Elvis starts working as warehouseman, then truck driver and trainee electrician at Crown Electric.
Nov. 1	'Mystery Train' by Little Junior's Blue Flames (i.e. Junior Parker) released on Sun Records.

1954

Apr.	'Shake, Rattle And Roll' by Big Joe Turner released on Atlantic Records.
May	'Rock Around The Clock' by Bill Haley and His Comets released as the B-side to 'Thirteen Women'; goes virtually unnoticed. One year later the song is re-released to coincide with the movie *Blackboard Jungle* and goes to Number One.
May 25	The Starlite Wranglers, with Scotty Moore on guitar and Bill Black on bass, record 'No She Cares No More for Me' at Sun Records studio.

Part Three: RAISING THE STORM – THE SUN YEARS

"There is low-down people and high-up people, but all of them get the kind of feeling this rock and roll music tells about."

"I was an overnight sensation. A year after they heard me the first time they called me back."

"My career as a singer started by accident. I went into a record shop to make a record for my mother, just to surprise her. Some man in there heard me sing and said he might call me some time. He did — a year and a half later. He was Sam Phillips, the owner of Sun Records, and I made a couple of records for him."

"All I know is I hung up and ran fifteen blocks to Mr Phillips before he'd gotten off the line."

"A lot of people ask me where I got my singing style. Well I didn't copy my style from anybody."

"I jump around because it is the way I feel. In fact, I can't even sing with a beat at all if I stand still."

"Rock and roll has been around for many years. It used to be called rhythm and blues. And as far as I can remember it's been very big. Personally I don't think it'll ever die out because they're gonna have to get something mighty good to take its place."

"I never took any singing lessons, and the only practising I did was on a broomstick before my Dad bought me my first guitar."

"It's hard to explain rock and roll. It's not what you call folk music. It's a beat that gets you. You feel it."

"It's not like when you hear it on the radio, when you do it on stage you have to put on a show for people."

"I never thought of it as being suggestive. That's just my way of expressing the songs."

"My very first appearance after I started recording was doing a show in Memphis where I started, a big show in an outdoor auditorium. I came to the stage and I was scared stiff. It was my first big appearance in front of an audience. I came out and I was doing a fast type tune, one of my first records, and everyone started hollering and I didn't know what they were hollering at. Then I came off stage and my manager told me that everyone was hollering because I was wiggling. So I did a little more and the more I did, the more I got."

Introduction

The beginnings of Elvis Presley's extraordinary singing career have inevitably become clouded in myth. In common with other 'mythic' figures everyone, it seems, wants their own version of the Elvis story, as a keepsake or a role model. The rags to riches archetype demands that the Presleys be as poor as possible, that Elvis should be down to his last dime, and then one day open his mouth and start singing. The world should then take one listen and beat a path to his door. As with all legends, the truth turns out to be a lot more interesting.

Historical research has rescued Elvis from being a hapless figure, who just happened to be in the right place at the right time, whose God-given talents were recognized by other people, and who was molded by forces outside his control. Instead we now see a man with a vision of his own destiny and the determination to carry it through. Above all Elvis was a man who was not buffetted by fate, but who made choices about his music, his career, his life.

One of the great myths of the Sun years covers the recording of Elvis's first single 'That's All Right' on July 5, 1954. After trying a few ballads, the recording session wasn't getting anywhere. Elvis stood on the brink of falling at the first hurdle. During a break Elvis started fooling around with an old rhythm and blues song giving it an edgy, jumped-up sound. Bill Black joined in, then Scotty Moore. The rest is history. A new musical form was created by accident. But what if, as seems just as likely, Elvis knew exactly what he was doing. He could see that the ballads weren't getting to Sam Phillips. He knew Sun's reputation for recording rhythm and blues — but he didn't feel in a strong enough position to introduce jumped up R 'n' B into the session. So he waited for the break, and then went at it. Far from being a lucky accident, Elvis might easily have decided this was the way to go. The one thing that's never been in doubt, was that it was Elvis who first started playing 'That's All Right'. It was his choice and it worked.

And what about Elvis's first appearances? Legend tells us he was scared to death before he went on stage — there's little reason to doubt that. But at his first real performance at Overton Park Shell, Memphis in July he started moving around while he was singing. He always said he couldn't help it, it was the effect of the music. The crowd loved it, and they kept on loving it. But was Elvis's electrifying stage show (there's never been anything like it before or since) pure reaction as he always claimed? As he stood in the wings at Overton Park Shell on that first hot summer night, the odds are that he knew exactly what he was going to do. He might have been nervous over whether it would work out — would he make a fool of himself? — but he chose to do it anyway. When asked about his movements, he naturally said they were instinctive in order to avoid accusations that he was being deliberately sexually provocative. But we needn't take his comments at face value.

Elvis may not have manipulated the start of his career in quite the calculating way all this implies. But it seems probable that he was neither simply the victim, nor the passive beneficiary of circumstance.

That's All Right

The events of July 1954

In retrospect, the career of Elvis Presley may seem like a story of talent easily, triumphantly and inevitably achieving recognition. But there were plenty of hurdles to cross on the way, and plenty of setbacks to balance the breakthroughs. The strength of Elvis's determination to succeed is always underestimated. The long hot July of 1954 was, however, the moment when all things became possible for Elvis. That one recording session could have changed popular music forever is perhaps too strong a notion. But this was indeed a defining moment, and the joy of those who created it still comes across every time we hear the energy and the yearning of 'That's All Right' and 'Blue Moon Of Kentucky.'

"We thought it was exciting, but what was it? It was just so completely different."
Scotty Moore on listening to the first playback of 'That's All Right.'

On Sunday July 4, 1954, Elvis Presley pulled up outside Scotty Moore's house on Belz Street. Marion Keisker at the Memphis Recording Service had kept his name and number on file for a year, and Scotty rang him at the suggestion of Marion's boss Sam Phillips. Sam was looking for a singer to try out a new song and he wanted Scotty's opinion. Scotty got his friend from the Starlite Wranglers, bass-player Bill Black, to come along too. The three of them played a few ballads together and nothing much happened. But after talking to Scotty on the phone that night, Sam Phillips decided that it was worth getting the three of them into the studio together the next evening.

And so on July 5, 1954, Elvis Presley, Scotty Moore, and Bill Black turned up at Sam Phillips' Sun Studios. As the world now knows, they spent a long time trying out the ballads that seemed to suit Presley's voice, without getting satisfactory results. Then, during a break, Elvis started playing a song he'd heard years before, by Arthur Crudup. Bill Black joined in, then Scotty. They started playing around with 'That's All Right', upping the tempo, changing the beat. Sam Phillips knew this was something else entirely. They worked the song over until the exuberance and originality shone through on the recording. Even when they heard it played back they didn't know what they'd done. 'We thought it was exciting, but what was it? It was just so completely different.' Scotty Moore's reaction anticipated the world's response. In the end, nobody cared what exactly it was — it was exciting, it was different, and it was enough to shake the world.

Sam Phillips cut an acetate of 'That's All Right' on his studio lathe and had radio DJ Dewey Phillips come by to listen.

'Daddy–O–Dewey' took it away to play on his *Red Hot and Blue* show on WHBQ Radio the following Thursday, July 8. Sam phoned Elvis and told him to listen in. He tuned the radio, but it seems his nerves got the better of him and he just couldn't wait. He went out to the Suzore movie house on North Main Street instead. Gladys and Vernon listened though, and after an hour and a half's wait came the moment they, and the rest of the world (though it didn't yet know it), had been waiting for. The first Elvis Presley record was played over the air at 9:30 p.m. on July 8, 1954, and things were never quite the same again.

Gladys immediately got a call from Dewey, asking her to get her son down to the station — the phone lines were going crazy. Gladys and Vernon rushed to get Elvis out of Suzore's. The legend holds that he ran the length of Main Street to the Chisca Hotel and

Inside Sun
The now famous Sun Studio consists of a small front office, one large studio (small by today's standards) and a control room. The photo below shows Sam Phillips in the control room with Elvis, Bill and Scotty looking in through the glass panel. The equipment was basic, but included two Ampex taping machines wired together. The delay of the signal passing between them gave an echo or 'slapback' effect. Millions of dollars have since been spent trying unsuccessfully to recreate this characteristic Sun sound.

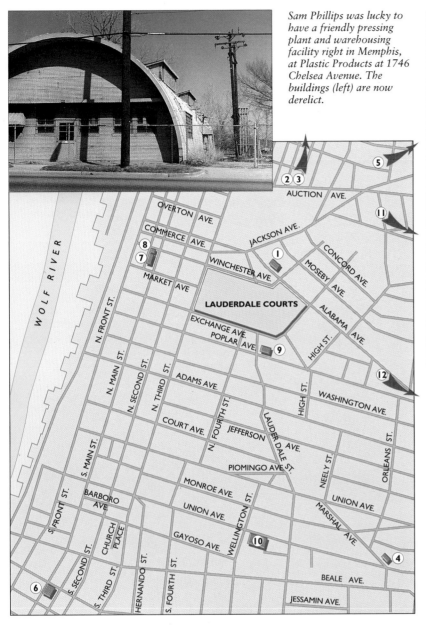

Sam Phillips was lucky to have a friendly pressing plant and warehousing facility right in Memphis, at Plastic Products at 1746 Chelsea Avenue. The buildings (left) are now derelict.

Locations in Memphis July 1954

1. **462 Alabama Avenue**, Elvis's home in July 1954.
2. **Scotty Moore's house** on Belz Street. Elvis, Bill Black, and Scotty met up here to rehearse on July 4.
3. **Bill Black's house**, 3 doors from Scotty Moore. Scotty had moved onto Belz Street to be near to Bill. The men were close friends and both members of the Starlite Wranglers.
4. **Sun Studio**, Elvis's first recording session was on July 5, 1954 .
5. **Plastic Products**, 1746 Chelsea Avenue. Pressing plant for Sun records. The owner, Robert 'Buster' Williams, was an important factor in Sun's foundation, providing distribution capital and warehousing as well as pressing facilities.
6. **Chisca Hotel**, WHBQ studios. Dewey Phillips played the first Presley record from here.
7. **Suzore Theater.** Elvis was found here by his parents and rushed round to WHBQ on the night of July 8.
8. **Charlie's Records.** The first Elvis Presley record was purchased here, or...
9. **Poplar Tunes.** Vies with Charlies for honor of selling first copy of an Elvis record.
10. *Memphis Press–Scimitar* Offices, scene of Elvis's first interview, July 28, 1954.
11. **Bon Air Club**, 4862 Summer Avenue. Elvis sang his two songs in the interval of a set by Doug Poindexter on July 17, 1954.
12. **Overton Park Shell.** Elvis, Scotty and Bill made their first advertised appearance on a bill headlined by Slim Whitman, July 30, 1954.

The Sun Studio building (right) has survived the redevelopment of central Memphis. The tiny building sits at the corner of Marshall and Union avenues. The Studio is used for recording at night and for tours during the day. Much of it is preserved as it was in the 1950s.

was interviewed before he had time to get his breath back. In response to the calls and telegrams that poured in, Dewey played the record seven times that night.

After the events of July 8, Sam Phillips knew that he had to get another side recorded and get a record out as soon as possible. The trio came back into the studio and tried another raft of songs before trying a rockabilly version of 'Blue Moon Of Kentucky.' The result is a delicious combination of raucous energy and emotive vocals. A disc was pressed at Plastic Products in Memphis and 'That's All Right/Blue Moon Of Kentucky' was issued as Sun catalog number 209 on July 19.

Meanwhile, Elvis gave his first 'real' performance. He sang his two songs in the interval of a Starlite Wranglers show at the Bon Air Club. Eight days later, growing interest in the record prompted Marion Keisker to take him over to the *Memphis Press–Scimitar* office for his first interview. It appeared next day, accompanied by a photo. Then on July 30, came the first advertised concert. Sam had managed to get Presley on the bill of a concert headlined by SlimWhitman at the Overton Park Shell.

In the space of a month, they had gone from unsuccessful rehearsals in Scotty's living room to recordings, radio and a major concert venue. The storm was beginning to break.

Hometown Boy

Memphis performances 1954 through 1955

Although Elvis Presley created the archetypal rock and roll singer's career, in one respect at least his start was unique. Before he made a record he had hardly sung in public. The most he'd done was sing a few numbers at amateur clubs and concerts. The Elvis Presley sound was created not by countless one-night stands in smoky clubs, but in the studio. But without a stage act there would be no record sales and no music career. Now he had to get up and show the people who heard the records what he could do on stage. In doing so he surprised himself, and eventually turned America upside down. But things started slowly...

Presley's first performance as a semi-professional singer actually happened two days before his first record was released, though demo discs had been playing on radio stations in Memphis for over a week. Scotty Moore and Bill Black were both members of a country hillbilly band called the Starlite Wranglers. They were headed by singer Doug Poindexter and had regular work at a club called the Bon Air out in east Memphis. On Saturday July 17, 1954, Sam Phillips took Elvis out to the club. While the rest of the band took an intermission break, Scotty and Bill stayed on stage and Elvis made his first attempts to sing his two new songs for an audience. He was nervous as hell beforehand and completely deflated afterwards, though by all accounts the short session went well. It's not hard to imagine what it might have been like for the young Presley. The biggest moment in his life passed by in an instant, and without, it seemed, anyone noticing. The crowd kept on talking and drinking and shouting and having a time, the other musicians trooped back on stage and the whole thing got going again. The world hadn't stopped turning after all.

The next part of Sam's and Scotty's strategy was to get Elvis on the bill of an upcoming Slim Whitman concert. By Friday July 30, interest in the young Presley had grown enough to get an interview and photo in the *Memphis Press–Scimitar*. The record 'That's All Right' was getting good airplay on rhythm and blues stations, while the flip side, 'Blue Moon Of Kentucky', was doing business with country audiences. Before the Overton Park Show, Scotty Moore said that Elvis's knees were knocking so loud you could hear them on stage. They were all nervous and vulnerable behind their little trio of instruments. But as soon as they started into the first chords of 'That's All Right', something started to hap-

pen. Elvis stood on the balls of his feet and leaned into the microphone. His legs started moving in time to the music. It was like he was tapping his foot with the whole lower half of his body. The crowd went wild. When they'd played their two songs, they had to go

The old Eagle's Nest is still a thriving music venue, now called the Americana, at the corner of Lamar Avenue and Winchester Road. Youngsters used to use the club as a changing room for the nearby swimming pool. Rumour has it that they used to sneak in to catch Elvis's act, then leave when the house band came on. The regular bookings at the Eagle's Nest were an important first step for Presley.

> "I hadn't thought of him in terms of a physical specimen ... I wasn't thinking, 'Is he going to look good on stage, is he going to be a great performer?' I was just looking for something nobody could categorize."
> Sam Phillips

> "It was a real eye-opener. He just automatically did things right."
> Bob Neal

Memphis concerts 1954 to 1961

1. **Bon Air Club**, 4862 Summer Avenue at Summer and Medenhall, now parking lot for Rally's Hamburgers.
2. **Bel Air Motel**, 1850 South Bellevue Boulevard. Played sometime in July 1954.
3. **Firestone Workers' Union Hall**, Firestone Boulevard. Played some time in July 1954.
4. **Overton Park Municipal Shell**. First advertised concert supporting Slim Whitman, July 30, 1954. Supported Webb Pierce in front of 4,000 fans on August 5, 1955.
5. **KWEM Radio**, West Memphis. Possible brief appearance on Doug Poindexter's show.
6. **Eagle's Nest**, Lamar Avenue at Winchester Road. First date August 7, 1954, also their first headline. Then September 18, 24, 25, October 1, 6, 9, 13, 20, 29, 30, November 17, December 10.
7. **Bellevue Park**, Bellevue and South Parkway. Baseball benefit, August 8, 1954.
8. **Kennedy Hospital**, Getwell Road, benefit show, August 29, 1954.
9. **St. Mary's**, rehearsals and unpaid shows.
10. **Lamar-Airways Shopping Center**, 2256 Lamar Avenue. Opening of new shopping center, September 9, 1954.
11. **Memphis State University** blood donation drive, November 8, 1954.
12. **Ellis Auditorium**. Played two shows in the North Hall supporting Faron Young, February 6, 1955, as musical intro to a 'Wrestling Program', December 19, 1955.
13. **Ellis Auditorium**. Cotton Festival, May 15, 1956. Shared top billing with Hank Snow, played to 7,000 fans in both halls at the same time.
14. **Russwood Park Baseball Stadium**, 914 Madison Avenue (now Baptist Hospital). Benefit concert on July 4, 1956.
15. **Ellis Auditorium North Hall**. Two concerts, February 25, 1961.

The parking lot for the Lamar–Airways shopping center (below) was the scene of Elvis's first performance from the back of a truck — though not the last. The grand opening was on September 9, 1954. The sign for the Bel Air

Motel (bottom) still stands on Bellevue Boulevard (now Elvis Presley Boulevard) in Memphis. The motel is gone, together with the club where Elvis, Scotty and Bill played in July and August 1954. The Overton Park Shell (above)

is practically unchanged since July 30, 1954, when Elvis thrilled an audience for the first time ever. It is the most accessible of all the venues he played, allowing anyone to go and stand on the open air stage.

back for an encore, so they did them both again. After Overton Park Elvis never got nervous again.

After the Overton Park show, Scotty Moore, Elvis's manager at this time, didn't have to look too hard for work for Elvis, Bill and himself in Memphis. Soon they were booked as the regular intermission band at the Eagle's Nest, a country music club out on Lamar Avenue (now called the Americana). Sleepy-Eyed John, a DJ on WHHM, was the booker for the club, and his band was the principal act. He'd been critical of Presley's record on his radio show, but he had the sense to book him anyhow. Scotty and Bill virtually quit the Starlite Wranglers at this point, as the band was falling apart anyhow. From now on it was the three of them, all or nothing. Youngsters came just to see Elvis at the Eagle's Nest, and walked out when the house band started up. It was a taste of things to come, and an indication of how Elvis created a kind of music that hadn't been heard, and couldn't be categorized.

The trio were still working full time in the day through the summer of 1954, so performances were restricted to the Memphis area. They played some clubs, including the Bel Air, took part in a benefit, and played off the back of truck at the opening of a shopping center. All the time their confidence grew, as they became ready to head further afield.

First Time on the Road

The 1954 concerts

Elvis, Scotty, and Bill continued to work full-time at their day jobs until October 1954, when they signed a contract with the *Louisiana Hayride* radio show. Any performances up to then had to be fitted in around the working day. Scotty Moore booked shows in and around Memphis, but this wasn't easy while he was working. Bob Neal, a local DJ and promoter who had emceed the Overton Park show, started to take them under his wing. Their area of operation started to expand, first into Arkansas, then, on the back of the *Hayride*, into Louisiana and then Texas — the state that really took the young singer to its heart. This was the start of two and a half years of almost continual travel, which would take them to nearly every state in the country.

"Nobody knew what rock and roll was in those days. It's not like you hear it on the radio, when you do it on stage you have to put on a show for people."
Elvis Presley

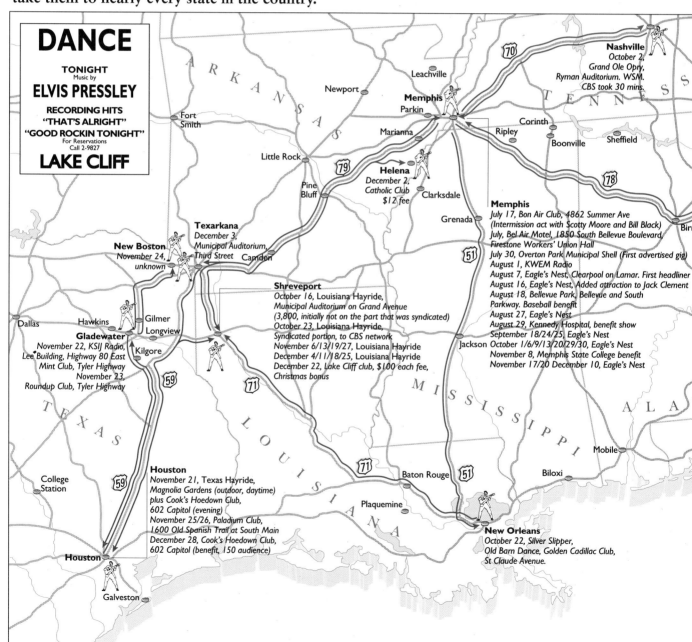

DANCE
TONIGHT
Music by
ELVIS PRESSLEY
RECORDING HITS
"THAT'S ALRIGHT"
"GOOD ROCKIN TONIGHT"
For Reservations
Call 2-9827
LAKE CLIFF

Nashville
*October 2,
Grand Ole Opry,
Ryman Auditorium. WSM.
CBS took 30 mins.*

Helena
*December 2,
Catholic Club
$12 fee*

Memphis
*July 17, Bon Air Club, 4862 Summer Ave
(Intermission act with Scotty Moore and Bill Black)
July, Bel Air Motel, 1850 South Bellevue Boulevard,
Firestone Workers' Union Hall
July 30, Overton Park Municipal Shell (First advertised gig)
August 1, KWEM Radio
August 7, Eagle's Nest, Clearpool on Lamar. First headliner
August 16, Eagle's Nest, Added attraction to Jack Clement
August 18, Bellevue Park, Bellevue and South
Parkway. Baseball benefit
August 27, Eagle's Nest
August 29, Kennedy Hospital, benefit show
September 18/24/25, Eagle's Nest
October 1/6/9/13 20/29/30, Eagle's Nest
November 8, Memphis State College benefit
November 17/20 December 10, Eagle's Nest*

Texarkana
*December 3,
Municipal Auditorium,
Third Street*

New Boston
*November 24,
unknown*

Shreveport
*October 16, Louisiana Hayride,
Municipal Auditorium on Grand Avenue
(3,800, initially not on the part that was syndicated)
October 23, Louisiana Hayride,
Syndicated portion, to CBS network
November 6/13/19/27, Louisiana Hayride
December 4/11/18/25, Louisiana Hayride
December 22, Lake Cliff club, $100 each fee,
Christmas bonus*

Gladewater
*November 22, KSIJ Radio,
Lee Building, Highway 80 East
Mint Club, Tyler Highway
November 23,
Roundup Club, Tyler Highway*

Houston
*November 21, Texas Hayride,
Magnolia Gardens (outdoor, daytime)
plus Cook's Hoedown Club,
602 Capitol (evening)
November 25/26, Paladium Club,
1600 Old Spanish Trail at South Main
December 28, Cook's Hoedown Club,
602 Capitol (benefit, 150 audience)*

New Orleans
*October 22, Silver Slipper,
Old Barn Dance, Golden Cadillac Club,
St Claude Avenue.*

Getting out of Memphis

Bob Neal had seen Elvis right at the start and was smart enough to know that the boy had real potential. He started by booking the trio into halls in the area around Memphis — any place they could drive to after work. Neal promoted the shows on his radio program on WMPS and his wife sold tickets on the door. There was no need to do any other advertising, so unfortunately there are no written records of many of these early shows. It seems likely that they played places around Memphis in the summer of 1954, particularly in September when they missed their regular slot at the Eagle's Nest for a few weeks.

Presley's first documented performance outside Memphis was, astonishingly, on the *Grand Ole Opry* in Nashville. Sam Phillips pulled the stops out to get the trio booked onto the show, but even he was surprised when they were invited on within three months of releasing their first record. On October 2, 1954, Sam Phillips drove over to Nashville with Elvis, Scotty, and Bill. Unknown to them Marion Keisker also came over, as did Bobbie Moore and Evelyn Black, Scotty and Bill's wives. According to legend Elvis sang one song, 'Blue Moon Of Kentucky', and didn't go down too well with the audience of country fans or the show's management. In contrast, the song's author Bill Monroe seems to have taken to Elvis's treatment of it well enough to re–record it in 4/4 time. The story is that the producer of the *Opry*, Jim Denny, told Elvis to go back to driving a truck. Later versions say he was more diplomatic. In any event, one thing is for sure — Elvis was not invited back on the show.

Fortunately there was already an invitation in from the *Opry's* rival, the *Louisiana Hayride* broadcast out of Shreveport. Within two weeks the three musicians were on air again, and this time everything went according to plan. They were radio performers to stay. Given their revolutionary treatment of the well-loved 'Blue Moon of Kentucky', it's not so surprising that they didn't suit the *Opry* — maybe it's more notable that the *Hayride* took them on. Once they gave up their jobs they were able to push further afield. There were concerts in Atlanta, in Gladewater, in Texarkana, and all the way down to Houston. Over the next 12 months they were to play in hundreds of towns all over the South, but the state of Texas was their first real stomping ground. Highway 79 became their path to the future.

How good is the evidence?

There are written advertisements for only a few Elvis shows in 1954. Lake Cliff, in Shreveport, was a club and motel at which Elvis played, probably on November 19, as was the Paladium Club in Houston (see below) on Thanksgiving weekend, November 25 and 26. The Catholic Club in Helena, Arkansas, on December 2 is definitely documented. Appearances on the *Hayride* and at the Eagle's Nest, Memphis are documented, but beyond that it's a matter of eyewitness reports and deduction. The show in New Orleans seems a little unlikely, whereas the *Texas Hayride* in Houston was almost definitely played by Elvis, probably on November 21. The trio played at least one and maybe two shows in Gladewater. Local residents say that Elvis played Texarkana on December 12, but again, there is no written record.

Chattanooga

(78)

Atlanta
October 8, Silver Slipper, Conley, Highway 42, south of Atlanta

M A

Posters for Elvis's 1954 concerts are rare items. The promoters of the Houston show (left) may have been a little premature in calling 'Elvis Pressley' 'America's Great Singing Star', but there's no doubt that the Louisiana Hayride gave him an eager audience in Texas.
The photo (above) shows Elvis somewhat later, but it captures his innocence before the world took him over.

Good Rockin' Tonight

The Louisiana Hayride 1954-56

Live radio was the most powerful force in southern music over the thirty years leading up to Presley's debut on the *Louisiana Hayride*. Radio both tapped the vein of southern music and brought it to a wide audience. For his first shows on the *Louisiana Hayride* in October 1954 Presley received $18 per show, with Scotty Moore and Bill Black getting $12 dollars each. By the time he completed his contractual obligation, for a total of fifty shows, in December 1956 he had earned $430,000 just from record royalties. KWKH Radio of Shreveport, Louisiana had signed him as a virtually unknown hillbilly singer and seen him become the biggest recording artist in history. The *Louisiana Hayride* played a significant role in that transformation.

"Well I'd like to say how happy we are to be out here. We're gonna do a song for you we got on the Sun record, it goes something like this." Elvis's first words on the *Louisiana Hayride*.

The *Louisiana Hayride* was a close cousin of the *Grand Ole Opry* broadcast by WSM in Nashville. The show went out live every Saturday night, from KWKH Radio in the town of Shreveport, Louisiana, broadcast from the town's Municipal Auditorium. Having started on April 3, 1948 the show had become one of the most important showcases for country musicians throughout the South. Cowboy artists like Gene Autrey had made their big break on the Louisiana Hayride. By the time Elvis appeared in 1954 it was transmitted by 190 other radio stations across the region. Elvis appeared on the Lucky Strike section of the show which was for new talent. His original contract was for 52 appearances, to be fulfiled as and when the station managers decided. The booking was a huge boost for Presley's career, even though the fee was only $18 per show. Getting on to live radio meant that he could sing his latest songs (his second single was released 3 weeks before his first *Louisiana Hayride* appearance) and promote his concerts week after week.

On March 5, 1955 Presley appeared on the section of the show broadcast on local television in the Shreveport area. Unfortunately no record exists of this first ever TV appearance.

In November 1955 Presley's *Hayride* contract was renewed at $200 per show. Elvis was now earning enough from his concerts and getting enough airplay on other stations

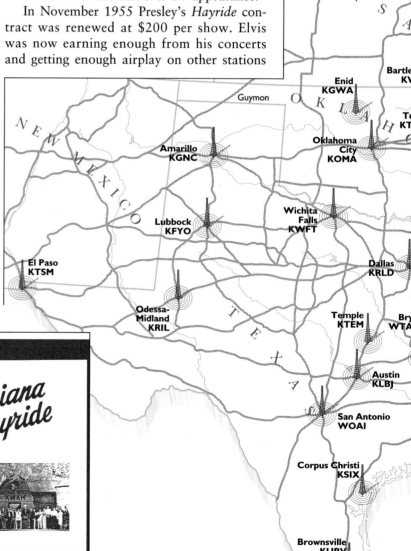

The CBS Radio Network and the Louisiana Hayride

The Louisiana Hayride was broadcast from Radio KWKH in Shreveport, Louisiana. A half hour portion of the show, sponsored by Lucky Strike cigarettes, was syndicated via the CBS network to 190 stations throughout Texas and the South (map below), making almost the whole population of the region a potential audience.

to want to get out of his obligation to KWKH. To do this he had to pay a fee of $400 for each show he missed. In fact he missed very few weekly shows up until April 1956.

Elvis's last show on the Hayride was a special benefit concert on December 15, 1956, recorded live at the Louisiana Fairgrounds in front of 9,000 fans. At that time the LP *Elvis* was at Number One on the Billboard Chart, three of his singles had gone gold and *Love Me Tender* was the biggest grossing film in the country. Elvis arrived in Shreveport in style, driving overnight from Memphis in a white Lincoln Continental with the band following behind in a stretch Cadillac. A lot of things had changed in 26 months.

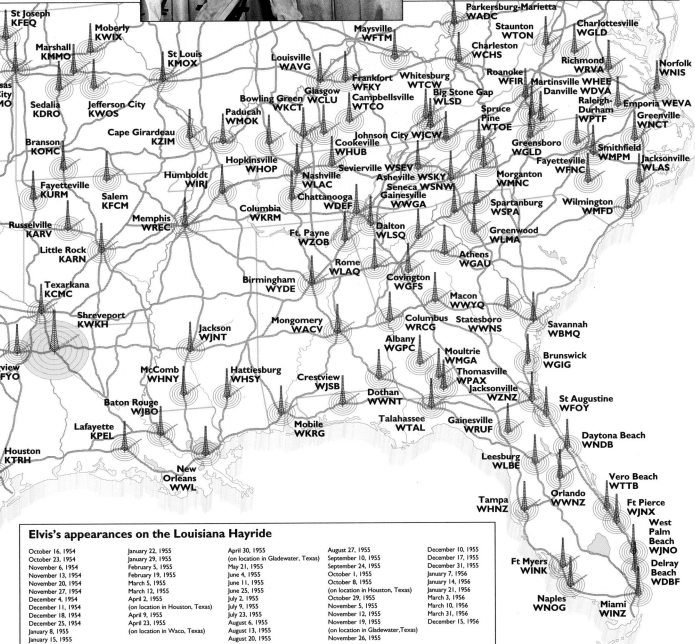

Elvis's appearances on the Louisiana Hayride

October 16, 1954	January 22, 1955	April 30, 1955	August 27, 1955	December 10, 1955
October 23, 1954	January 29, 1955	(on location in Gladewater, Texas)	September 10, 1955	December 17, 1955
November 6, 1954	February 5, 1955	May 21, 1955	September 24, 1955	December 31, 1955
November 13, 1954	February 19, 1955	June 4, 1955	October 1, 1955	January 7, 1956
November 20, 1954	March 5, 1955	June 11, 1955	October 8, 1955	January 14, 1956
November 27, 1954	March 12, 1955	June 25, 1955	(on location in Houston, Texas)	January 21, 1956
December 4, 1954	April 2, 1955	July 2, 1955	October 29, 1955	March 3, 1956
December 11, 1954	(on location in Houston, Texas)	July 9, 1955	November 5, 1955	March 10, 1956
December 18, 1954	April 9, 1955	July 23, 1955	November 12, 1955	March 31, 1956
December 25, 1954	April 23, 1955	August 6, 1955	November 19, 1955	December 15, 1956
January 8, 1955	(on location in Waco, Texas)	August 13, 1955	(on location in Gladewater, Texas)	
January 15, 1955		August 20, 1955	November 26, 1955	

Trying To Get To You

January to February 1955

At the start of 1955 Elvis Presley had been a recording artist and professional singer for just five months. His progress in that time had been extraordinary, but there was a lot of work still to do in order to make the big time. With Bill Black's bass strapped to the roof of their car, Elvis, Scotty and Bill criss-crossed Texas and the South playing high school halls, night clubs and road houses, returning to Memphis for recording sessions, and to Shreveport for radio broadcasts. They lit a slow fuse in the South which eventually was to explode all over America and the world. But for the time being they were just a touring act, working hard for their money.

"I jump around because its the way I feel. I can't even sing with a beat at all if I stand still".

On January 1, 1955 Bob Neal became Presley's full time manager. Neal had been arranging most of the concerts in any case, and had acted as emcee and promoter for most of those in the Memphis area. Now that he had a solid arrangement Neal worked hard to get publicity for the out-of-town concerts, often travelling with the three musicians to arrange pre-concert radio slots and newspaper adverts.

Neal's cause was helped by Elvis's weekly appearances on the *Louisiana Hayride*. As well as providing promotion, the *Hayride* was used as the basis for touring packages, where a host of acts would travel together. As his popularity increased, Presley's touring schedule became less haphazard — he didn't have to drive 1,000 miles to do a one-off concert when he could sell-out a number of venues.

The tour packages became an increasing feature of his touring through 1955. To begin with this brought him in front of pure country audiences, who had come to see acts like the Carter Sisters and Jim Ed and Maxine Brown. The crowds were often bemused by Presley's music, which was even more raucous than his recordings, and his stage act which was increasingly explosive. Bill Black had sometimes to come to the trio's rescue by acting the comic on stage. Later on, the tour packages worked the other way, as the country acts were disregarded and often abused by the thousands of young fans who had come just to see Elvis. By the end of 1955 it was impossible to get any name artists to go on a bill with Presley — the hysteria surrounding his live performances didn't give anyone else a chance. Within six weeks of becoming Presley's manager Bob Neal arranged Elvis's introduction to the man who would eventually assume that role, in one of the most famous relationships in showbusiness.

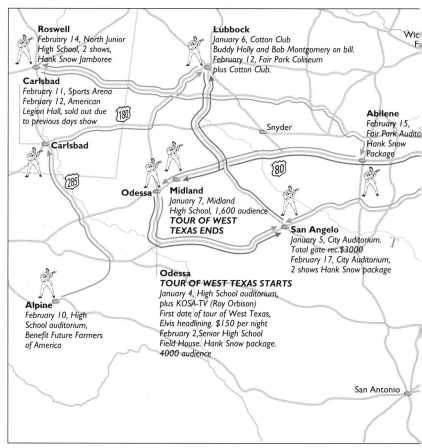

Roswell
February 14, North Junior High School, 2 shows, Hank Snow Jamboree

Lubbock
January 6, Cotton Club Buddy Holly and Bob Montgomery on bill. February 12, Fair Park Coliseum plus Cotton Club.

Wic F

Carlsbad
February 11, Sports Arena February 12, American Legion Hall, sold out due to previous days show

Carlsbad

Snyder

Abilene
February 15, Fair Park Audito Hank Snow Package

Odessa

Midland
January 7, Midland High School, 1,600 audience
TOUR OF WEST TEXAS ENDS

San Angelo
January 5, City Auditorium. Total gate rec.$3000 February 17, City Auditorium, 2 shows Hank Snow package

Alpine
February 10, High School auditorium, Benefit Future Farmers of America

Odessa
TOUR OF WEST TEXAS STARTS
January 4, High School auditorium, plus KOSA-TV (Roy Orbison) First date of tour of West Texas, Elvis headlining. $150 per night February 2, Senior High School Field House. Hank Snow package. 4000 audience

San Antonio

Meeting the Colonel

On Sunday February 6, 1955 Elvis, along with Scotty Moore and Bill Black, played two shows at the Ellis Auditorium in Memphis — on North Main Street between Poplar and Exchange.

Between the 3 p.m. and 8 p.m. shows Elvis met with Colonel Tom Parker for the first time, in Palumbo's Cafe at 85 Poplar Street. Also present at this momentous occasion were Parker's aides Tom Diskin and Oscar Davis, while Elvis had Sam Phillips and Scotty and Bill with him. With all those people there, we can assume the importance of the meeting was well understood. In fact they were there to discuss the upcoming tour of west Texas and New Mexico. For the first time Elvis was to tour with Hank Snow, a popular country artist with a number of hits to his name. Snow was managed by Parker in a complex arrangement in which they were co-owners of a company called Hank Snow-Jamboree Attractions. The company was based in Madison Tennessee, and operated particularly in Florida and the southeast, arranging and promoting tours.

Parker had been viewing Presley's rising popularity with interest, and it seems that Elvis in return began to see Parker as his route to the big time.

Concerts, January—February 1955

➤ Tour of west Texas. Jan 4, Odessa to Jan 7, Midland. Produced by Tillman Franks and Billy Walker of the *Louisiana Hayride*. Elvis headlined above Billy Walker, Jimmy and Johnny (a comic singing duo), and comedian Peach Seed Jones. Pay was $150 per day plus $10 gas money, split between Elvis, Scotty and Bill.

➤ Tour of region around Memphis. Billed as the Louisiana Hayride Jamboree. Jan 12, Clarksdale MS to Jan 21, Sikeston MO. Support included Jim Ed and Maxine Brown, Bob Neal also performed. Local acts were added to the bill in different towns.

➤ Tour of east Texas. Jan 24, Hawkins, to Jan 28, Gaston. Booked by Tom Perryman of KSIJ Radio in Gladewater. Elvis headlined supported by the Browns. The pay was $150 per show plus $10 a day expenses.

➤ Tour of east Texas and New Mexico. Feb 10, Alpine TX, to Feb 18, West Monroe LA. First part of tour Elvis support was Duke of Paducah, Charlene Arthur and Jimmie Rodgers Snow. Feb 14 Roswell, joined Hank Snow Jamboree, played third on the bill for rest of the tour.

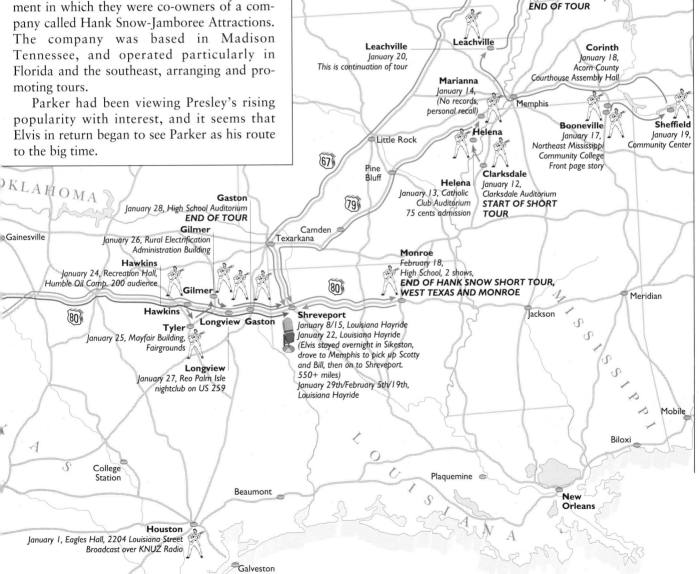

Sikeston
January 21,
National Guard Armory
END OF TOUR

Poplar Bluff

Corinth
January 18,
Acorn County
Courthouse Assembly Hall

Leachville
January 20,
This is continuation of tour

Leachville

Marianna
January 14,
(No records,
personal recall)

Memphis

Booneville
January 17,
Northeast Mississippi
Community College
Front page story

Sheffield
January 19,
Community Center

Little Rock

Helena

Pine Bluff

Helena
January 13, Catholic
Club Auditorium
75 cents admission

Clarksdale
January 12,
Clarksdale Auditorium
START OF SHORT TOUR

OKLAHOMA

Gaston
January 28, High School Auditorium
END OF TOUR

Gainesville

Gilmer
January 26, Rural Electrification
Administration Building

Camden
Texarkana

Monroe
February 18,
High School, 2 shows,
**END OF HANK SNOW SHORT TOUR,
WEST TEXAS AND MONROE**

Hawkins
January 24, Recreation Hall,
Humble Oil Camp. 200 audience

Gilmer

Hawkins

Longview   Gaston

Jackson

Meridian

Tyler
January 25, Mayfair Building,
Fairgrounds

Shreveport
January 8/15, Louisiana Hayride
January 22, Louisiana Hayride
(Elvis stayed overnight in Sikeston,
drove to Memphis to pick up Scotty
and Bill, then on to Shreveport.
550+ miles)
January 29th/February 5th/19th,
Louisiana Hayride

Longview
January 27, Reo Palm Isle
nightclub on US 259

MISSISSIPPI

Mobile

College Station

LOUISIANA

Biloxi

Beaumont

Plaquemine

New Orleans

Houston
January 1, Eagles Hall, 2204 Louisiana Street
Broadcast over KNUZ Radio

Galveston

Three For Texas

Live shows February through April 1955

Things weren't just getting busy, they were frantic. Elvis, Scotty, and Bill played nearly 50 shows in just over two months from February 19 to the end of April, ranging from Cleveland, Ohio, to Odessa, Texas. In addition they found time to fly to New York for a TV audition and to release a fourth single 'Baby Let's Play House'/'I'm Left You're Right, She's Gone'. Most of their work was done in Texas, where Elvis was creating enough of an impression to move up the bill in some major venues. The TV rejection must have rankled, though. In the end it wasn't going to be enough to be a star in Texas and the South, he needed more than that. And although the live shows were going well, his records weren't selling as well as he knew they could.

"There was never a country act that could follow him. With this type of show he would have a big crowd, and then when he appeared, he just tore them up completely."
Bob Neal

Those lucky enough to see an Elvis Presley show in the early part of 1955 remember, above everything else, the initial shock — caused by both the music and the performance. This was in some ways the golden age of Presley shows. The music was fresh and raucous and different, the performances were spontaneous and outrageous. In a few months time the teenage crowds would get so hysterical that you couldn't hear the music, and Elvis himself would begin to get worn down by the same routines. But for now it was a strange, bewildering, and exhilarating spectacle.

"Just a real raw cat singing like a bird. First thing he came out and spat out a piece of gum. His diction was real coarse, like a truck driver's. I can't overemphasise how shocking he looked and seemed that night." That's how Roy Orbison remembers Presley's appearance in Odessa, Texas. The strangest thing was the contrast between the polite and mild-mannered young man off-stage and the sneering, snarling, gyrating figure behind the microphone. Bob Neal put it down to competition. Elvis might like and admire his fellow artists, but he wanted to be the best, he wanted the audience to love him more than it loved anyone else — more than it had loved anyone else before. For country-music fans in small towns in Texas this was sometimes hard to take, but the reaction of other performers indicates that Elvis was doing what he wanted to — he was blowing them off the stage. Singers like Hank Snow felt angry, but what could they do?

Cleveland and New York
Elvis, Scotty, and Bill, together with manager Bob Neal, drove up to Cleveland on February 26 to play the Circle Theater Jamboree. They carried a stack of records in the trunk, because

Sun's distribution didn't reach that far north. This was the first time that Elvis, Scotty, and Bill had played in the north. They were hoping it would be a home from home. A lot of southerners — black and white — had moved up to industrial northern cities like Cleveland

---

Live Shows, February 19 to April 30, 1955

↗ Week long tour of Arkansas and Louisiana: February 20, Little Rock, to February 25, Texarkana. Package billed as the 'WSM Grand Ole Opry Show'. Elvis third on bill to Duke of Paducah and Mother Maybelle and the Carter Sisters. Colonel Parker co-promoted the shows.

↗ Performances local to Memphis and Shreveport: March 2, Newport, to March 12, Shreveport. Variety of support acts, including Jimmy Work and Betty Amos.

↗ Memphis to Houston via College Station to play Grand Prize Jamboree, broadcast over KPRC Radio: March 19, 20. Fourth on *Louisiana Hayride* package bill at College Station. Topped bill at Houston Jamboree.

↗ Arkansas and Texas shows: March 29, Parkin, to April 2, Houston. Support was Onie Wheeler. Houston show was live remote broadcast for *Louisiana Hayride* in front of a capacity crowd at the City Auditorium.

↗ Weekend of long drives: April 7, Corinth, to April 9, Shreveport.

↗ Week of concerts in Texas: April 10, Houston, to April 16, Dallas. Elvis headlined, supported by Onie Wheeler.

↗ String of shows out from Mississippi to west Texas: April 20, Grenada, to April 30, Gladewater. From April 23 Elvis appeared on a bill with Dub Dickerson, Chuck Lee and Gene Kay and the Walking A Ranch Hands. Highlight was the remote broadcast of the *Louisiana Hayride* from Gladewater. Slim Whitman and Jim Reeves headlined in front of 3,000 fans.

On April 16, 1955 Elvis was the special attraction at the Big D Jamboree in Dallas, headlined by Sonny James. The jamboree was Radio KRLD's answer to the Louisiana Hayride, and was also partly broadcast over the CBS network. Presley's billing (right) was a sign of his growing popularity in Texas.

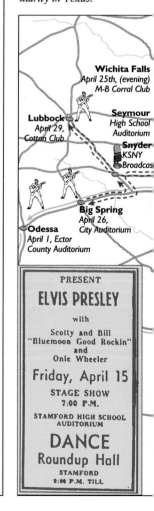

PRESENT

ELVIS PRESLEY

with

Scotty and Bill
"Bluemoon Good Rockin"
and
Onie Wheeler

Friday, April 15

STAGE SHOW
7:00 P.M.

STAMFORD HIGH SCHOOL
AUDITORIUM

DANCE

Roundup Hall

STAMFORD
9:00 P.M. TILL

BIG "D"
JAMBOREE
SPORTATORIUM
April 16—Saturday—8 P. M.
Dallas, Texas

Elvis Presley
SUN RECORDING STAR
"THAT'S ALL RIGHT MAMA"

SONNY JAMES

HANK LOCKLIN

CHARLINE ARTHUR

BELEW TWINS

JIMMY COLLIE

DOUG BRAGG

LAFAWN PAUL

ORVILLE COUCH

RILEY CRABTREE

JOE BILL

PLUS MANY
OTHER STARS
and
THREE BANDS

NO ADVANCE
IN PRICES
STILL

Adults   Children
60   .30

after the war, and there was a keen interest in rhythm and blues, and in hillbilly music. Cleveland had been the base of the legendary DJ Alan Freed, and now another presenter, Bill Randle, was making waves there. Bob Neal met up with Randle and played him Elvis's records — none of which he'd heard before. Randle was impressed with the music and with Bob Neal. He promised him help to get Elvis onto Arthur Godfrey's *TV Scouts*, a New York TV show.

This must have worked, because two weeks later they were on a flight to New York, heading for an audition. It was the first time Elvis or Bill had flown. They never even got to see Godfrey, and were turned down at the first attempt. They were disappointed at the outcome and at the waste of the money they'd saved to make the trip. The northern entertainment establishment just didn't care for southern hillbillies. It seemed the only way to make them notice you was to raise a big enough storm to batter their doors down, then they'd have to let you in. So that's what Elvis went and did.

Newport
March 2, Armory plus Porky's Rooftop Club

Poplar Bluff
March 9, Armory

Sikeston

Corinth
April 7, Court House Meeting Room, two shows 3.30 p.m. and 8.00 p.m.

Tulsa

Pine Bluff
February 23, Watson Chapel High School, two shows

Newport

Parkin
March 29

Memphis

Corinth

Little Rock
February 20, Robinson Auditorium
First of week tour with wsm Grand Ole Opry show.
Mother Maybelle & Carter Sisters top the bill

Parkin

Helena
March 8, Catholic Club

Hope
February 2, City Hall Not close to a full house

Helena

Pine Bluff

Clarksdale

Clarksdale
March 10, City Auditorium

Wichita Falls

Gainesville
April 14, Owl Park baseball field

Gladewater
April 30, Remote for Louisiana Hayride, Elvis headlined. High School gymnasium 3,000 country fans

De Kalb
March 4, High School

Texarkana

Camden
Eldorado

Grenada
April 20, American Legion Hut

anford

Dallas

Gladewater

Eldorado
March 30, High School Auditorium

Camden
February 21, City Auditorium

Meridian

eckenridge
ril 13, High School Auditorium st review

nford
5, 7.00 p.m.
School Auditorium
p.m. Roundup Hall

Longview
March 31, Reo Palm Isle

Shreveport   Rushton

Bastrop
February 24, South Side Elementary School, two shows

Jackson

Waco
April 23, Heart O' Texas Coliseum, remote broadcast for Louisiana Hayride, 5,000 spectators

Texarkana
February 25, City Hall City Auditorium
End of Grand Ole Opry tour
April 22, Arkansas Municipal Stadium

Baton Rouge

Biloxi

Dallas
April 16, Big D Jamboree, Sportarium. 8.00 p.m. to 12.00, broadcast on KRLD

Shreveport
February 19, March 5, televised in Shreveport area March 12, April 9, Louisiana Hayride

College Station
March 19, G. Rolle White Coliseum, Texas A&M University 8.00 p.m.

n Antonio

Houston

New Orleans
May 1, travels to join Hank Snow Jamboree

Houston
March 19, Eagle's Hall Broadcast over KORC radio 8 to 11.00 p.m.,
March 20, Afternoon two shows at Magnolia Gardens, evening Cook's Hoedown
April 2, City Auditorium. Big capacity crowd, remote broadcast for Louisiana Hayride
April 10, Magnolia Gardens (afternoon), Cook's Hoedown (evening)
April 24, Magnolia Gardens (afternoon), Cook's Hoedown (evening)

TEXAS
LOUISIANA
MISSISSIPPI

Moving Up A League

The Hank Snow All-Star Jamboree, May 1955

In retrospect Florida in May 1955 may have been *the* moment when the Elvis Presley bandwagon became unstoppable. Sure, he still had a long way to go to become the biggest entertainer of the century. But the incredible popularity that he generated on this tour, and the scenes of hysteria that greeted him wherever he went, meant that from now on the music industry simply could not afford to ignore him. One aspect of this sensationally successful tour was definitely not lost on the young Presley — it was entirely arranged and promoted by the one man who seemed to hold the key to the real big time, Colonel Tom Parker.

"What really stole the show was this 20 year-old sensation, Elvis Presley, a real sex box as far as the teenage girls are concerned."
Orlando Sentinel, May 16.

Hank Snow was an established country singer, an RCA recording artist and was, not coincidentally, managed by Tom Parker. Florida was Parker's real stomping ground and this tour gave him a chance to show what he could do. The touring package was worked by grouping a number of established country singers together to build up bigger audiences, as well as introducing new talent lower down on the bill. Artists might join the tour for just a few shows, or stay with it right through. At various times the package split into two sections, each playing a different location on the same night.

The May 1955 Hank Snow's All Star Jamboree certainly lived up to its name. As well as Snow, the tour included at various times Faron Young, Slim Whitman, Martha Carson, the Davis Sisters and Mother Maybelle and the Carter Sisters, as well as a host of younger talent. To avoid the problems encountered on previous package tours, it was decided to put the younger artists on in the first half of the show, with Presley closing before the interval. It seems that the audience reaction to Elvis made this impossible after the first night, and he closed the show for the rest of the tour.

As the publicist for the Florida area Parker had a real ace in the hole. Mae Axton will go down in history as the co-writer of Presley's first mainstream pop hit 'Heartbreak Hotel', but she was also a perceptive analyst of musical trends, and a champion of 'hillbilly' music when it was widely derided by the mainstream entertainment industry. When she interviewed Presley as part of the publicity for the Daytona Beach concert, one of her questions demonstrated the difficulty people were having in classifying his strange but electrifying style. "Elvis you are sort of a bebop artist more than anything else aren't you? Is that

what they call you?" Elvis replied "I have never given myself a name, but a lot of the disc jockeys call me bopping hillbilly and bebop, I don't know what else." Although the term 'rock and roll' existed it was never applied to Presley at this stage of his career. He was still widely known as a country artist, presumably because he was white. Later in the tour Mae Axton was the publicist for the biggest concert that Presley had yet played, and another turning point in his career — Jacksonville, Florida, Friday May 13, 1955.

Hysteria at Jacksonville

The newly built baseball park in Jacksonville was the venue for the two final concerts of the Florida section of the tour. At the end of the Friday concert, in front of 14,000 fans Presley innocently but impishly said, "I'll see you all backstage girls." Around half the audience (thats how it felt anyhow) took him at his word. Girls broke through police lines and into the dressing room, where Mae Axton and

Tom Parker were counting the takings. The police regrouped and Elvis got out in one piece, but without his coat, shirt or boots. Thousands of teenage girls wrote or scratched their names, phone numbers and messages all over his Lincoln Continental. It was a riot, and unlike anything seen before in America. From now on the crowds changed from enthusiastic to hysterical, from a mixture of ages to almost exclusively teenage girls. Colonel Parker saw the reaction and in Mae Axton's words "got dollar marks in his eyes". Hank Snow was firmly pushed aside as Parker began to concentrate exclusively on Elvis Presley. Country music was losing out to rock and roll.

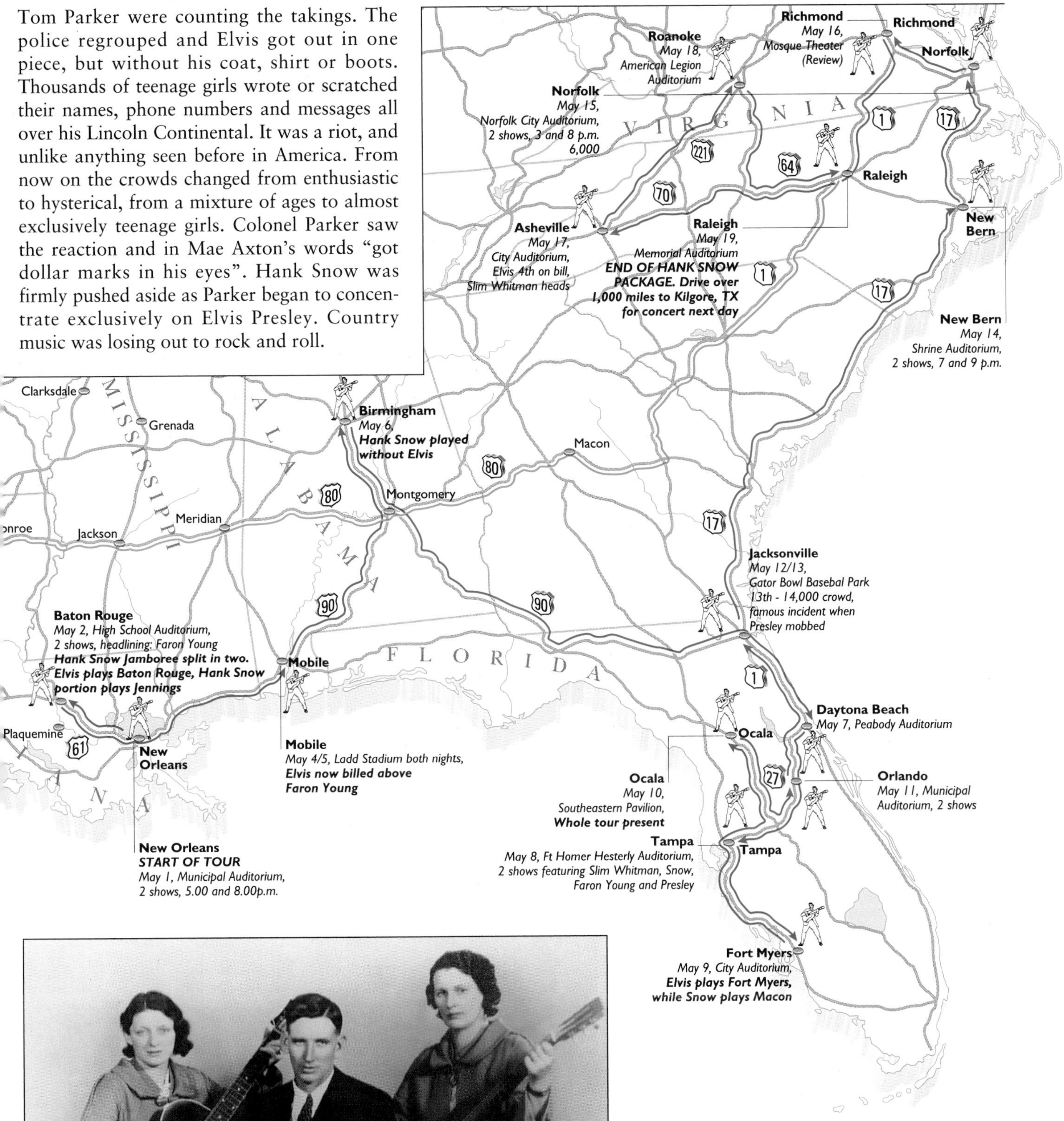

Richmond
May 16, Mosque Theater (Review)

Richmond

Roanoke
May 18, American Legion Auditorium

Norfolk

Norfolk
May 15, Norfolk City Auditorium, 2 shows, 3 and 8 p.m. 6,000

V I R G I N I A

221

64

70

Raleigh

1

New Bern

17

Asheville
May 17, City Auditorium, Elvis 4th on bill, Slim Whitman heads

Raleigh
May 19, Memorial Auditorium
END OF HANK SNOW PACKAGE. Drive over 1,000 miles to Kilgore, TX for concert next day

1

17

New Bern
May 14, Shrine Auditorium, 2 shows, 7 and 9 p.m.

Clarksdale

M I S S I S S I P P I

Grenada

A L A B A M A

Birmingham
May 6, **Hank Snow played without Elvis**

Macon

80

Montgomery

80

Meridian

17

onroe

Jackson

Jacksonville
May 12/13, Gator Bowl Baseal Park
13th - 14,000 crowd, famous incident when Presley mobbed

90

90

1

Baton Rouge
May 2, High School Auditorium, 2 shows, headlining: Faron Young
Hank Snow Jamboree split in two. Elvis plays Baton Rouge, Hank Snow portion plays Jennings

Mobile

F L O R I D A

Daytona Beach
May 7, Peabody Auditorium

Plaquemine

61

New Orleans

A
N
A

Ocala

27

Ocala
May 10, Southeastern Pavilion, **Whole tour present**

Orlando
May 11, Municipal Auditorium, 2 shows

Mobile
May 4/5, Ladd Stadium both nights, **Elvis now billed above Faron Young**

Tampa
May 8, Ft Homer Hesterly Auditorium, 2 shows featuring Slim Whitman, Snow, Faron Young and Presley

Tampa

New Orleans
START OF TOUR
May 1, Municipal Auditorium, 2 shows, 5.00 and 8.00p.m.

Fort Myers
May 9, City Auditorium, **Elvis plays Fort Myers, while Snow plays Macon**

After this tour it became increasingly difficult for Presley to share a bill with country artists like Hank Snow (above left) and the Carter Sisters, though he continued to play with the Carters until well into 1956. Mother Maybelle was a surviving member of the Carter Family, one of the country music's legends dating from the 1920's. The picture (left) shows her with A.P. Carter seated and his wife Sara. The Carter Sisters were daughters Anita, Helen and June. June Carter later married Elvis's fellow Sun recording artist Johnny Cash.

Like Nothing Ever Seen Before

Tours and concerts May to July 1955

It was around this time that Elvis and those around him began to realize that he was going to have to get out of Memphis sooner rather than later. He didn't need to move physically of course — in fact he more or less remained in Memphis till the end of his life. But he was no longer a Memphis phenomenon, while both his record company and his manager were. Sun's distribution was having trouble keeping pace with the demand the concerts were generating even in the South. And while Bob Neal was doing a good job, he was hooking up with other promoters who could see Elvis's real potential. Presley was getting noticed nationally, while his records were still big regional sellers but were doing modestly in the national charts. Something was going to have to give.

In contrast to the Florida tours, the shows in Texas and Louisiana were often just Elvis, Scotty, and Bill, with some local acts in support, as these posters show, (below). At least Elvis was top of the bill, even if they didn't always spell his name correctly.

After the phenomenally successful tour of Florida in May 1955, the pace, if anything, increased. The band played around 48 shows in 44 days from late May through to the early part of July, when they took a two-week vacation. Included in this maelstrom of activity was a planned 800-mile drive from Memphis to Stamford, Texas, on June 16. Unfortunately, after a stop in Hope, Arkansas, Elvis's beautiful pink Cadillac caught fire somewhere near Texarkana. Elvis sat under a tree and watched it go up in smoke. An engaged parking brake may have been to blame.

Elvis got a lift to Texarkana and the band played a set there that night while figuring out how to get to Stamford. They put all the instruments in Scotty's Chevy, and while Bill and Scotty drove, Elvis took a chartered flight to Abilene, then a taxi on to their destination. The distances weren't unusual — in the previous week they had played five venues strung out over a distance of 2,000 miles. And the week before that had included an epic journey up through the Texas panhandle to play the town of Guymon in western Oklahoma. No wonder the cars were giving out. Elvis often drove to a new venue at night, as he couldn't sleep after the excitement of a live show.

All this must have started to lose its appeal. It's fine to bust yourself driving thousands of miles around the country for a few months. But when you've seen thousands of kids going wild for you in Florida, the endless two lane blacktops of west Texas must start to feel like a grind. At least there were the shows, which always seemed to give the guys a lift. But they needed that vacation in July, and in the background things were beginning to happen that would change their lives forever.

The Jimmie Rodgers festival

On May 25 and 26, 1955, Elvis, Scotty, and Bill played the third Jimmie Rodgers Memorial Festival in Meridian Mississippi. Over 600 performers and musicians played to thousands of country music fans, who came from all over Texas and the South. Rodgers, who had died of tuberculosis in 1933 at the age of 35, was, like Elvis, a musical innovator, but in an entirely different age. Rodgers fused the traditions of cowboy music and the blues. His revolutionary phrasing and his clear, unmannered and haunting vocal style laid the foundations for country music. Though he wasn't yet born when Rodgers died, Elvis would undoubtedly have heard his songs over the radio and absorbed elements of his highly distinctive style. The festival confirmed acceptance of Elvis by many country music promoters and fans, while he himself was creating a different kind of music.

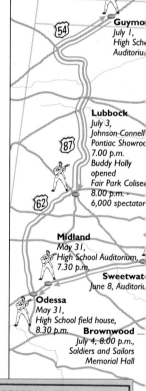

Guymo
July 1,
High Schc
Auditoriu

Lubbock
July 3,
Johnson-Connell
Pontiac Showroo
7.00 p.m.
Buddy Holly
opened
Fair Park Colise
8.00 p.m. -
6,000 spectator

Midland
May 31,
High School Auditorium,
7.30 p.m.

Sweetwat
June 8, Auditoriu

Odessa
May 31,
High School field house,
8.30 p.m.

Brownwood
July 4, 8.00 p.m.,
Soldiers and Sailors
Memorial Hall

IN PERSON
† Elvis ★
PRESLEY
SCOTTY and BILL
The Blue Moon Boys

AT THE
Slavonian Lodge
Sunday Night June 26
For One Big Show
And Dance
Show Time 8:00 p.m.
Dance 9:00 'Til 1:00 a.m.
In The New
Air-Conditioned Auditorium

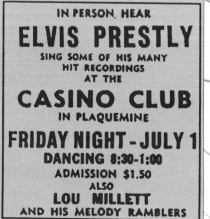

IN PERSON, HEAR
ELVIS PRESTLY
SING SOME OF HIS MANY
HIT RECORDINGS
AT THE
CASINO CLUB
IN PLAQUEMINE
FRIDAY NIGHT - JULY 1
DANCING 8:30-1:00
ADMISSION $1.50
ALSO
LOU MILLETT
AND HIS MELODY RAMBLERS

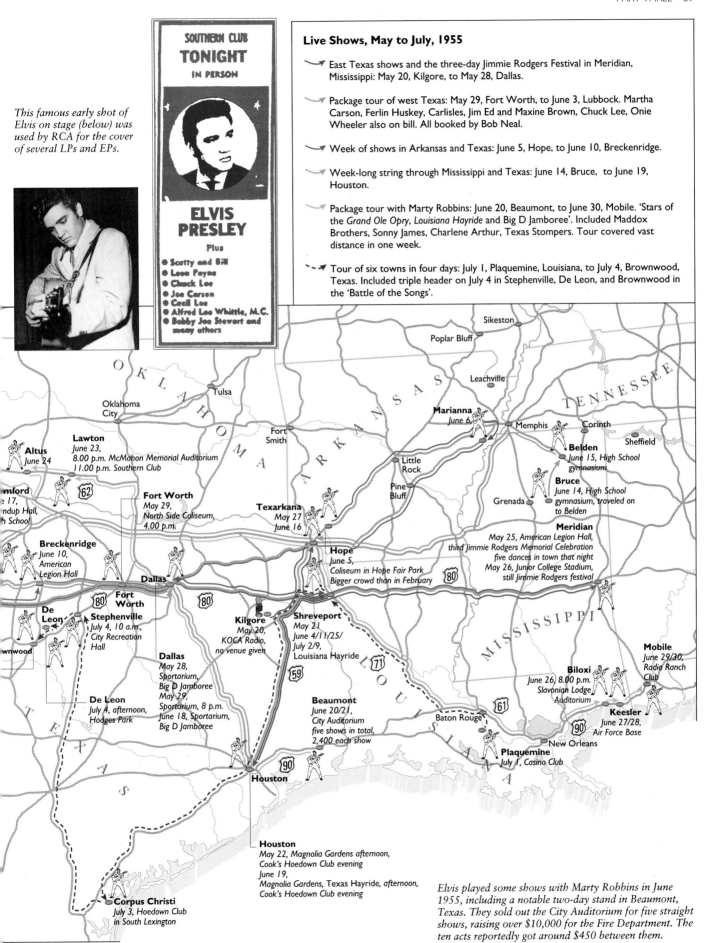

This famous early shot of Elvis on stage (below) was used by RCA for the cover of several LPs and EPs.

SOUTHERN CLUB
TONIGHT
IN PERSON

ELVIS PRESLEY
Plus
● Scotty and Bill
● Leon Payne
● Chuck Lee
● Joe Carson
● Cecil Lee
● Alfred Lee Whittle, M.C.
● Bobby Joe Stewart and many others

Live Shows, May to July, 1955

East Texas shows and the three-day Jimmie Rodgers Festival in Meridian, Mississippi: May 20, Kilgore, to May 28, Dallas.

Package tour of west Texas: May 29, Fort Worth, to June 3, Lubbock. Martha Carson, Ferlin Huskey, Carlisles, Jim Ed and Maxine Brown, Chuck Lee, Onie Wheeler also on bill. All booked by Bob Neal.

Week of shows in Arkansas and Texas: June 5, Hope, to June 10, Breckenridge.

Week-long string through Mississippi and Texas: June 14, Bruce, to June 19, Houston.

Package tour with Marty Robbins: June 20, Beaumont, to June 30, Mobile. 'Stars of the *Grand Ole Opry*, *Louisiana Hayride* and Big D Jamboree'. Included Maddox Brothers, Sonny James, Charlene Arthur, Texas Stompers. Tour covered vast distance in one week.

Tour of six towns in four days: July 1, Plaquemine, Louisiana, to July 4, Brownwood, Texas. Included triple header on July 4 in Stephenville, De Leon, and Brownwood in the 'Battle of the Songs'.

Sikeston

Poplar Bluff

OKLAHOMA

Tulsa

Leachville

Oklahoma City

TENNESSEE

Marianna
June 6

Memphis

Corinth

Fort Smith

Sheffield

Belden
June 15, High School gymnasium

Little Rock

Altus
June 24

Lawton
June 23,
8.00 p.m. McMahon Memorial Auditorium
11.00 p.m. Southern Club

...mford
...e 17,
...ndup Hall,
...h School

62

Pine Bluff

Grenada

Bruce
June 14, High School gymnasium, traveled on to Belden

Fort Worth
May 29,
North Side Coliseum,
4.00 p.m.

Texarkana
May 27
June 16

ARKANSAS

Meridian
May 25, American Legion Hall, third Jimmie Rodgers Memorial Celebration five dances in town that night
May 26, Junior College Stadium, still Jimmie Rodgers festival

Breckenridge
June 10,
American
Legion Hall

Dallas

Hope
June 5,
Coliseum in Hope Fair Park
Bigger crowd than in February

80

80

Fort Worth

80

80

MISSISSIPPI

De Leon

Stephenville
July 4, 10 a.m.,
City Recreation
Hall

...wnwood

Kilgore
May 20,
KOCA Radio,
no venue given

Shreveport
May 21
June 4/11/25/
July 2/9,
Louisiana Hayride

59

71

Mobile
June 29/30,
Radio Ranch
Club

Dallas
May 28,
Sportarium,
Big D Jamboree
May 29,
Sportarium, 8 p.m.
June 18, Sportarium,
Big D Jamboree

Biloxi
June 26, 8.00 p.m.
Slavonian Lodge
Auditorium

LOUISIANA

61

Keesler
June 27/28,
Air Force Base

De Leon
July 4, afternoon,
Hodges Park

Beaumont
June 20/21,
City Auditorium
five shows in total,
2,400 each show

Baton Rouge

90

New Orleans

TEXAS

Plaquemine
July 1, Casino Club

90

90

Houston

Houston
May 22, Magnolia Gardens afternoon,
Cook's Hoedown Club evening
June 19,
Magnolia Gardens, Texas Hayride, afternoon,
Cook's Hoedown Club evening

Elvis played some shows with Marty Robbins in June 1955, including a notable two-day stand in Beaumont, Texas. They sold out the City Auditorium for five straight shows, raising over $10,000 for the Fire Department. The ten acts reportedly got around $450 between them.

Corpus Christi
July 3, Hoedown Club
in South Lexington

Going with the Colonel

Live performances July to September 1955

The period from July to September 1955 saw a number of events that pushed Elvis on to greater glory, and that have become part of the Presley legend. In July, while in the middle of a supposed two-week vacation, Elvis once again went through the doors of 706 Union Avenue, Memphis, to lay down one of the greatest rock and roll tracks ever. In August, after weeks of fencing around, Elvis also signed a contract with Tom Parker, whereby the latter would act as his 'special adviser'. The contract tied Parker in to any future success Presley might have. This was the incentive Parker needed, and he set about plotting the singer's career with consummate skill. They were going places together.

"It was the greatest thing I ever did on Elvis. At the end Elvis was laughing because he didn't think it was a take, but I'm sorry, it was a masterpiece." Sam Phillips on the recording of 'Mystery Train' on July 11, 1955.

Elvis had been whipping up a storm on the road, and now it was time to follow that up with some recorded output. He owed it to Sam Phillips to get some songs that Sun could issue. Quite apart from record sales, he could reach much bigger audiences through radio than even the most successful tours would bring. But radio needed records.

A session was set up for July 11 with Scotty, Bill, and drummer Johnny Bernero. (Bernero worked at the Memphis Light, Gas, and Water Company across the street. If you look out from the present-day Sun Studio Cafe, you can see the old building with MLGW written above the gateway.) All of Elvis's Sun sessions were problematic. Once they had tasted the magic with 'That's All Right', they might expect to be able to re-create the formula. But that was the problem — there wasn't a formula. Each and every Presley record on Sun was achieved by practically starting from scratch. Although the ten recordings that were issued invented a whole new kind of music, they are all stylistically quite different from each other. This isn't surprising when you realize the different kinds of songs that they started with at each session.

At this July session they recorded a country ballad written for the occasion, a blues lament that Sam Phillips had previously recorded with Junior Parker and an old rhythm and blues hit that they'd made attempts at before — all with that unmistakable Sun sound. Of these, 'Mystery Train' was the masterpiece — Presley's voice floating over a driving hypnotic rhythm. 'Trying To Get To You' wasn't released at the time, though it is a wonderful take — the song ideally made for Presley's yearning vocal style. The Stan Kesler song 'I Forgot To Remember' is memorable for Elvis's vocal and the tear-drenched tone of

Scotty Moore's remarkable guitar break. After several months of playing almost every night, the band had honed their skills. They were, without question at the height of their musical powers.

After another week off, the trio went back on the road, and were back in Florida by the end of July. This time Elvis was an added attraction on the Andy Griffith Show tour. Griffith was a comedian with a huge national following, whose most recent record had sold half a million copies. Elvis was put on the tour as an 'Extra Attraction'.

Tours, July to September, 1955

➤ Local shows on the way to *Louisiana Hayride*: July 20, Cape Girardeau, to July 23, Shreveport.

➤ Florida Tour: July 25, Fort Myers, to July 31, Tampa. Elvis was a late addition to a tour by nationally popular comedian Andy Griffith. Also billed were Marty Robbins, Jimmy Farmer, Ferlin Huskey, Jimmie Rodgers Snow, Glenn Reeves. Tour arranged by Colonel Parker.

➤ Webb Pierce package tour: August 1, Tupelo, to August 5, Memphis. Pierce should have headlined, but Presley closed the show in Muscle Shoals, and possibly elsewhere. Bill included Johnny Cash and Wanda Jackson.

➤ Tour of east Texas: August 8, Tyler, to August 12, Kilgore. Support by Jim Ed and Maxine Brown. Booked through Tom Perryman of KSIJ Radio.

➤ Mid Texas Tour: August 22, Wichita Falls, to August 26, Gonzales. *Louisiana Hayride* package including Johnny Horton, Betty Amos.

➤ Jamborees: September 1, New Orleans Hillbilly Jamboree; September 2, Texarkana, with Johnny Cash, Charlene Arthur, Floyd Cramer; September 3, Big D Jamboree, Dallas.

➤ Package tour: September 5, Forrest City, to September 8, Clarksdale. Elvis headlined with support from Johnny Cash, Bud Deckelman and Eddie Bond, his old Memphis co-musician.

Wichita Falls
August 22,
Sudder Park baseball field
Stage on flat bed truck

Fort Worth

Stephenville

T E

X A

S

Waco

Brya
August 2.
Saddle Clu

Austin
August 25,
Sportcenter

Gonzales
August 26,
Baseball Park

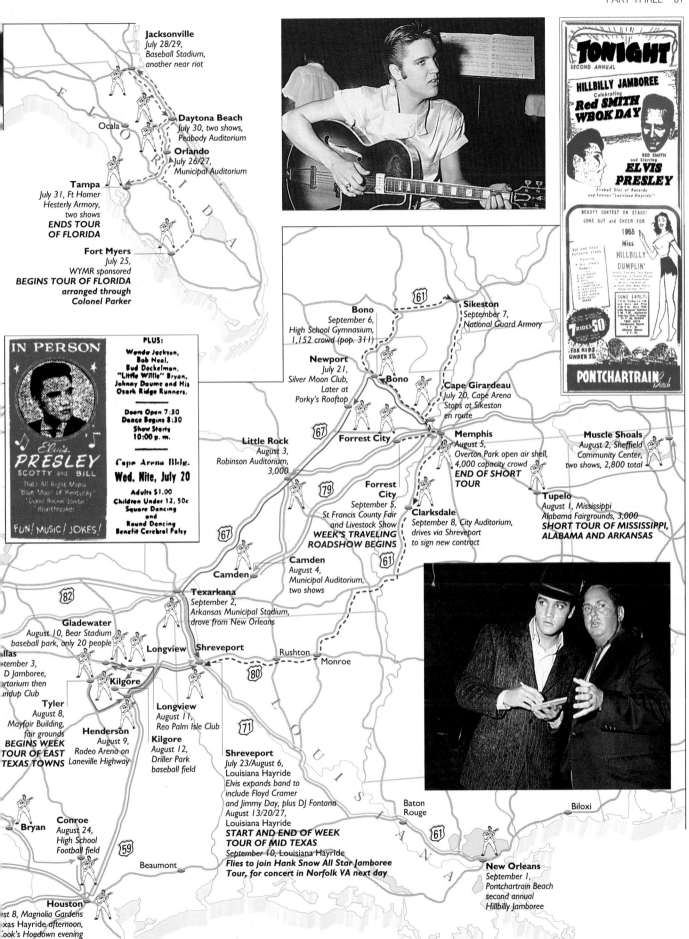

Jacksonville
July 28/29,
Baseball Stadium,
another near riot

Daytona Beach
July 30, two shows,
Peabody Auditorium

Ocala

Orlando
July 26/27,
Municipal Auditorium

Tampa
July 31, Ft Homer
Hesterly Armory,
two shows
**ENDS TOUR
OF FLORIDA**

Fort Myers
July 25,
WYMR sponsored
BEGINS TOUR OF FLORIDA
arranged through
Colonel Parker

IN PERSON

Elvis
PRESLEY
SCOTTY and BILL

Thats All Right Mama
"Blue Moon of Kentucky"
"Good Rockin' tonite"
Heartbreaker

FUN! MUSIC! JOKES!

PLUS:
Wanda Jackson,
Bob Neal,
Bud Deckelman,
"Little Willie" Bryan,
Johnny Daume and His
Ozark Ridge Runners.

Doors Open 7:30
Dance Begins 8:30
Show Starts
10:00 p. m.

Cape Arena Bldg.
Wed. Nite, July 20

Adults $1.00
Children Under 12, 50c
Square Dancing
and
Round Dancing
Benefit Cerebral Palsy

Bono
September 6,
High School Gymnasium,
1,152 crowd (pop. 311)

Sikeston
September 7,
National Guard Armory

Newport
July 21,
Silver Moon Club,
Later at
Porky's Rooftop

Bono

Cape Girardeau
July 20, Cape Arena
Stops at Sikeston
en route

Little Rock
August 3,
Robinson Auditorium,
3,000

Forrest City

Memphis
August 5,
Overton Park open air shell,
4,000 capacity crowd
**END OF SHORT
TOUR**

Muscle Shoals
August 2, Sheffield
Community Center,
two shows, 2,800 total

**Forrest
City**
September 5,
St Francis County Fair
and Livestock Show
**WEEK'S TRAVELING
ROADSHOW BEGINS**

Clarksdale
September 8, City Auditorium,
drives via Shreveport
to sign new contract

Tupelo
August 1, Mississippi
Alabama Fairgrounds, 3,000
**SHORT TOUR OF MISSISSIPPI,
ALABAMA AND ARKANSAS**

Camden
August 4,
Municipal Auditorium,
two shows

Texarkana
September 2,
Arkansas Municipal Stadium,
drove from New Orleans

Gladewater
August 10, Bear Stadium
baseball park, only 20 people

Longview

Shreveport

Rushton

Monroe

Dallas
September 3,
?D Jamboree,
?rtarium then
?undup Club

Kilgore

Tyler
August 8,
Mayfair Building,
fair grounds
**BEGINS WEEK
TOUR OF EAST
TEXAS TOWNS**

Henderson
August 9,
Rodeo Arena on
Laneville Highway

Longview
August 11,
Reo Palm Isle Club

Kilgore
August 12,
Driller Park
baseball field

Shreveport
July 23/August 6,
Louisiana Hayride
Elvis expands band to
include Floyd Cramer
and Jimmy Day, plus DJ Fontana
August 13/20/27,
Louisiana Hayride
**START AND END OF WEEK
TOUR OF MID TEXAS**
September 10, Louisiana Hayride
**Flies to join Hank Snow All Star Jamboree
Tour, for concert in Norfolk VA next day**

Baton
Rouge

Biloxi

Conroe
August 24,
High School
Football field

Bryan

Beaumont

New Orleans
September 1,
Pontchartrain Beach
second annual
Hillbilly Jamboree

Houston
?st 8, Magnolia Gardens
?xas Hayride afternoon,
?ook's Hoedown evening

Moving Out Of The Deep South

Concerts September to October, 1955

At first glance it may seem that Elvis was still grinding out the miles on the road, slowly but surely increasing his audience through personal appearances. But while he was treading the boards a much bigger game was being played out in the background. Colonel Tom Parker was intent on raising Presley's profile in the national music scene, so that the big record companies, RCA in particular, would come up with the cash needed to buy out his contract from Sun. The colonel got a big boost when Elvis played on equal billing with one of the country's biggest stars, Bill Haley, at a time when Presley hadn't yet had a single national hit record.

The Bill Haley/Elvis Presley concert was in Oklahoma City on October 16, 1955. The country's top rock and roll act shared billing with the nation's fastest rising young singer. It was a coup for Parker and within two weeks the Colonel was putting together the deal that would make popular music history, and take Presley on to the national stage.

In-between, Elvis went north to Cleveland again, to play on a pure country bill headed by Roy Acuff and Kitty Wells. While in Cleveland, Elvis, Scotty, and Bill performed at a special live show that was filmed for a short movie. Bill Randle, the local DJ, was involved once again, and Pat Boone, Bill Haley, and the Four Lads were also on the bill. A second concert was arranged but never took place, and the film was never issued. Randle apparently eventually sold the portion of the film showing Elvis for nearly $2 million in 1992, but it has mysteriously failed to surface since.

Back in Memphis, Sam Phillips at Sun was getting tired of Colonel Parker seeming to invite offers for a recording contract that he didn't own, and which Phillips had not formally put up for sale. Parker wasn't even officially Elvis's manager at this point, though few doubted that it was only a matter of time. Eventually Parker got Phillips to name the price that he would want for the remaining two years of Elvis's contract with Sun. He named $35,000, plus the $5,000 that he owed to Presley in back royalties. In late October, Parker managed to squeeze an offer of $25,000 out of RCA, and armed with that he came to Memphis on October 29 to haggle. Colonel Parker met Sam Phillips in

the Holiday Inn on South Third Street, next door to the studios of WHER, Phillips' new radio station. It is clear that the two men most influential in Elvis Presley's career did not get along at all well. Phillips disliked the deal-making and back-stabbing side of the music business, which was meat and drink to Parker. Parker probably aimed to bargain. Sam, however, did not lower his price. Instead Parker agreed to pay an unrefundable $5,000 for a month's option, to be taken up by December 1, 1955. The Colonel had, after weeks of talking Presley up to other people, put his own money on the table. Now he had some work to do to get it back.

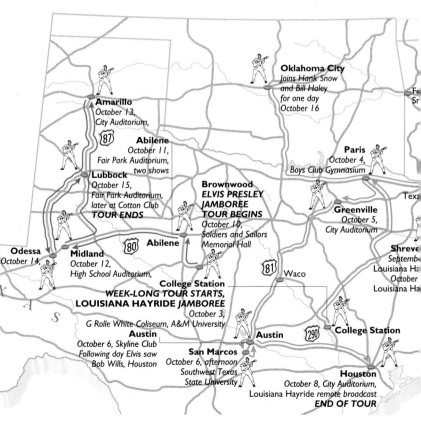

The poster (below right) shows Elvis as the extra added attraction to a Grand Ole Opry package in the country-loving northern city of Cleveland. Roy Acuff did more than almost anyone else to make the Opry into a national institution, and make Nashville the center for country music. Kitty Wells was billed as 'The Queen of Country Music'.

Concerts, September to October, 1955

➤ Hank Snow All-Star Jamboree tour: September 11, Norfolk, to September 22, Kingsport. Elvis headlined the package this time. Support included the Louvin Brothers, Alabama Sand Boys, Cowboy Copas, Hank Snow's Rainbow Ranch Boys.

➤ *Louisiana Hayride* Jamboree tour of Texas: October 3, College Station, to October 8, Houston. Presley topped the bill of a seven-act troupe including Jimmy and Johnny, Johnny Horton, Betty Amos.

➤ Elvis Presley Jamboree tour of west Texas: October 10, Brownwood, to October 15, Lubbock. Support included Johnny Cash, Floyd Cramer, Wanda Jackson, Jimmy Newman. Buddy Holly opened in Lubbock as part of Buddy and Bobby.

➤ October 16, Oklahoma City, to October 29, Shreveport. Variety of shows with Bill Haley (Oklahoma City), Roy Acuff and Kitty Wells (Cleveland) and the Greater Gulf States Fair (Prichard)

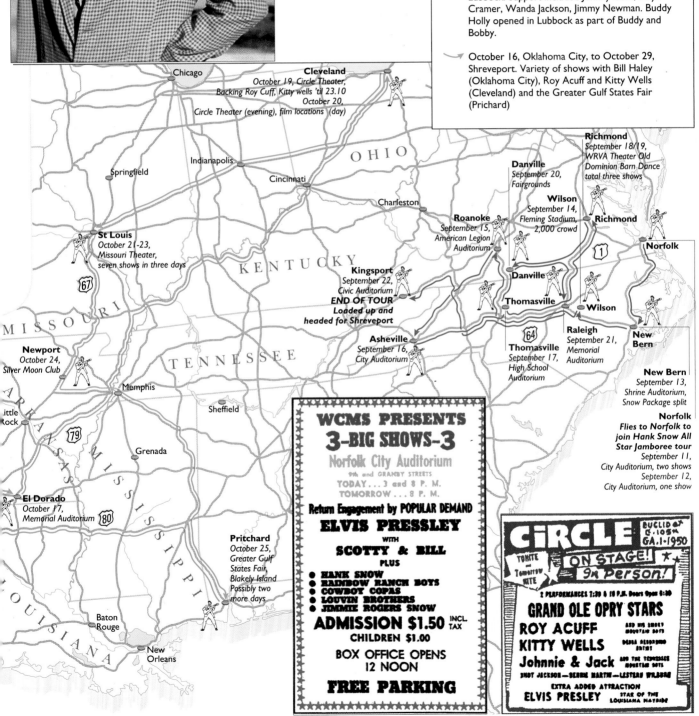

Last Of The Local Boy

Live shows from November 1955 to January 1956

In November 1955 it seems that everyone finally got what they wanted — well, almost everyone. Elvis wanted to record for a big record label, and he wanted a big-time manager. Now the record deal with RCA came through. The Colonel had won his gamble and at the same time he became Presley's full-time manager. Sam Phillips got enough money to pay off his debts and set Sun Records on course for some remarkable years to come. Only Bob Neal, Presley's manager until November 1955, was left out in the cold. But he had the grace to acknowledge that things had grown beyond his league. And then there was Scotty Moore and Bill Black. Without the patronage of Sam Phillips their position was uncertain. The men who had helped to create the Presley sound didn't figure too heavily in Colonel Parker's plans.

"By releasing his contract to RCA–Victor we will give Elvis the opportunity of entering the largest organization of its kind in the world, so his talents can be given the fullest opportunity."
Sam Phillips,
November 21, 1955.

In the midst of an ever more hectic touring program, two crucial events took place in this period of Presley's career. In late October Colonel Tom Parker, who was not yet Elvis's manager, had bought an option on his recording contract. Now he had to get RCA to come up with enough cash to take up the option — and he had to do it fast. At the start of November there was still a $10,000 gap between what RCA would pay and what Sam Phillips would accept.

A convention for DJs from all over the region was held in Nashville on November 10 and 11, 1955. It was a real music industry get-together, with regional record company reps showing their head office executives what a good job they were doing, and the DJs meeting up and swapping notes about records, musical trends and everything else. Tom Parker was there of course, and he made sure that Elvis attended, along with the right people from RCA. He wanted them to see for themselves what kind of impact Elvis was having on the music business in the South. This must have been an anxious time for Parker. RCA wasn't bidding against anyone else and Phillips wasn't going to lower his price.

Parker's strategy paid off and RCA bit the bullet and paid up. On November 21 the tiny Sun Records studio at 706 Union Avenue Memphis was full of men in suits and ties. Parker came with his right hand man Tom Diskin and Hank Snow. Steve Sholes, the head of RCA's Country and Western Division, came along with RCA's attorney and his regional distributor. Sam Phillips was there with Elvis, Gladys and Vernon Presley, and Bob Neal, still Elvis's manager at this time. As well as the deal between Sun and RCA, the

Colonel also executed a contract with publishers Hill and Range, whereby Elvis would automatically get a cut of the publishing rights of every song he recorded — as long as it came from them. Last but not least, Tom Parker became Elvis's manager, with Bob Neal finally bowing out of the picture. From January 1, 1956, Elvis Presley was an RCA recording artist and the most expensive buy in music business history.

The wisdom of the deal for Sam Phillips has often been questioned, but just as often been confirmed. Sun Records was badly in debt to the extent that he was unable to pay Elvis's back royalties. If he wanted to carry on he had to get some money from somewhere, and fast. He must have thanked the day that

he had had the wisdom to sign Elvis for three years, because this in the end saved his company. With the money he got for the Elvis contract, Phillips was able to look for other artists to develop, with the luxury of a little more time to work in. He was able to record Carl Perkins, Roy Orbison, Johnny Cash, and Jerry Lee Lewis all in the next two years. In the early days of the studio Sam, had recorded the track that is often described as the first rock and roll record — 'Rocket 88' by Jackie Brenston. In 1958 he recorded Jerry Lee's greatest ever track, 'Whole Lotta Shakin'. In between there were 'Mystery Train', 'Blue Suede Shoes' and 'I Walk The Line' and a whole lot of other classic cuts. While there were other great record producers around at the time, there wasn't anyone who worked with the variety of performers that Phillips did. His track record confirms his status as the greatest of all the record producers.

Live shows, November 1955 to January 1956

↱ Week-long circuit of east Texas and the South, November 5 to 12. Included non-singing appearance at DJ convention in Nashville (November 10, 11) and mill opening in Carthage, Texas, on November 12.

↱ Western Swing Jamboree tour: November 13, Memphis, to November 18, Longview, then remote broadcast for *Louisiana Hayride* from Gladewater on November 19. Elvis shared top billing with Hank Thompson and the Brazos Valley Boys. Charlene Arthur and Carl Perkins supported.

↱ Shows throughout Texas, the South and Indianapolis: November 25, Port Arthur, to December 19, Memphis. Included Hank Snow package in both Indianapolis and Louisville, and Talent Show in Montgomery, ending with a musical wrestling show at the Ellis Auditorium in Memphis.

↱ Week of shows from January 1, St Louis, to January 7, Shreveport. Then to Nashville for first RCA recording session.

By late 1955, Elvis was becoming a universally recognized figure. Life in his hometown of Memphis was changing, and as the pressure from fans increased he would find he had no alternative but to retreat further and further from them.

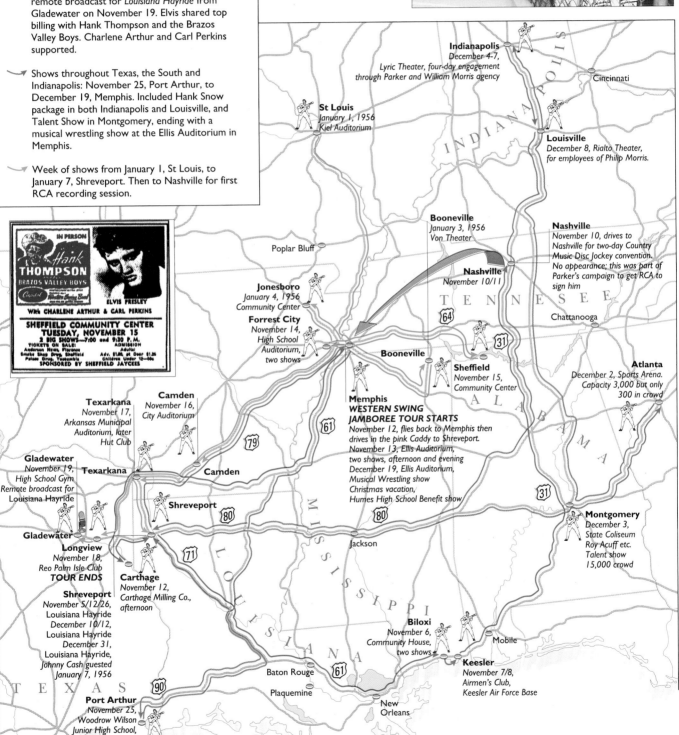

Chronology

July 1954–December 1955

1954

July 2	Funeral for two members of the Blackwood Brothers gospel quartet held in Ellis Auditorium.
July 4	At Sam Phillips' suggestion Elvis meets up with Scotty Moore and Bill Black at Scotty's home.
July 5	Elvis, Scotty and Bill record 'That's All Right' at the Sun studio.
July 8	'That's All Right' is played on radio WHBQ by Dewey Phillips.
July 9–11	Elvis, Scotty and Bill return to the studio to record 'Blue Moon Of Kentucky'
July 12	Scotty Moore becomes Elvis's official manager.
July 17	Elvis plays interval slot at Bon Air Club.
July 19	First Elvis Presley record, Sun Catalog No. 209, 'That's All Right'/'Blue Moon Of Kentucky' is released.
July 28	Interview with Elvis appears in Memphis Press-Scimitar.
July 30	First advertized appearance at Overton Park Shell.
Aug. 7	Billboard gives the Presley single a positive review. First of a string of shows at the Eagle's Nest club.
Aug. 8	Brief appearance on Doug Poindexter's KWEM radio show.
Aug. 18	Baseball benefit concert at Bellevue Park.
Aug. 29	Benefit show at Kennedy Hospital, Getwell Road
Sept. 9	Opening of Lamar-Airways Shopping Center. Trio play from back of a truck.
Sept. 10	Recording session produces 'Good Rockin' Tonight' and 'I Don't Care If The Sun Don't Shine'.
Sept. 27	Second single is released. 'Good Rockin' Tonight'/'I Don't Care If The Sun Don't Shine'.

Oct. 2	Only appearance on the Grand Ole Opry.
Oct. 8	Show at the Silver Slipper, Atlanta.
Oct. 16	First appearance on the Louisiana Hayride.
Nov. 6	Signs contract for regular appearances on the Louisiana Hayride.
Nov. 8	Memphis State University blood donation drive
Nov.	Quits work at Crown Electric to concentrate on singing career.
Nov. 21	Plays Texas Hayride and Cook's Hoedown Club, Houston
Nov. 22/23	Concerts in Gladewater, Texas
Nov. 25/26	Paladium Club, Houston
Dec.	Presleys move to 2414 Lamar Avenue, as Elvis begins to earn more.
Dec. 2	Trio play the Catholic Club, Helena, Arkansas
Dec. 20	Recording session produces 'Milkcow Blues Boogie' and 'You're A Heartbreaker'.
Dec. 28	Return to Houston, Cook's Hoedown Club

1955

Jan. 1	Bob Neal becomes Elvis's manager.
Jan. 4	Starts week's tour of west Texas.
Jan. 8	Third single released, 'Milkcow Blues Boogie'/You're A Heartbeaker'.
Jan. 12–21	'Louisiana Hayride' tour of region around Memphis.
Jan. 24–28	Tour of towns in east Texas, through KSIJ of Gladewater.
Feb. 5	Elvis, Scotty and Bill record 'Baby Let's Play House'.
Feb. 6	Plays Ellis Auditorium, Memphis. Meets Colonel Parker.
Feb. 10	Begins tour of west Texas and New Mexico.
Feb. 14	Joins Hank Snow package for Texas tour.
Feb. 20–25	'Grand Ole Opry' tour of

	Louisiana and Arkansas, co-promoted by Colonel Parker.
Feb. 26	The trio play the 'Circle Theater Jamboree' in Cleveland, Ohio.
Mar. 5	Trio record 'I'm Left, You're Right, She's Gone' with drummer Jimmie Lott.
Mar. 6–11	Tour of area west of Memphis.
Mar. 15	Elvis, Scotty and Bill fly to New York to audition for 'Arthur Godfrey's Talent Scouts' television show.
Mar. 19– Apr. 16	Shows in Texas, Arkansas, Mississippi and Louisisana.
Apr. 16	Elvis headlines Big D Jamboree in Dallas Sportarium.
Apr. 23	Remote broadcast for Louisiana Hayride from Waco in front of 5,000.
Apr. 30	Fourth single, 'Baby Let's Play House'/'I'm Left, You're Right, She's Gone' released.
May 1	Elvis, Scotty and Bill join Hank Snow Jamboree tour of Florida and the southeast. Promoted by Colonel Parker.
May 13	Crowd riot at Jacksonville, Florida when Elvis is mobbed by teenagers.
May 29– June 3	Tour of mid and west Texas.
June 20–30	Tour with Marty Robbins from Texas to Alabama.
July	Presleys move to rented house at 1414 Getwell Road in the eastern part of Memphis.
July 4	Triple header at Stephenville, De Leon and Brownwood, Texas.
July 11	Recording session at Sun produces 'Mystery Train', 'I Forgot To Remember To Forget' and 'Trying To Get To You'.
July 25–31	Tour of Florida as part of Andy Griffith package. Tour arranged by Colonel Parker.
Aug. 1–5	Webb Pierce package tour, Mississippi and Tennessee.
Aug. 5	Country jamboree at Overton Park Shell, Memphis.
Aug. 6	Fifth and final Sun single released, 'I Forgot To Remember To Forget'/ 'Mystery Train'.
Aug. 8–12	Tour of east Texas towns. Booked through KSIJ Radio.
Aug. 15	Elvis signs Colonel Parker as a 'Special Adviser'.
Aug. 22–26	Tour of mid Texas, Louisiana Hayride package.
Sept. 1	New Orleans Hillbilly Jamboree
Sept. 3	Big D Jamboree, Dallas.
Sept. 5–8	Local tour with Johnny Cash among support
Sept. 11–22	Hank Snow All-Star Jamboree tour of east coast states.
Oct. 3–8	Louisiana Hayride Jamboree tour of Texas.
Oct. 10–15	Elvis Presley Jamboree tour of west Texas.
Oct. 16	Plays on bill with Bill Haley, currently the nation's most poular act, in Oklahoma City.
Oct. 19	Plays on bill with Roy Acuff and Kitty Wells in Cleveland.
Oct. 20	Plays in scenes for rock and roll film in Cleveland. Film has never been seen.
Oct. 29	Tom Parker and Sam Phillips meet to agree terms for selling of Elvis's recording contract to RCA.
Nov. 5–9	Circuit of east Texas and the South.
Nov. 10–11	Attends Country Music Disc Jockey Convention, Nashville.
Nov. 13–18	Western Swing Jamboree tour, Arkansas.
Nov. 21	Triple contract signing in Memphis: Colonel Parker becomes Elvis's manager, RCA buys his recording contract, effective January 1, 1956, and Hill and Range give him a cut of publishing rights in exchange for exclusivity of material.
Nov. 25 to Dec.	Shows throughout Texas, the South and Indianapolis
Dec. 2	RCA re-release 'I Fogot To Remember To Forget'/ 'Mystery Train'.
Dec. 19	Plays in musical introduction wrestling show at the Ellis Auditorium, Memphis.

Part Four: THE WORLD CAPITULATES
– RCA, TELEVISION AND THE MOVIES, 1956–1958

"I wasn't known at all until Colonel Parker started managing me, and then I got on RCA Victor and on television. I was known in certain sections, but I wasn't known all over."

"Singing rhythm and blues really knocks it out. I watch my audiences and I listen to them and I know that we're all getting something out of our system but none of us knows what it is."

"People want to know why I can't stand still while I'm singing. Some people tap their feet, some people snap their fingers, and some people just sway back and forth. I just started doing them all together, I guess."

"Everything is going so fine for me that I can't believe it's not a dream. I hope I never wake up."

"I'm afraid to wake up each morning. I can't believe all this has happened to me. I just hope it lasts."

"When I sang hymns back home with Mom and Pop, I stood still and I looked like you feel when you sing a hymn. When I sing this rock and roll, my eyes won't stay open and my legs won't stand still. I don't care what they say, it ain't nasty."

"Rock and roll music if you like it, you can't help but move to it. That's what happens to me. I can't help it."

"I've been blamed for just about everything wrong in this country."

"I don't see that any type of music would have a bad influence on people. It's only music. I can't figure it out. In a lot of the papers they say rock and roll is a big influence on juvenile delinquency. I don't think that it is, juvenile delinquency is something, I don't know how to explain it, but I don't see how music has anything to do with it at all."

"I've been scratched and bitten. I just accept it with a broad mind because actually they don't intend to hurt you. They want pieces of you for souvenirs."

"Besides records and personal appearances I'm looking forward to making a movie. I took a screen test and Paramount Picture signed me to a contract. I may make a picture before the end of the year."

"Touring is the roughest part. It's really rough. You're in a town, you do a show, you come off, you ride in a car, you go on to the next town. I get all keyed up after a show. It's hard to relax."

Introduction

In the 27 months between signing up with RCA records on January 1, 1956 and going into the Army in March 1958, Elvis was the most famous singer America and the world had ever seen. The shy, polite, god-fearing boy from Tennessee became a symbol of sexual license and rebellion for most of the world's youth. In the first 18 months of his career, from July 1954 to the end of 1955, he had played hundreds of shows and released five singles. But virtually all of his shows had been in Texas and the South, while not one of his records had made it onto a national chart. Nevertheless he had taken the South by storm — and musically he had learned enough to know what he was going to do next.

In the years at Sun Elvis had been guided by Sam Philips in his choice of material and in the kind of sound they both wanted to create. Elvis's achievement in the next two years was not simply to go out and do the same thing virtually on his own, but to go one step further. What Elvis did at RCA was to take the bluesy rockabilly sound that he and Sam Phillips, together with Scotty Moore and Bill Black, had created at Sun and turn it into commercial dynamite. When he went to RCA there was absolutely no guarantee that he was going to be able to do that, and whatever is said about Sam Phillips discovering Elvis, tracks like 'Heartbreak Hotel', 'Hound Dog' and 'All Shook Up' are the product of Elvis's musical vision. In the end it was Elvis who made rock and roll a commercial goldmine — by his sexuality, by his performances, but mostly by his extraordinary musical gifts and judgement.

The fifties was the decade America discovered television. Before the fifties the only way you got to see someone performing was to go to a show, or see them on the movies. Movie stars were therefore the giants of the entertainment world. But television caught up fast. By 1956 most people could get to see a television program if they wanted, and in September eighty per cent of viewers tuned in to see Elvis on the *Ed Sullivan Show* — the biggest TV audience in history at the time. Television made Elvis a national star in 1956. But he didn't repay the compliment. Once he'd done everything that TV could offer, he went off to do what he really wanted — to be a movie star.

The four movies Elvis made before he went into the Army contain his best work, but the best moments in them are the musical set pieces. Elvis idolized the power that Marlon Brando and James Dean projected just, it seemed, by being on the screen. But both actors had undergone training and coaching to perfect their craft, and had Elvis done the same he might have made a better show of it. However admirable the early movies are, it's the music that matters.

In 1956 something happened to change Elvis's relationship with the world. At a definable point, newspapers stopped calling him Elvis Presley or Presley and he became simply 'Elvis'. Though this brought him a rare closeness to his fans, had he remained 'Presley', the world might have taken his movies more seriously.

The Other Music City

Nashville and the recording of 'Heartbreak Hotel', January 1956

Memphis and Nashville share the same state and the same obsession with music, but little else. In Memphis the music grows out of the life of the city. But Nashville is where the music industry rules. Elvis had first come to the self–proclaimed home of country music as a promising young singer in October 1954. He was politely but coolly received by both audience and management at the Grand Ole Opry back then, and felt he had been rejected by the country music industry. Now here he was, fifteen months later, the hottest thing in showbusiness. RCA brought their new singer to Nashville in the hope that the surroundings would be more familiar than a New York studio. But Nashville wasn't going to be any easier this time than it was back in 1954.

Elvis's first recording session for RCA took place at the company's old studio on McGavock Street, which they rented from the Methodist TV and Radio Commission. This was Elvis, Scotty and Bill's first try at recording outside of the Sun studio, and their first time without the reassuring presence of Sam Phillips behind the controls. And that expensive signing fee carried with it a lot of responsibility. How were they going to start to pay back what RCA had paid out?

It's worth remembering that even at this apparently triumphant stage of Elvis's career, there were a lot of doubts about the wisdom of RCA's decision to take him on. Quite apart from the young singer's own career prospects, the recording industry still wasn't sure whether rock and roll was going to be any more than a passing phase. And then there was the studio work. Was the industry giant RCA, with studios full of the latest and best equipment, going to be able to capture the Presley magic in the same way that Sun had? There was even talk of hiring Sam Phillips to produce Elvis for RCA. When news of this filtered through to Phillips he put it down to nerves on RCA's part and urged them to relax. He told Steve Sholes from RCA to just let Elvis be what he was, not to force him into some pre–determined role. The advice was sound, though to Sholes it must have sounded frustratingly vague. To make things worse Sam Phillips had just issued Sun's most successful single to date — Carl Perkins' 'Blue Suede Shoes'. Its combination of rock and roll vitality and commercial sound was exactly what RCA was looking for from Elvis.

The musicians at the Nashville session were Elvis, Scotty and Bill, with DJ Fontana on drums and Floyd Cramer on piano. Chet Atkins, legendary country guitarist and RCA's man in Nashville, had arranged the session, and played rhythm guitar. The players assembled in the early afternoon — an unusual and not especially relaxing time for a recording session. Everyone was edgy at the start of the proceedings – Sholes and Chet Atkins just as much as Elvis's regular band. According to reports, Elvis himself was perfectly at ease. Once the band got warmed up, they went into Ray Charles' 'I Got A Woman', and the tension fell away. An indication of how things were going comes from Chet Atkins. He said that between takes he went out and called his wife to come down to the studio 'Because it

Nashville Locations
Though Elvis was very definitely a Memphis man, he visited Nashville frequently, and recorded here throughout his career from 1956 onwards. In 1956 RCA rented studio space in a building on McGavock Street. On Elvis's return from the army he first recorded at RCA's new Studio B on March 20, 1960. He continued to record here throughout the rest of his career.
In 1954 Elvis played the Grand Ole Opry in the Ryman Auditorium, staying over for the Midnight Jamboree at Ernst Tubb's record store on Broadway. He visited backstage at the Grand Ole Opry on December 21, 1957. Nashville is now full of music memorabilia. The Car Collector's Hall Of Fame has an Elvis Cadillac, while the Country Music Hall Of Fame goes one better and has his one and only gold Cadillac.

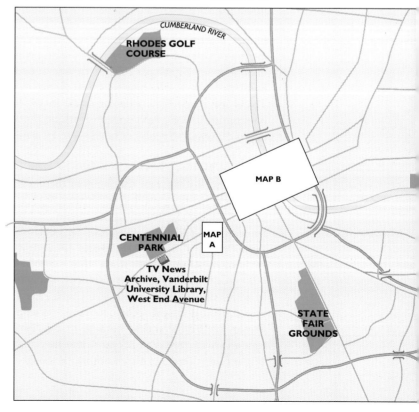

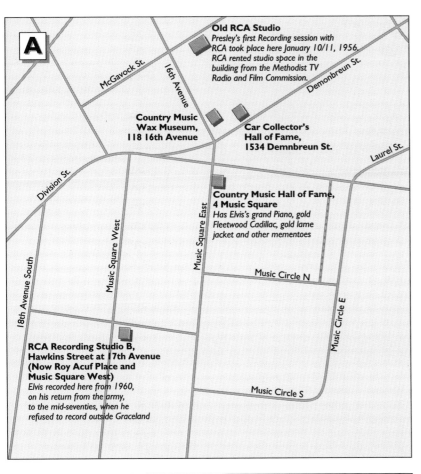

A

Old RCA Studio
Presley's first Recording session with RCA took place here January 10/11, 1956. RCA rented studio space in the building from the Methodist TV Radio and Film Commission.

McGavock St.

16th Avenue

Demonbreun St.

Country Music Wax Museum, 118 16th Avenue

Car Collector's Hall of Fame, 1534 Demnbreun St.

Laurel St.

Division St.

Music Square West

Music Square East

Country Music Hall of Fame, 4 Music Square
Has Elvis's grand Piano, gold Fleetwood Cadillac, gold lame jacket and other mementoes

Music Circle N

18th Avenue South

Music Circle E

RCA Recording Studio B, Hawkins Street at 17th Avenue (Now Roy Acuf Place and Music Square West)
Elvis recorded here from 1960, on his return from the army, to the mid-seventies, when he refused to record outside Graceland

Music Circle S

Grand Ole Opry
The most famous radio show in America came about after its originator, George Dewey Hay visited a hoedown and decided to capture and broadcast a similar atmosphere. He moved to Nashville from Chicago to work for WSM, where he started the Opry. In 1941 the show moved to the Ryman Auditorium (below) where it remained until 1972.

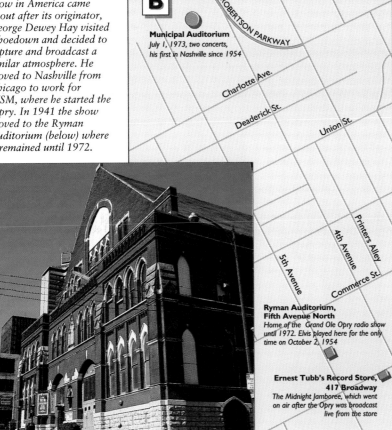

B

JAMES ROBERTSON PARKWAY

Municipal Auditorium
July 1, 1973, two concerts, his first in Nashville since 1954

Charlotte Ave.

Deaderick St.

Union St.

Printers Alley

4th Avenue

5th Avenue

Commerce St.

Ryman Auditorium, Fifth Avenue North
Home of the Grand Ole Opry radio show until 1972. Elvis played here for the only time on October 2, 1954

Ernest Tubb's Record Store, 417 Broadway
The Midnight Jamboree, which went on air after the Opry was broadcast live from the store

was so damned exciting.' It appears that Nashville hadn't seen anything quite like Elvis and his band in full swing. Everyone was happy with their treatment of 'I Got A Woman', but Steve Sholes was after something more commercial than the bluesy rocker for Elvis's first RCA single.

The previous November Elvis had been in Nashville for a DJ convention. Mae Axton, Tom Parker's north Florida publicist who had got to know Elvis pretty well, was also in town. One afternoon she went up to Elvis's hotel room and played him the demo of a song she'd just written especially for him. She and Tommy Durden got the inspiration for it after reading a newspaper report of a suicide case. The man had left a note saying 'I walk a lonely street.' They turned that one unforgettable phrase into 'Heartbreak Hotel'.

Elvis was hooked by the strange mournful quality of the lyric and the melody. He told Mae he was going to record the song. Two months later he kept his promise. Steve Sholes and RCA were unsure about 'Heartbreak Hotel' at first. It was unlike anything Elvis had previously recorded. The sound was muddy and unclear. How would Presley's teenage audience take its morbid sentiments? In fact, despite the musicians' eventual enjoyment, the session had not been an obvious success for Sholes and RCA. He returned to New York with a rock and roll cover, a muddy depressing blues, and a straight ballad. 'Heartbreak Hotel' went to Number One on the nation's pop, blues and country charts and sold a million copies in the first eight weeks. Elvis's musical instincts were once again exactly in tune with his audience.

Slapback and reverb

One of the things that Steve Sholes had realized was the need to get some of the reverb or slapback, that so characterized Elvis's Sun sound, into the RCA mix. Sam Phillips had achieved this by relaying the track between two tape players after it had been recorded. The RCA engineers rigged up a system where a mike and amp stood at opposite ends of the outside corridor of the McGavock Street studio. The sound was then fed back into the room, so that the reverb was created as the musicians were playing. The resulting sound has the echo of the Sun sound, but loses the crispness of the treble notes. Contrast the muddy, though atmospheric, sound of RCA's 'Heartbreak Hotel', with the clear but impressively deep sound of Sun's 'I'm Left, You're Right, She's Gone'.

Bright Lights, Big City

TV Shows and Hound Dogs, New York 1956

1956 was the year that saw Elvis turn from a Southern phenomenon into a national and then international star. This was done principally through the medium of television. New York was the center of American TV. All the major networks were based there, as were the major power brokers. New York was also the center of the recording industry, and it was in New York in 1956 that Elvis recorded the tracks for RCA that established him as the major musical force in America. Elvis's first 1956 visit to New York was also the last time he was able to walk the streets of a major city without being recognized. It was his last taste of freedom in a town he didn't return to until 1972 when he broke the attendance record at Madison Square Garden.

The trip to New York was symbolic. Elvis, the Hillbilly Cat, had paid his dues playing around the Southern States, building up a following. And now here he was storming the barricades of the entertainment establishment. Many of them weren't happy about having him on TV, but his overwhelming popularity forced even the reluctant Ed Sullivan to book him on his show.

His first six national TV appearances were on *Stage Show* a CBS–TV variety show hosted by the Dorsey Brothers. The shows went out opposite the Perry Como Show, and got 20 per cent of the national TV audience in January and February 1956. In contrast Elvis's first Ed Sullivan show, broadcast on October 28 was watched by an audience of 80 per cent — a staggering 43 million people. Elvis was by then the biggest thing ever to hit the American music business.

Elvis would visit New York only twice more, to join his army ship bound for Germany and to play Madison Square Garden in 1972.

New York City Locations

Warwick Hotel, 65 West 54th Street.
This was the base for the trips to New York in 1956. Elvis first stayed here on January 28, the night of his first national TV appearance.

CBS Studio 50 (*now* **Ed Sullivan Theater**), 1697 Broadway (between 53 & 54th St).
Stage Show the variety show hosted by the Dorsey Brothers was broadcast live from this studio at prime time on Saturday evenings.

RCA Studios, 155 East 24th Street.
Elvis first recorded here on January 30, 1956. This was his second session for RCA having cut 'Heartbreak Hotel' in Nashville on January 10 and 11. Tracks recorded in the first session included 'Blue Suede Shoes', 'My Baby Left Me' and 'Tutti Frutti'. Elvis returned here on July 2 to record 'Hound Dog', 'Don't Be Cruel' and 'Anyway You Want Me'. The studio was in RCA's New York headquarters building.

Hudson Theater, 44th Street.
The *Steve Allen Show*, broadcast live on July 1, 1956 was transmitted from this midtown Manhattan theater.

Maxine Elliott Theater, 39th Street.
Site of the broadcast of the *Ed Sullivan Show* on October 28, 1956. This was Elvis's second appearance on the show, though his first from New York.

"We'd like at this time to introduce you to a young fellow who, like many performers came out of nowhere to be an overnight big star. This young fellow we saw for the first time while making a movie short. We think tonight he's going to make television history for you. We'd like you to meet him now — Elvis Presley."
Bill Randle introducing Elvis's first television appearance on *Stage Show*, January 28, 1956.

Elvis's acoustic guitar and Bill Black's slap bass looked out of place in a TV studio, where orchestras were the standard fare. But once they got started that didn't worry them – or the audience.

Paramount Theater, Broadway and 43rd Street.
Elvis's first film, *Love Me Tender*, was premiered here on November 16, 1956.
Penn Station, 7th Avenue and 31st Street.
Elvis liked to travel by train whenever possible. The old Penn station was his point of entry to and exit from New York City in 1956.
National Foundation for Infantile Paralysis, 120 Broadway.
Elvis recorded an interview for the annual charity event the 'March Of Dimes'. The interview was issued as part of a disc for use by radio stations.

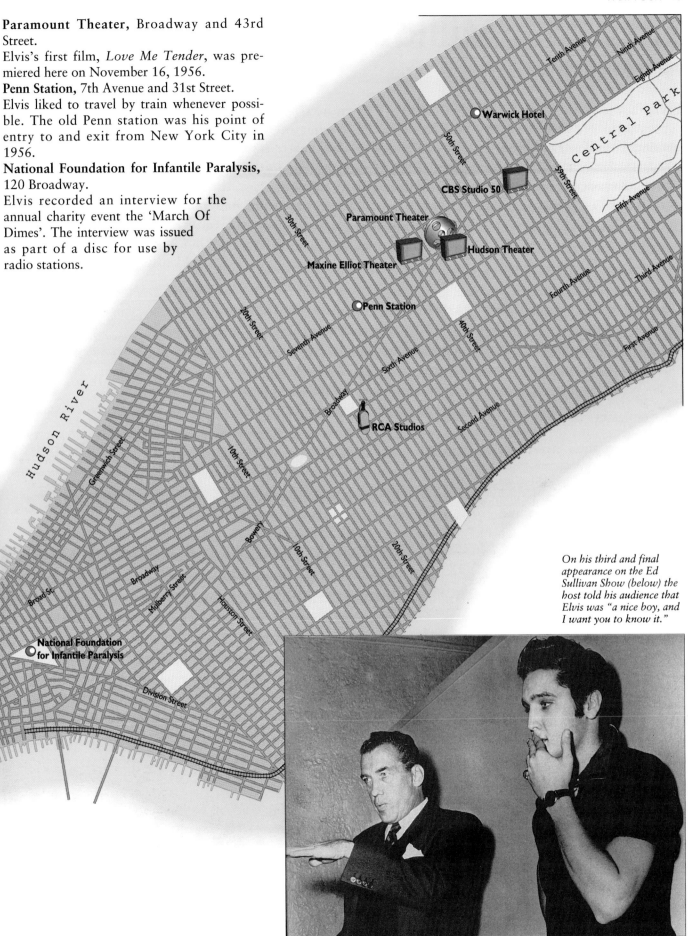

On his third and final appearance on the Ed Sullivan Show (below) the host told his audience that Elvis was "a nice boy, and I want you to know it."

Fifty Four Million Fans Coast To Coast

The explosion in TV audiences

Elvis first played to a truly national audience when he stood on the stage of the CBS studio on Broadway on January 28, 1956. That night he was seen by around 13 million people — more than he could ever play to in a lifetime of live concerts. But that was just the beginning. Although his initial run on *Stage Show* saw only a modest increase in the audience figures, over the next few months Elvis became the biggest draw that American television had ever seen. After appearances on the Milton Berle and Steve Allen shows, Elvis made it onto the top slot — the *Ed Sullivan Show*. His first appearance drew an audience share of over eighty per cent, with an estimated viewing public of 43 million — the biggest audience in television history at that time.

There are lots of reasons why there will never be anyone quite like Elvis ever again, but technology certainly has something to do with it. Elvis came at a very particular time in technological development, which allowed him first to be heard across a wide stretch of the country, and then to be seen performing live by audiences undreamed of by singers from previous decades.

Radio had given Elvis his first big break. As soon as he got a contract to appear weekly on the Louisiana Hayride he was able to turn professional. Apart from the money, the radio show gave him exposure and promotion. There were around 100 million radio sets in use in the US in the mid-fifties.

Then there were changes in the record industry. In Elvis's early days at Sun and then RCA his singles were released as 78s. But RCA had been experimenting for some time with a new smaller format — a seven-inch disc that was played at 45 rpm. The new format was much cheaper to produce, and therefore cheaper for customers to buy. The 45 started to take over from 78s at the height of Elvis's popularity. And at the same time cheap electric record players were coming on to the market, putting record collecting in reach of millions of households. In addition to all this the 1950s were the most prosperous in American history. Though there was still poverty, there was plenty of work, with good wages and an abundance of cheap manufactured goods. The fact that a relatively poor working man like Vernon Presley was able to buy his seventeen year old son a used car, says something about the realities and expectations of Americans in the fifties. This widespread prosperity affected the young generation more than anyone. They had money to

spend, and wanted new things to buy.

Of all the technological changes to sweep the country in the fifties, television was the most pervasive. In 1950 around ten per cent of homes had a television set; by 1960 the figure was eighty-five per cent. Though each major city had, and still has, its own local station, the key to success was to join one of the national networks. The growth of the three television networks gave the country a nationally shared popular entertainment, and made TV stars like Lucille Ball as big as the Hollywood idols of the forties.

But the content of fifties television was a reflection of the conservatism of the times. Because the entertainment was designed to cater for the widest possible audience it was generally bland and unchallenging. The sponsors of the shows also had a strong influence over the content, blocking anything that might cause offense. In the same way he had stormed through the school halls and music clubs of the South, Elvis erupted onto this comfortable scene like a volcano. Over on

Television ratings
For his appearances on 'Stage Show' in January, February and March of 1956, Elvis attracted around 20 per cent of the viewing audience. He wasn't a nationally known figure at this time, and his appearances did little to alter the decline of the show, which was seen as outdated in its concept. Its hosts, the Dorsey Brothers had passed their peak of popularity in the forties. Milton Berle was more in tune with Elvis, and by the time Elvis appeared on his show 'Heartbreak Hotel' had topped every chart in the country. You would have had to be from Mars not to know who Elvis was. The second Berle show caused a storm of controversy after Elvis performed the last verse of 'Hound Dog' at half-pace but with full throttle. That must have pepped up the audience for the record-breaking 'Ed Sullivan show' on September 9.

1956

January 28th,
Stage Show,
New York
Rating: 18.4%
(Perry Como 34.6%)

February 4th,
Stage Show,
New York
Rating: 18.2%
(Perry Como 38.4%)

February 11th,
Stage Show,
New York

February 18th,
Stage Show,
New York

Ed Sullivan hadn't wanted Elvis on his show, but the success of the Steve Allen Show *worried Sullivan deeply. He called Colonel Parker immediately after that broadcast and fixed a deal. Sullivan wasn't present at the first show, which was hosted by Charles Laughton from the CBS Los Angeles studios. Elvis's third and final appearance was on January 6, 1957.*

NBC Perry Como strolled down a curved staircase, crooning to the strains of an off camera orchestra. While on CBS, Elvis came at the camera like a tornado with a bad attitude. With unkempt greasy hair that kept falling over a face heavy with eye make-up, long sideburns and a parody of a coat, shirt and tie, Elvis looked like every parent's vision of the youth from hell. But more than that was his posture, his singing and his movements — oh, his movements.

For his first appearance Elvis chose not to sing his RCA single 'Heartbreak Hotel'. Instead he went into a jittery version of Joe Turner's 'Shake Rattle and Roll' that segued into 'Flip, Flop And Fly'. If anyone ever doubted where Elvis was coming from, now they knew. Respectable white musicians like Bill Haley had already scored hits with toned down versions of black rhythm and blues songs. But here was a white boy, looking very unrespectable, and goosing the songs up for all he was worth.

In the next few months he was to perform material as diverse as 'Tutti Frutti' and 'Peace In The Valley'. The range of his influences and material was demonstrated on television, and by bringing such a diversity of American musical styles into the mainstream, he changed popular music forever.

March 17th,
Stage Show,
New York

March 24th,
Stage Show,
New York
Rating: 20.9%
(Perry Como 30.1%)

April 3rd,
Milton Berle, San Diego
Rating: 30%

June 5th,
Milton Berle, LA
Rating 30% plus

September 9th,
Ed Sullivan Show, LA
Rating: 82.6%, 54 million audience.
Biggest ever for a variety show at that time.

September 28th,
Ed Sullivan Show, NY
Rating: 80%

Back On The Road

Tours of the east coast states, February 1956

The first months of 1956 might have been designed to test any group of musicians to destruction. Having completed a potentially disastrous, but ultimately triumphant first recording session for RCA, Elvis, Scotty and Bill headed off for Texas, via the Louisiana Hayride at Shreveport. After driving around 2,500 miles in 8 days, they flew to New York for the all-important television debut. Further TV shows in February were fitted in between tours of the east coast. These involved playing two or three shows a night before driving on to another town. The weather was bad, and the crowds were often hysterical. Some of the other musicians on the tours were getting jealous of the success of the boy wonder. All that was exhausting enough, but then every Saturday they drove or flew back up to New York to do another TV show. Where, they must have wondered, was it all going to lead?

"It's all happening so fast, there's so much happening to me that some nights I just can't fall asleep. It scares me you know, it just scares me."
Elvis Presley, 1956

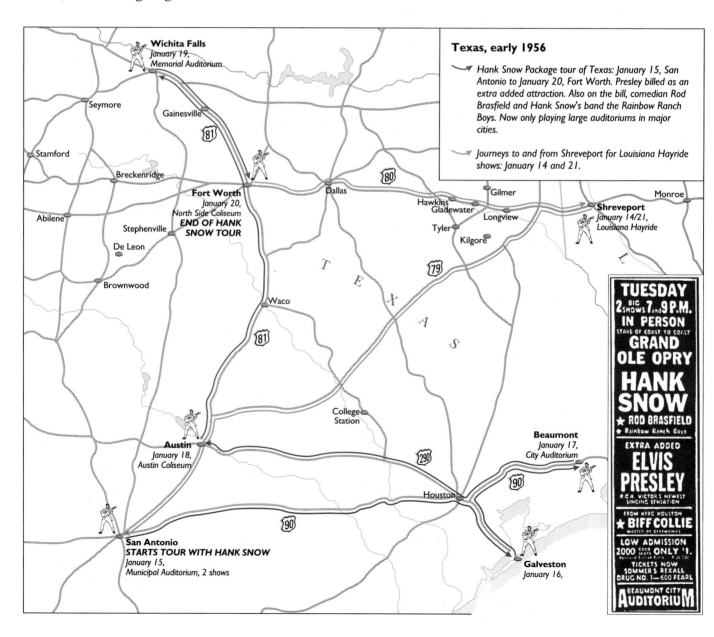

Wichita Falls
January 19,
Memorial Auditorium

Seymore

Gainesville

Stamford

Breckenridge

Fort Worth
January 20,
North Side Coliseum
END OF HANK SNOW TOUR

Abilene

Stephenville

De Leon

Brownwood

Waco

Dallas

Hawkins
Gladewater

Tyler

Kilgore

Gilmer

Longview

Monroe

Shreveport
January 14/21,
Louisiana Hayride

T E X A S

College
Station

Austin
January 18,
Austin Coliseum

Beaumont
January 17,
City Auditorium

Houston

San Antonio
STARTS TOUR WITH HANK SNOW
January 15,
Municipal Auditorium, 2 shows

Galveston
January 16,

Texas, early 1956

Hank Snow Package tour of Texas: January 15, San Antonio to January 20, Fort Worth. Presley billed as an extra added attraction. Also on the bill, comedian Rod Brasfield and Hank Snow's band the Rainbow Ranch Boys. Now only playing large auditoriums in major cities.

Journeys to and from Shreveport for Louisiana Hayride shows: January 14 and 21.

TUESDAY
2 BIG SHOWS 7 and 9 P.M.
IN PERSON
STARS OF COAST TO COAST
GRAND OLE OPRY
HANK SNOW
★ ROD BRASFIELD
★ Rainbow Ranch Boys
EXTRA ADDED
ELVIS PRESLEY
R.C.A. VICTOR'S NEWEST SINGING SENSATION
FROM KPRC HOUSTON
★ BIFF COLLIE
MASTER OF CEREMONIES
LOW ADMISSION
2000 GOOD SEATS ONLY $1.
TICKETS NOW
SOMMER'S REXALL
DRUG NO. 1— 600 PEARL
BEAUMONT CITY
AUDITORIUM

Over the next couple of years, which saw most of Presley's best selling releases, RCA's biggest worry was getting him off the road or off the movie set, and into the recording studio. The relationship between Steve Sholes, head of RCA's Country and Western division and Colonel Parker started badly and remained that way. Parker knew that Sholes needed Elvis's product, and Parker controlled that product. For a man like Sholes it was a humiliating position to be in, and one that was exploited by Parker. Sholes had to plead for time to be allowed in Elvis's schedule for recording. Parker wasn't stupid, he knew that Elvis had to release records to keep his fans happy, and to keep making money, but he just loved to keep everyone on edge.

To start with, Sholes re-released all of Presley's Sun singles on RCA. Their biggest success was 'I Forgot To Remember To Forget' which reached Number One on Billboard's Country and Western Singles Chart on February 15, 1956, giving Elvis his first Number One record on any national chart. By that time RCA had released the first single Elvis had actually recorded with them. On January 27, 1956 'Heartbreak Hotel' hit the nation's record stores and juke boxes. By March 7 it was on top of the Country and Western Chart where it stayed for 17 weeks. It reached Number One on the Billboard Singles Chart on April 25, and stayed there for seven weeks.

The trouble with touring

The tours of the east coast states were set up so that Elvis, together with Scotty and Bill, would be able to get back to New York for their Saturday night TV shows. But this reckoned without the vagaries of the northeastern winter. On February 11, Elvis drove the 500 miles from Charlotte, North Carolina to New York. On the way they hit a snow storm, which ought to have prevented the journey. They carried on though and Elvis made the TV studio minutes before the broadcast of Stage Show started. The next week a plane was hired to fly Elvis, Scotty and Bill from Winston-Salem to New York. Elvis wasn't to escape difficulties by flying though. In April the band nearly crashed when a charter plane stalled after take off from El Dorado, Arkansas. In March 1956 Carl Perkins was nearly killed in an auto crash in similar circumstances — the driver fell asleep while driving through the night to New York for a TV appearance. Showbusiness was getting dangerous.

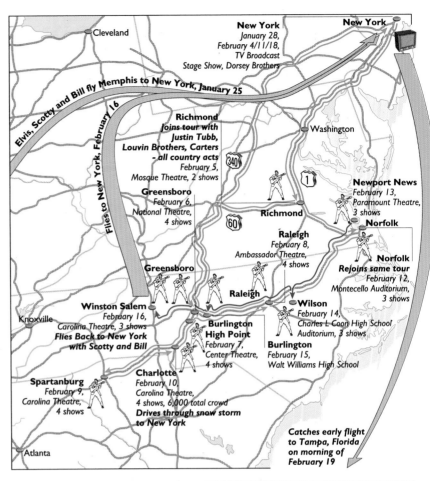

New York
January 28,
February 4/11/18,
TV Broadcast
Stage Show, Dorsey Brothers

Elvis, Scotty and Bill fly Memphis to New York, January 25

Flies to New York, February 16

Richmond
*Joins tour with
Justin Tubb,
Louvin Brothers, Carters
– all country acts*
February 5,
Mosque Theatre, 2 shows

Greensboro
February 6,
National Theatre,
4 shows

Raleigh
February 8,
Ambassador Theatre,
4 shows

Newport News
February 13,
Paramount Theatre,
3 shows

Norfolk
Rejoins same tour
February 12,
Montecello Auditorium,
3 shows

Winston Salem
February 16,
Carolina Theatre, 3 shows
*Flies Back to New York
with Scotty and Bill*

**Burlington
High Point**
February 7,
Center Theatre,
4 shows

Wilson
February 14,
Charles L Coon High School
Auditorium, 3 shows

Burlington
February 15,
Walt Williams High School

Spartanburg
February 9,
Carolina Theatre,
4 shows

Charlotte
February 10,
Carolina Theatre,
4 shows, 6,000 total crowd
*Drives through snow storm
to New York*

**Catches early flight
to Tampa, Florida
on morning of
February 19**

Cleveland Washington Knoxville Atlanta

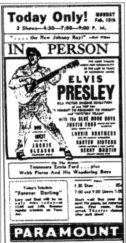

Today Only! MONDAY Feb. 13th
3 Shows—4:30—7:00—9:00 P. M.

"...the New Johnny Ray!"—Les' Wren

IN PERSON

ELVIS
PRESLEY
RCA VICTOR SINGING SENSATION

"I FORGOT TO REMEMBER TO FORGET" and "MYSTERY TRAIN"
with the BLUE MOON BOYS
JUSTIN TUBB
LOUVIN BROTHERS
CARTER SISTERS
BENNY MARTIN

Tennessee Ernie Ford ... plus
Webb Pierce And His Wandering Boys

Today's Schedule
"Forever Darling"

PARAMOUNT

East coast states, February 1956

⤻ Tour of Virginia and Carolinas: February 5, Richmond to February 10, Charlotte. Elvis headed a bill which included Justin Tubb (son of Ernest), the Louvin Brothers and Mother Maybelle and the Carter Sisters.

⤻ Continuation of east coast tour: February 12, Norfolk to February 16, Winston-Salem.

Elvis, Scotty and Bill did get to play Texas, on a Hank Snow package, but for most of early 1956 they were tied to the east coast by their six contracted TV shows from New York.

From Florida To Hollywood

Screen tests, TV and live shows; February to March 1956

Elvis started this period of the momentous year of 1956 in the familiar theaters of Florida. He ended it in the unfamiliar surroundings of California, and most unbelievable of all, on a movie set in Hollywood. Florida had always been hot for Elvis. His 1955 tours there had seen the first teenage hysteria, and had been the real beginning of his relationship with Tom Parker. Now he was back there with his own touring package as the hottest thing in showbusiness. But more than that, Elvis had turned a whole new generation into music fans. At the height of his popularity he could have done — more or less — anything he wanted. And what he wanted more than anything else, was to be a movie actor.

Elvis was becoming a seasoned television performer, as well as a veteran of some 300 live shows. By the end of his run on Stage Show he was totally in control, manipulating the studio audience in the same way he pulled at the emotions of the fans at his concerts. Gone was the frantic style of the first appearance. But a little vital energy was being lost, as Presley became more assured. He was becoming a consummate entertainer, and in order to do so he had to ease away from being the 'Hilbilly Cat'. In some ways he started to parody himself even at this early part of his career. On the television recordings he laughs with the audience at his own mannerisms, as if to say 'Let's see you scream at this'.

All this was the inevitable result of his growing confidence and his changing relationship with his audience. He was now the most popular singer in America — a fact that was shortly to be confirmed by his holding the Number One spot on the Billboard chart for 18 out of the last 36 weeks of 1956. At most of his concerts the audience were making a

"Hot as a $1 pistol"
As Elvis wound up his Florida tour at the end of February, he had his first national Number One as 'I Forgot To Remember To Forget' reached the top of the Country and Western charts. Though recorded during Elvis's time at Sun, it needed RCA's marketing and distribution strength to become a national hit. More significantly 'Heartbreak Hotel' entered the Billboard singles chart in the first week of March. Presley was, as Billboard magazine said that week, as "hot as a $1 pistol."

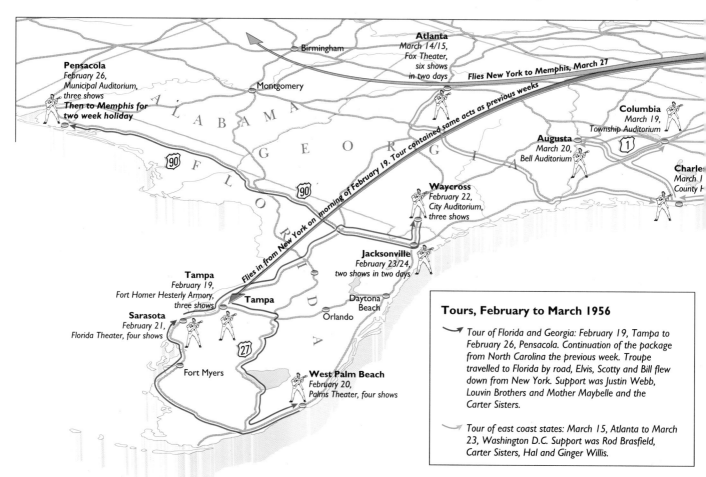

Atlanta
March 14/15,
Fox Theater,
six shows
in two days

Flies New York to Memphis, March 27

Birmingham

Pensacola
February 26,
Municipal Auditorium,
three shows
**Then to Memphis for
two week holiday**

Montgomery

A L A B A M A

G E O R G I A

F L O R I D A

Columbia
March 19,
Township Auditorium

Augusta
March 20,
Bell Auditorium

Charle
March 1
County H

Tour contained same acts as previous weeks

Waycross
February 22,
City Auditorium,
three shows

Flies in from New York on morning of February 19.

Jacksonville
February 23/24,
two shows in two days

Tampa
February 19,
Fort Homer Hesterly Armory,
three shows

Tampa

Daytona
Beach

Orlando

Sarasota
February 21,
Florida Theater, four shows

Fort Myers

West Palm Beach
February 20,
Palms Theater, four shows

Tours, February to March 1956

Tour of Florida and Georgia: February 19, Tampa to February 26, Pensacola. Continuation of the package from North Carolina the previous week. Troupe travelled to Florida by road, Elvis, Scotty and Bill flew down from New York. Support was Justin Webb, Louvin Brothers and Mother Maybelle and the Carter Sisters.

Tour of east coast states: March 15, Atlanta to March 23, Washington D.C. Support was Rod Brasfield, Carter Sisters, Hal and Ginger Willis.

louder noise than the musicians. It was becoming difficult to hear the music, which seemed to be irrelevant to the proceedings. The fans, mostly teenage girls, were there to take part in an adoration, at the center of which stood Elvis Presley. It was impossible for him to remain as he was, or to take this new role entirely seriously. So he acted up for the audience and for his own sake — and probably for the sake of his sanity. The result was, that by the time the world discovered Elvis Presley he was no longer the genuinely free spirit that first set the South on fire.

March 15, 1956 was another notable date in Elvis's career. Although Colonel Tom Parker had been effectively managing his career for several months, Bob Neal's contract ran out on this date and the Colonel now officially became Elvis's manager.

There has been a great deal of discussion about Parker's influence on Presley's career, and whether Elvis might have been better off without him in the long run. But there was never any doubt about Elvis's own view of the matter. In the few interviews he gave he occasionally referred to his early career. Before the Colonel came along, he always said, he wasn't really getting anywhere, he was just a local boy wonder.

material as singles and albums, was a fairly undeveloped strategy. On top of that Colonel Parker's intransigence in letting them have enough studio time, and the likely fickleness of his teenage audience made it sensible to get what they could while the going was good.

Apart from 'Heartbreak Hotel', which succeeded against RCA's expectations, the first part of 1956 did not produce any breakthrough commercial recordings. At sessions in New York on January 30 and February 3, Elvis had recorded a version of 'Blue Suede Shoes', together with cover versions of other rhythm and blues songs ('Lawdy Miss Clawdy', 'My Baby Left Me', 'Tutti Frutti', 'Shake Rattle and Roll', 'So Glad You're

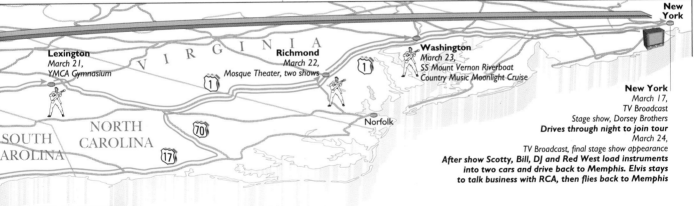

Lexington
March 21,
YMCA Gymnasium

V I R G I N I A

Richmond
March 22,
Mosque Theater, two shows

Washington
March 23,
SS Mount Vernon Riverboat
Country Music Moonlight Cruise

New York

NORTH
CAROLINA

Norfolk

SOUTH
AROLINA

New York
March 17,
TV Broadcast
Stage show, Dorsey Brothers
Drives through night to join tour
March 24,
TV Broadcast, final stage show appearance
After show Scotty, Bill, DJ and Red West load instruments into two cars and drive back to Memphis. Elvis stays to talk business with RCA, then flies back to Memphis

Music matters
The first signs of RCA's anxiety to cash in on Elvis's current popularity began to appear. Although in retrospect their decision to put out anything and everything that Elvis recorded at the time seems like short term planning, there were arguable reasons. They really did not know how long Presley's popularity would last. After all he was different from anything that went before, so RCA, along with everyone else, was in a totally new situation. Also, the management of an artist's career through the planned release of new

Mine' etc.). None of these was suitable for a single release for the pop market. Elvis himself was unsatisfied with 'Blue Suede Shoes', which he said would never be as good as the original. But on March 13 RCA Victor released the song as the feature of an EP. On the same day they released an LP and a double EP. All three records were titled simply *Elvis Presley*. The records did good business, but RCA were desperate for a hot new single. In the end Elvis turned to a song they'd been performing on stage for some time — the song that was to become his trade mark.

Hollywood to Las Vegas

Live shows April 1956

The tours of April 1956 were sandwiched by two locations which were to play overwhelming roles in Elvis Presley's later life — Hollywood and Las Vegas. On April 1 Elvis turned up for a screen test at Paramount Studios. For the benefit of Hal Wallis he sang Blue Suede Shoes and acted out a scene from a yet-to-be made movie called The Rainmaker. There wasn't much doubt that Elvis would pass the test — there was too much money riding on it for Wallis to fail him. Elvis probably didn't care too much about that — whatever anyone said, he was going to be a movie actor. Elvis's induction into mainstream American entertainment seemed to be complete when he was booked to play a fortnight at the New Frontier Hotel in Las Vegas. But things didn't turn out that way.

Although Elvis changed the rules concerning the culture of America and its youth, he was still a product of the times that he so decisively swept away. Before Elvis, young people — and young men in particular — wanted to look grown up and sophisticated. And when they dreamed, they dreamed of being movie stars up there on the huge screen in front of millions of adoring fans. The Hollywood system carefully cultivated the public image of its actors to perpetuate the 'Dream Factory'. The films had happy endings and the stars were idols, the moral guardians of the American dream. Every youngster wanted to be like them.

But after Elvis the young man's role model became the rock and roll singer, not the movie star. The aim then was not to look like your dad, but to look as different as possible from him. Not to be sophisticated, but raw, down to earth, honest. Not to look old and grown up and world weary, but young and impatient.

Elvis, the main progenitor of these massive changes in American culture was paradoxically caught between them. As a poorly dressed boy from a small town in Mississippi, part of him wanted to be like Clark Gable. But when he saw Marlon Brando in *The Wild One* and James Dean in *Rebel Without A Cause*, he knew along with millions of other teenagers that this was something different, something he felt part of. But then popular music replaced film as the major cultural force of the third quarter of the century — in large part because of the influence of Presley's immense popularity. The irony is that he got into film just as it was about to suffer the effects of its demotion in status.

Texas blues

Elvis's April tours of Texas and Oklahoma saw increasing crowd sizes and increasing hysteria. Up until April 17, Elvis had either shared top billing with Faron Young, a well-established country star, or been supported by true young talent like Wanda Jackson. But their part in the Presley roadshow became more and more unenviable. During a Faron Young set a mob of teenagers raced up and down in front of the stage searching for a glimpse of Elvis before he came on. From now on it became impossible to get any performers worth a dime to appear on the same bill. Henceforth it would be 'Elvis Presley and his Variety Show'. Texas, which had supported Elvis when he started out, now turned a little sour. Now the newspapers 'entertainment' reporters decided they should check out the Presley phenomenon they had missed when he was playing the school halls and gymnasiums. This gave them the opportunity to indulge in the favorite occupation of the narrow-minded members of the older generation, to belittle the enthusiasms of the young.

Vegas

Colonel Parker's decision to book Elvis into a hotel cabaret slot in Las Vegas in April can be seen as a rare blunder in an otherwise faultless promotional campaign. But Parker's long-term strategy was always to gently ease Elvis out of the teenage market, with all its dangers of passing fads and fancies, and into the established entertainment mainstream. His timing looks to have been wrong in this instance, but there's no doubt that he got what he wanted in the end. In the New Frontier Hotel the setting was all wrong.

Dangers of flying
After their April 13 show in Amarillo, Elvis, Scotty and Bill boarded a small charter plane for Nashville. They set off in the dark, got lost and landed for refuelling near El Dorado. When the plane took off again the engine died and the plane started to drop. The pilot found that fuel intake was switched to the empty tank, not the full one. The engine restarted OK. Elvis said afterwards 'I don't know if I'll ever fly again'. But next day he did.

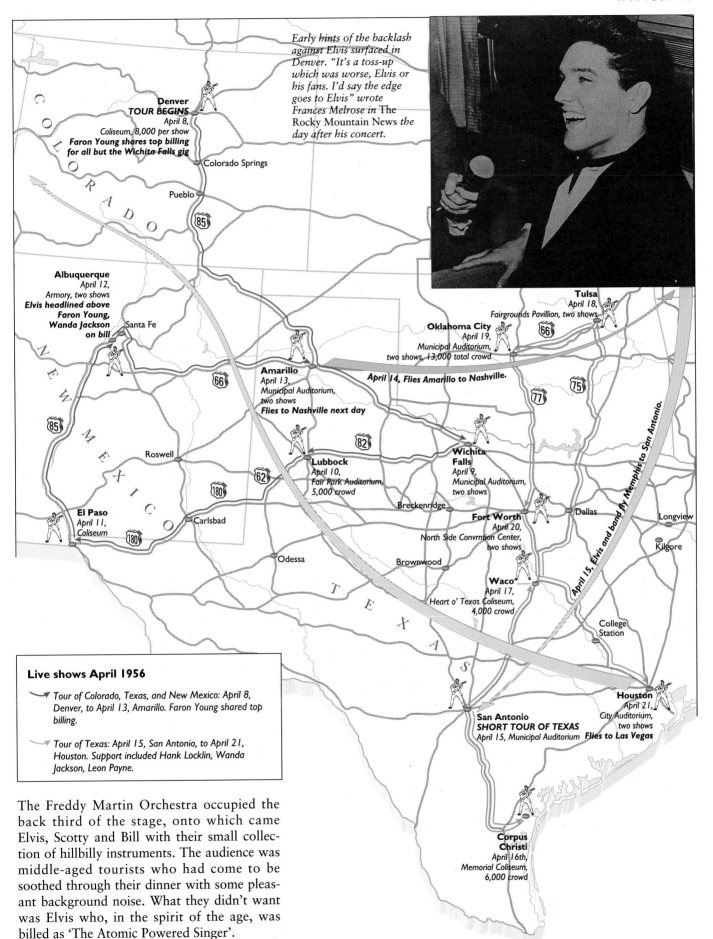

Early hints of the backlash against Elvis surfaced in Denver. "It's a toss-up which was worse, Elvis or his fans. I'd say the edge goes to Elvis" wrote Frances Melrose in The Rocky Mountain News the day after his concert.

Denver
TOUR BEGINS
April 8,
Coliseum, 8,000 per show
Faron Young shares top billing for all but the Wichita Falls gig

Colorado Springs

Pueblo

Albuquerque
April 12,
Armory, two shows
Elvis headlined above Faron Young, Wanda Jackson on bill

Santa Fe

Tulsa
April 18,
Fairgrounds Pavillion, two shows

Oklahoma City
April 19,
Municipal Auditorium,
two shows, 13,000 total crowd

Amarillo
April 13,
Municipal Auditorium,
two shows
Flies to Nashville next day

April 14, Flies Amarillo to Nashville.

Roswell

Lubbock
April 10,
Fair Park Auditorium,
5,000 crowd

Wichita Falls
April 9,
Municipal Auditorium,
two shows

Breckenridge

El Paso
April 11,
Coliseum

Carlsbad

Fort Worth
April 20,
North Side Convrntion Center,
two shows

Dallas

Longview

Kilgore

Odessa

Brownwood

Waco
April 17,
Heart o' Texas Coliseum,
4,000 crowd

College Station

April 15, Elvis and band fly Memphis to San Antonio.

Houston
April 21,
City Auditorium,
two shows
Flies to Las Vegas

Live shows April 1956

➤ Tour of Colorado, Texas, and New Mexico: April 8, Denver, to April 13, Amarillo. Faron Young shared top billing.

➤ Tour of Texas: April 15, San Antonio, to April 21, Houston. Support included Hank Locklin, Wanda Jackson, Leon Payne.

San Antonio
SHORT TOUR OF TEXAS
April 15, Municipal Auditorium

Corpus Christi
April 16th,
Memorial Coliseum,
6,000 crowd

The Freddy Martin Orchestra occupied the back third of the stage, onto which came Elvis, Scotty and Bill with their small collection of hillbilly instruments. The audience was middle-aged tourists who had come to be soothed through their dinner with some pleasant background noise. What they didn't want was Elvis who, in the spirit of the age, was billed as 'The Atomic Powered Singer'.

Conquering America
Tours of the Midwest and California, May to June 1956

By May 1956 'Heartbreak Hotel' was the nation's Number One single, and *Elvis Presley* the Number One LP. In the two years since that first short appearance at the Bon Air Club in Memphis, Elvis had played hundreds of concerts to increasingly enthusiastic audiences. But there were still large areas of the country that had never had the chance to see an Elvis Presley live show. Elvis's geographic and musical roots were in the South. He had quickly branched out into Texas, then took Florida by storm. Virginia and the Carolinas followed after that. California had to wait until April 1956. Now following the pause in Las Vegas, Elvis finally hit the Midwest — but the reaction wasn't quite up to expectations.

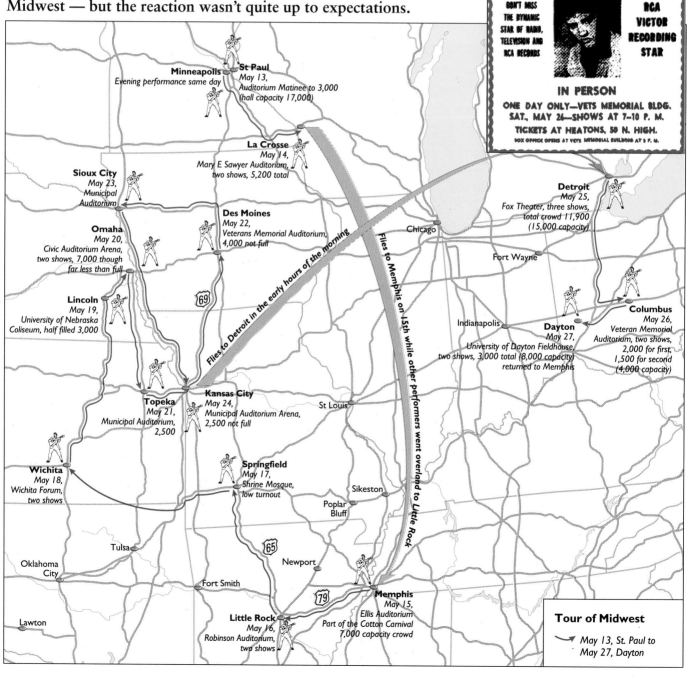

RECORD DEALERS WELCOME
Elvis Presley
TO COLUMBUS

DON'T MISS THE DYNAMIC STAR OF RADIO, TELEVISION AND RCA RECORDS

RCA VICTOR RECORDING STAR

IN PERSON
ONE DAY ONLY—VETS MEMORIAL BLDG.
SAT., MAY 26—SHOWS AT 7–10 P. M.
TICKETS AT HEATONS, 50 N. HIGH.
BOX OFFICE OPENS AT VETS MEMORIAL BUILDING AT 5 P. M.

Minneapolis
Evening performance same day

St Paul
May 13,
Auditorium Matinee to 3,000
(hall capacity 17,000)

La Crosse
May 14,
*Mary E Sawyer Auditorium,
two shows, 5,200 total*

Sioux City
May 23,
Municipal
Auditorium

Des Moines
May 22,
*Veterans Memorial Auditorium,
4,000 not full*

Detroit
May 25,
*Fox Theater, three shows,
total crowd 11,900
(15,000 capacity)*

Chicago

Omaha
May 20,
*Civic Auditorium Arena,
two shows, 7,000 though
far less than full*

Fort Wayne

Indianapolis

Columbus
May 26,
*Veteran Memorial
Auditorium, two shows,
2,000 for first,
1,500 for second
(4,000 capacity)*

Lincoln
May 19,
*University of Nebraska
Coliseum, half filled 3,000*

Dayton
May 27,
*University of Dayton Fieldhouse,
two shows, 3,000 total (8,000 capacity)
returned to Memphis*

Flies to Detroit in the early hours of the morning

Flies to Memphis on 15th while other performers went overland to Little Rock

Topeka
May 21,
*Municipal Auditorium,
2,500*

Kansas City
May 24,
*Municipal Auditorium Arena,
2,500 not full*

St Louis

Wichita
May 18,
*Wichita Forum,
two shows*

Springfield
May 17,
*Shrine Mosque,
low turnout*

Sikeston

Poplar
Bluff

Tulsa

Oklahoma
City

Newport

Memphis
May 15,
*Ellis Auditorium
Part of the Cotton Carnival
7,000 capacity crowd*

Fort Smith

Lawton

Little Rock
May 16,
*Robinson Auditorium,
two shows*

Tour of Midwest

→ May 13, St. Paul to
May 27, Dayton

The fifteen day tour of May 1956 took in six-teen cities in eleven states. The package was built around Elvis with the support acts some-times listed as including the Blue Moon Boys and the Jordanaires, who were also part of Elvis's act. Although the sizes of the audiences were as good as on many previous tours, the shows were mostly booked into vast concert halls, that didn't get filled. There was an obvi-ous expectation on the part of Colonel Parker and the booking agency that the hysteria sur-rounding Elvis would enable them to fill any hall and charge any price for tickets. In the event this was to be the only tour that Elvis played after signing for RCA which didn't get close to selling out.

While it is easy to explain why Elvis's appearances in Las Vegas in April 1956 were less than successful, this tour is more debat-able. The tickets might have been priced too high for the teenage audience. Poor advance publicity has been blamed too. Elvis's sexual image may also have prompted parents into keeping their daughters away. Certainly the age of Presley's audience seems to be reflected in the attendances at La Crosse, Wisconsin on May 14 — the 7.00 p.m show was a 4,000 sell-out, while the 9.30 show got only 1200.

Those fans who did turn up certainly did their utmost to make up for the empty seats around them. The first show of the tour was at the city auditorium in St Paul, Minnesota.

Tour of California and Arizona

➤ June 3, Oakland, to June 10, Tucson

Oakland: the Benny Stron Orchestra and Paul Desmond supported. Two shows to total crowd of 6,500
Interrupted tour to play 'Milton Berle Show' live from Los Angeles.
Support for section from San Diego to Tucson — Flair Sextet, Jackie Little, Frankie Connors and Phil Maraquin. Phoenix and Tucson shows were at outdoor arenas, Elvis arriving on stage in a Cadillac.

Oakland
June 3,
Auditorium Arena,
2 shows, 6,500
in total crowd

San Francisco

Los Angeles
June 5,
TV Broadcast,
Milton Berle show
ABC TV
June 8,
Shrine Auditorium

Long Beach
June 7,
Municipal Auditorium,
4,000 sellout

San Diego
June 6,
San Diego Arena,
2,500 sellout

Flies to Phoenix on June 9

Phoenix
June 9,
State Fairground,
5,000 crowd

Tucson
June 9,
Rodeo Grounds

Three thousand fans turned out on the afternoon of May 13 in a hall that could comfort-ably hold 17,000. Nevertheless Elvis had to be got out of the place by a platoon of local police officers, and still managed to get his coat ripped in half on the way.

Elvis had visited California in April, to do a screen test and to appear on the Milton Berle Show. This was broadcast on April 3, live from the deck of the aircraft carrier USS Hancock, docked in San Diego. Elvis, Scotty, Bill and DJ then played the San Diego Arena on April 4 and 5, in front of 5,000 fans each night. Now they were back to do a full tour of California. After the Oakland show, which brought an outraged review from the local newspaper, Elvis appeared on his second Milton Berle Show, on which he did his noto-rious and electrifying performance of 'Hound Dog' with its provocative slowed-down end-ing. The numbers recovered when Elvis returned briefly to his old haunts in Memphis and Little Rock. The Memphis show was again at the Ellis Auditorium, as part of the city's annual Cotton Festival. The Memphis Press-Scimitar, the paper that carried Elvis's first ever interview in July 1954, carried the concert review on the front page. Headlined "7,000 Yell Praise For Elvis Presley", the story's first paragraph ran, "Two of the proudest persons in Memphis today are Mr and Mrs Vernon Presley, who last night saw their son Elvis greeted with one of the greatest ovations and demonstrations of popularity in Memphis history, as some 7,000 fans jam-packed both the north and south halls of the Ellis Auditorium."

"Elvis stood one of the greatest indoor crowds in Memphis history on its ears last night as both halls of the Ellis Auditorium were packed to about 7,000 capacity when he made his typical slouching appearance pandemonium set in. Perspiration was rolling down his face as he whipped out the songs which have made him a national idol. He joked, clowned and you could sense the understanding between him and those who so eagerly follow him. It was a happy spirited crowd ...
Elvis had a triumphant home-coming."
Memphis Press-Scimitar
May 16, 1956

Teenage Mayhem

TV, recordings and live shows, June through August 1956

One song seems to encapsulate the story of the late summer of 1956. Elvis had been singing 'Hound Dog' in his live act for a number of months, often using it to close the show. He had caused a national sensation when he performed it, or rather performed to it, on the Milton Berle television show in early June. In response to that, his next television appearance, on the Steve Allen Show on July 1, featured Elvis performing a toned down version of the song to a basset hound. The following day he went into RCA's New York studio and at last recorded 'Hound Dog'. It was released as a double A-side single with 'Don't Be Cruel' on July 13. Within 18 days it had sold over a million copies. It reached Number One and stayed on the Billboard top 100 until January 1957.

Elvis got back where he felt comfortable for his concerts in June and August — Georgia, the Carolinas, Memphis and Florida. And in between he managed to get a vacation near Biloxi on the Gulf Coast of Mississippi. The events of July 1956 in particular were captured in a remarkable series of photographs by a young New Yorker called Alfred Wertheimer. He managed to take Elvis at his most relaxed moments and to capture the hysteria surrounding him from Elvis's own angle. Quite apart from the photos, Wertheimer's account of the recording of 'Hound Dog' gives one of the most revealing insights into Elvis's concern for his music, and his fanatical attention to detail.

The session took place at RCA Studio 1 in their headquarters building at East 24th Street, New York. The band, consisting of Elvis, Scotty Moore, Bill Black, DJ Fontana and Shorty Long on piano, went for 'Hound Dog' first. Elvis had warmed up by singing some spirituals with the Jordanaires while the others tuned their instruments. At previous RCA sessions that he'd photographed, Wertheimer recalled, the producer had been in charge — he had always been the man to please. In this case, though Elvis never pushed himself forward, it became obvious that producer Steve Sholes was deferring to him. Most songs would need about seven or eight takes, but after 26 takes Elvis still wasn't happy. They did four more, then Elvis sat cross-legged in front of a speaker to listen to the playbacks. There was no splicing or overdubbing available then, even at RCA's ultra-modern studio. Each take had to be perfect or rejected. With enormous patience and concentration Elvis listened to the complete takes, then declared that the final cut was the one.

Straight after that Elvis, the band and the Jordanaires heard a demo of 'Don't Be Cruel', learned the song and came up with an arrangement (supervised by Elvis) within around 20 minutes. They recorded it in eight takes. Then they got 'Anyway You Want Me' in five. At the end of one of the best sessions Elvis was ever to do for RCA, he took away acetates of the three records. Next morning he quit New York for the South. He had Memphis on his mind.

While Elvis was recording Parker received a phone call from Ed Sullivan. After saying he would never have Elvis on his show Sullivan was bowing to commercial realities and offering Parker a deal.

"Elvis Presley sang his thanks to his hometown last night, and set off a demonstration of screaming affection such as Old Memphis has never witnessed. Wearing all black except for red tie and socks, Elvis used every magnetic bit of showmanship to give the crowd what it wanted."
Memphis Press — Scimitar, July 5, 1956

TODAY
2 SHOWS 2
4 and 8:15 P. M.

ELVIS PRESLEY

RCA Victor Recording Star, and his

VARIETY SHOW

General Admission $1.50
Box Office Opens 12 Noon
Call RA 7635 for Information
MUNICIPAL AUDITORIUM
Delightfully Air-Conditioned

The photo (left) shows Elvis at one of his most celebrated shows — Russwood Park Memphis, July 4, 1956. He'd played Memphis regularly as his fame grew, but this was the biggest show he gave there in the fifties. The old baseball stadium burned down several years later.

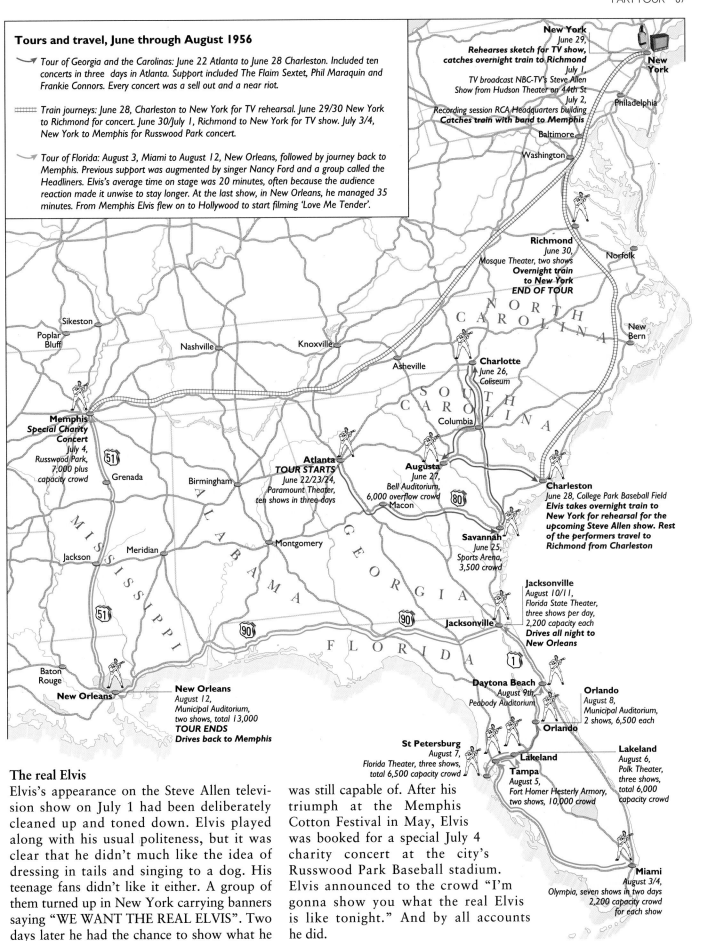

Tours and travel, June through August 1956

Tour of Georgia and the Carolinas: June 22 Atlanta to June 28 Charleston. Included ten concerts in three days in Atlanta. Support included The Flaim Sextet, Phil Maraquin and Frankie Connors. Every concert was a sell out and a near riot.

Train journeys: June 28, Charleston to New York for TV rehearsal. June 29/30 New York to Richmond for concert. June 30/July 1, Richmond to New York for TV show. July 3/4, New York to Memphis for Russwood Park concert.

Tour of Florida: August 3, Miami to August 12, New Orleans, followed by journey back to Memphis. Previous support was augmented by singer Nancy Ford and a group called the Headliners. Elvis's average time on stage was 20 minutes, often because the audience reaction made it unwise to stay longer. At the last show, in New Orleans, he managed 35 minutes. From Memphis Elvis flew on to Hollywood to start filming 'Love Me Tender'.

New York
June 29,
*Rehearses sketch for TV show,
catches overnight train to Richmond*
July 1
*TV broadcast NBC-TV's Steve Allen
Show from Hudson Theater on 44th St*
July 2,
*Recording session RCA Headquarters building
Catches train with band to Memphis*

New York

Philadelphia

Baltimore

Washington

Richmond
June 30,
Mosque Theater, two shows
*Overnight train
to New York
END OF TOUR*

Norfolk

N O R T H
C A R O L I N A

New
Bern

Sikeston

Poplar
Bluff

Nashville

Knoxville

Asheville

Charlotte
June 26,
Coliseum

S O U T H
C A R O L I N A

Columbia

Memphis
*Special Charity
Concert*
July 4,
Russwood Park,
7,000 plus
capacity crowd

Grenada

Birmingham

**Atlanta
TOUR STARTS**
June 22/23/24,
Paramount Theater,
ten shows in three days

Macon

Augusta
June 27,
Bell Auditorium,
6,000 overflow crowd

Charleston
June 28, College Park Baseball Field
*Elvis takes overnight train to
New York for rehearsal for the
upcoming Steve Allen show. Rest
of the performers travel to
Richmond from Charleston*

M I S S I S S I P P I

A L A B A M A

Jackson

Meridian

Montgomery

G E O R G I A

Savannah
June 25,
Sports Arena,
3,500 crowd

Jacksonville
August 10/11,
Florida State Theater,
three shows per day,
2,200 capacity each
*Drives all night to
New Orleans*

Baton
Rouge

New Orleans

New Orleans
August 12,
Municipal Auditorium,
two shows, total 13,000
TOUR ENDS
Drives back to Memphis

F L O R I D A

Jacksonville

Daytona Beach
August 9th,
Peabody Auditorium

Orlando
August 8,
Municipal Auditorium,
2 shows, 6,500 each

Orlando

St Petersburg
August 7,
Florida Theater, three shows,
total 6,500 capacity crowd

Lakeland

Tampa
August 5,
Fort Homer Hesterly Armory,
two shows, 10,000 crowd

Lakeland
August 6,
Polk Theater,
three shows,
total 6,000
capacity crowd

Miami
August 3/4,
Olympia, seven shows in two days
2,200 capacity crowd
for each show

The real Elvis

Elvis's appearance on the Steve Allen television show on July 1 had been deliberately cleaned up and toned down. Elvis played along with his usual politeness, but it was clear that he didn't much like the idea of dressing in tails and singing to a dog. His teenage fans didn't like it either. A group of them turned up in New York carrying banners saying "WE WANT THE REAL ELVIS". Two days later he had the chance to show what he was still capable of. After his triumph at the Memphis Cotton Festival in May, Elvis was booked for a special July 4 charity concert at the city's Russwood Park Baseball stadium. Elvis announced to the crowd "I'm gonna show you what the real Elvis is like tonight." And by all accounts he did.

Memphis Comes To Tinsel Town

Elvis's Hollywood in the fifties

Elvis's film career seemed to go wrong from the very start. By the time *Love Me Tender* was released, "introducing Elvis Presley", it was doing him a shocking disservice. It was demoting, not promoting him. By this point he was the most exciting item in the universe. Just to see his name in print set up a thrill in the brains, hearts and genitals of post-war youth. He was *it*. What the hell was he doing as a plowhand and married man, on the sidelines of a black-and-white historical drama, "starring" the unfamous, unyouthful, unexciting Richard Egan and a leading lady who'd been in mediocre Hollywood movies since 1948? *Love Me Tender* looked like, sounded like, creaked like, a B-movie. Hollywood's message was: we don't have a clue what to do with Elvis Presley.

"Is it a sausage? It is certainly smooth and damp-looking…"
The opening sentence of *Time* magazine's review of Elvis' acting debut in *Love Me Tender*

Love Me Tender was exactly the kind of film suddenly made hopelessly old-fashioned by the very impact of Elvis on the world. Yet Hollywood, Colonel Parker and RCA Victor perceived it as a triumph. It recouped its million-dollar cost in three days; 550 prints went on general release on November 21, 1956, days after a New York City premiere at which a giant cutout Elvis towered over the theater marquee, where 35 police and 20 extra ushers were needed to control the crowd; and the title-song had a million advance orders before it was even recorded.

This was terrific business: but it showed the short-sightedness, the fundamental misunderstanding on Colonel Parker's part about crap versus quality, that would plague Elvis's later career. If people stand in line to hand you their money and then you disappoint them greatly, you'll have fewer takers next time. Elvis's 1960s movies would prove this. After *Blue Hawaii* it was all downhill; as the films and their songs got worse, receipts and chart positions fell, and it grew ever harder to disguise this.

Even with *Love Me Tender*, Colonel Parker's business acumen was in doubt: was it wise for Elvis to take a flat fee ($100,000) for a movie so hugely profitable solely because of his presence?

20th Century Fox made that first film, but Parker had already concluded a deal with producer Hal Wallis and Paramount Pictures in April 1956: reportedly a seven-year, seven-film non-exclusive deal for $2.3 million; yet as with *Love Me Tender*, Elvis saw only a flat fee of $100,000 for his second film, *Loving You*.

Artistically, this was a big improvement: a starring role in a story that paralleled Elvis's

own, with terrific songs excitingly filmed, the whole package contemporary, exuberant and sexy. And in color. Released July 30, 1957, *Loving You* has worn well: still likeable, it's among Elvis's best movies.

The other pre-army films (both black-and-white) are also contenders: credible attempts to give Elvis real roles in real movies. MGM's tough-edged *Jailhouse Rock* came first, and includes compelling scenes about the record business, with strength and sexual tension between the punk hero and the female showbiz manager who takes him on. But… the famous song and dance routine built around the title number, praised by critics and much-excerpted on TV ever since, troubled rock and roll fans for exactly the reasons grown-ups liked it. The record itself is an uncompromising classic; to see Elvis turn it into a

(Above) from 1957's Loving You. *One of Elvis' co-stars in this and in 1958's* King Creole, *Dolores Hart, quit films to become a nun. She's now Mother Superior at the Regina Laudis Convent, Bethlehem, Connecticut. Judy Tyler,* Jailhouse Rock *co-star, was killed in a car-crash in July 1957. "All of us really loved that girl," said Elvis. "I don't believe I can stand to see the movie we made together now."*

Hollywood Musical set-piece was unwelcome.

So was the news that Elvis was to be drafted; a six-week deferment allowed him to finish *King Creole* for Paramount. This too holds up tolerably well and certainly seemed authentic at the time, with strong songs.

Elvis's private life in Hollywood was happy: he was pleased to be accepted as a star in the city of dreams. Other young actors like Dennis Hopper and Natalie Wood found him charmingly naïve.

Elvis working on the set of Love Me Tender, 1956. A BMG (RCA) video, Elvis In Hollywood, issued in 1993, deals with Elvis's four 1950s movies and includes extra fragments of footage. As fanzine-editor Trevor Cajiao comments: "After watching the real Elvis in Elvis In Hollywood, you'll wish the sixties had never happened."

Hopper says Elvis was troubled by having to hit Debra Paget in *Love Me Tender*: he didn't realize such stuff was simulated. Natalie Wood — young, lovely and a rebel herself — told Albert Goldman: "He was the first person of my age group... who said to me: 'How come you're wearing make-up? Why do you want to go to New York?'... It was like having the date I never had in high school."

She came to Memphis on October 31, 1956, met his family, saw the sights, and stayed four days. She didn't much like being at the center of a freak show. According to her sister she confided "He can sing but he can't do much else."

But other budding movie actors came to Hollywood on their own, and entered totally into the world of films, auditions, screen-tests and parties — they had to, in order to make their way in the business. Elvis, though, was already more famous than any of them could hope to be. Although Elvis was thrilled to be in the studios, he didn't aim to become part of Hollywood. Instead the degree to which Elvis brought Memphis to Hollywood is seen in the famous musical climax to *Loving You*. While Elvis is filmed dancing in the aisle of a packed theater, Gladis and Vernon Presley can be clearly seen among the crowd.

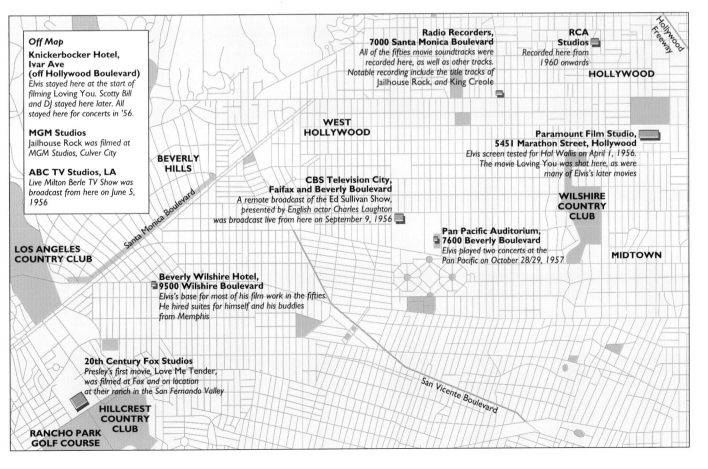

Movies And Mass Hysteria

Live shows September through December 1956

The last months of 1956 saw yet more significant events in the life and career of the 21-year-old Elvis Presley. After spending several weeks in the relative tranquillity of the 20th Century Fox film studios in Hollywood, Elvis returned to the mayhem of his live shows. He also made an emotional return to his home town of Tupelo to play in the same fairgrounds where he had first sung in public as a ten-year-old. Elvis played his biggest concert yet — in front of 26,500 fans at the Cotton Bowl in Dallas. At the end of the year another milestone came when Elvis said goodbye to live radio by playing the final show of his Louisiana Hayride contract.

"I've been looking forward to this home coming very much. I've been escorted out of these fairgrounds when I was a kid and snuck over the fence. This is the first time I've been escorted in." Elvis on his 1956 Tupelo show

Filming on *Love Me Tender* was supposed to be finished by late September. But Elvis had to make a special trip to fulfil a long-standing engagement in Tupelo, before returning to Hollywood. The occasion of his homecoming was the Mississippi-Alabama Fair and Dairy Show. In case the significance should be lost on anyone, Elvis was to perform on Children's Day, in an exact echo of the day when he stood on a chair as a ten-year-old in 1945 and sang 'Old Shep' to the crowd. Eleven years later the town held a parade in his honor, and both the mayor and the Governor of Mississippi turned out. Elvis drove down from Memphis with Vernon and Gladys, who were both overwhelmed by the reception. Gladys, it seems, felt uncomfortable about displaying their conspicuous wealth in a town where they had been so poor. Vernon, though, was just thrilled to see his old friends and talk over old times. Elvis gave an afternoon and evening show to a near-hysterical teenage audience. He had to stop the show several times to try to calm the crowd. More than 50,000 people tried to get in to a stadium that held 10,000. It was, all in all, a triumphant homecoming.

Love Me Tender

Elvis had sung the title song to his first movie on the Ed Sullivan show on September 9. Although RCA planned to release the single to coincide with the film's premiere, the demand forced them to go early. Some record stores had tapes of the TV performance running continually to hype up demand. The single was released on September 28, with advance orders of 856,000. RCA was busy flooding the market with as much Elvis product as possible. On August 31 they released all the tracks of his first LP in the form of six singles.

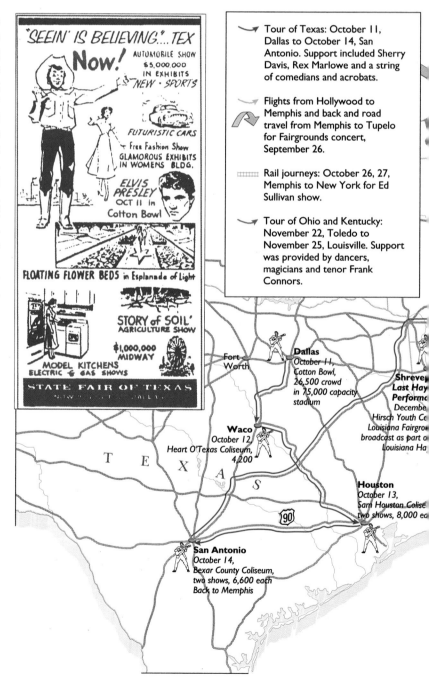

- Tour of Texas: October 11, Dallas to October 14, San Antonio. Support included Sherry Davis, Rex Marlowe and a string of comedians and acrobats.

- Flights from Hollywood to Memphis and back and road travel from Memphis to Tupelo for Fairgrounds concert, September 26.

- Rail journeys: October 26, 27, Memphis to New York for Ed Sullivan show.

- Tour of Ohio and Kentucky: November 22, Toledo to November 25, Louisville. Support was provided by dancers, magicians and tenor Frank Connors.

Fort Worth

Dallas
October 11,
Cotton Bowl,
26,500 crowd
in 75,000 capacity
stadium

Shreve
Last Hay
Performa
Decembe
Hirsch Youth Ce
Louisiana Fairgro
broadcast as part o
Louisiana Ha

Waco
October 12,
Heart O'Texas Coliseum,
4,200

T E X A S

90

Houston
October 13,
Sam Houston Colise
two shows, 8,000 ea

San Antonio
October 14,
Bexar County Coliseum,
two shows, 6,600 each
Back to Memphis

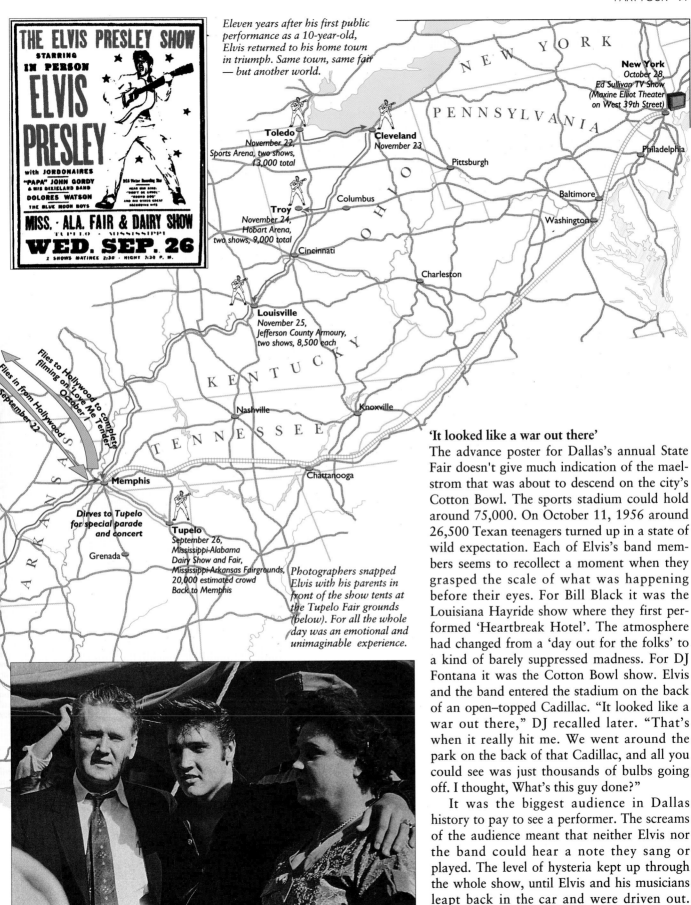

THE ELVIS PRESLEY SHOW
STARRING
IN PERSON
ELVIS
PRESLEY
with JORDONAIRES
"PAPA" JOHN GORDY
& HIS DIXIELAND BAND
DOLORES WATSON
THE BLUE MOON BOYS
MISS.-ALA. FAIR & DAIRY SHOW
TUPELO · MISSISSIPPI
WED. SEP. 26
2 SHOWS MATINEE 2:30 · NIGHT 7:30 P. M.

Eleven years after his first public performance as a 10-year-old, Elvis returned to his home town in triumph. Same town, same fair — but another world.

New York
*October 28,
Ed Sullivan TV Show
(Maxine Elliot Theater
on West 39th Street)*

Toledo
*November 22,
Sports Arena, two shows,
13,000 total*

Cleveland
November 23

Troy
*November 24,
Hobart Arena,
two shows, 9,000 total*

Louisville
*November 25,
Jefferson County Armoury,
two shows, 8,500 each*

Philadelphia

Pittsburgh

Baltimore

Washington

Charleston

Columbus

Cincinnati

Nashville

Knoxville

Chattanooga

Memphis

Flies to Hollywood to complete filming on Love Me Tender, October 1

Flies in from Hollywood September 22

Drives to Tupelo for special parade and concert

Grenada

Tupelo
*September 26,
Mississippi-Alabama
Dairy Show and Fair,
Mississippi-Arkansas Fairgrounds,
20,000 estimated crowd
Back to Memphis*

Photographers snapped Elvis with his parents in front of the show tents at the Tupelo Fair grounds (below). For all the whole day was an emotional and unimaginable experience.

'It looked like a war out there'

The advance poster for Dallas's annual State Fair doesn't give much indication of the maelstrom that was about to descend on the city's Cotton Bowl. The sports stadium could hold around 75,000. On October 11, 1956 around 26,500 Texan teenagers turned up in a state of wild expectation. Each of Elvis's band members seems to recollect a moment when they grasped the scale of what was happening before their eyes. For Bill Black it was the Louisiana Hayride show where they first performed 'Heartbreak Hotel'. The atmosphere had changed from a 'day out for the folks' to a kind of barely suppressed madness. For DJ Fontana it was the Cotton Bowl show. Elvis and the band entered the stadium on the back of an open–topped Cadillac. "It looked like a war out there," DJ recalled later. "That's when it really hit me. We went around the park on the back of that Cadillac, and all you could see was just thousands of bulbs going off. I thought, What's this guy done?"

It was the biggest audience in Dallas history to pay to see a performer. The screams of the audience meant that neither Elvis nor the band could hear a note they sang or played. The level of hysteria kept up through the whole show, until Elvis and his musicians leapt back in the car and were driven out. Whetever was going on here didn't seem to have much to do with music anymore.

End Of An Era

The 1957 tours

Whereas 1956 had been the year of RCA and television, Elvis's 1957 was dominated by the movies — and by the growing certainty of his induction into the US Army. Live shows became a lower priority now that Elvis's fans could see him at their local movie house, or occasionally on television. Nevertheless Elvis did play those parts of the US which hadn't yet had the chance to see him. 1957 was also his most successful on the Billboard singles chart — 'All Shook Up', 'Teddy Bear' and 'Jailhouse Rock' were at Number One for a total of 21 weeks.

"Ex-choir singer Presley pulls a monumental switch and warbles four sacred tunes with sincerity and commendable reverence." Billboard on the *Peace In The Valley* EP, released March 22, 1957

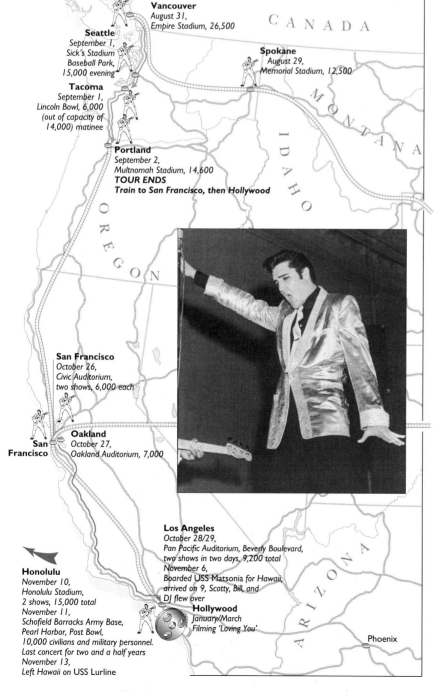

Vancouver
August 31,
Empire Stadium, 26,500

Seattle
September 1,
Sick's Stadium
Baseball Park,
15,000 evening

Spokane
August 29,
Memorial Stadium, 12,500

Tacoma
September 1,
Lincoln Bowl, 6,000
(out of capacity of
14,000) matinee

Portland
September 2,
Multnomah Stadium, 14,600
TOUR ENDS
Train to San Francisco, then Hollywood

San Francisco
October 26,
Civic Auditorium,
two shows, 6,000 each

Oakland
October 27,
Oakland Auditorium, 7,000

San Francisco

Los Angeles
October 28/29,
Pan Pacific Auditorium, Beverly Boulevard,
two shows in two days, 9,200 total
November 6,
Boarded USS Matsonia for Hawaii,
arrived on 9, Scotty, Bill, and
DJ flew over

Hollywood
January/March
Filming 'Loving You'

Honolulu
November 10,
Honolulu Stadium,
2 shows, 15,000 total
November 11,
Schofield Barracks Army Base,
Pearl Harbor, Post Bowl,
10,000 civilians and military personnel.
Last concert for two and a half years
November 13,
Left Hawaii on USS Lurline

Phoenix

The year started with good and less good news for Elvis. With his final appearance on the Ed Sullivan Show on January 6, he seemed deliberately to shake off the rebellious side of his public image. After exciting the audience with a spirited, though bodily static, version of 'Don't Be Cruel', he finished off with an acapella rendition of the gospel song '(There'll Be) Peace In The Valley' backed by the Jordanaires. After that Ed Sullivan came out and declared him to be "a real, decent fine boy". Parker's strategy of getting Elvis into the mainstream was working out nicely.

Within days of his return to Memphis from New York, on his twenty-second birthday Elvis was declared by the draft board to be A Profile and therefore draftable. He would be called up in six to eight months. Though he declared himself happy to serve, the prospect hung heavy on him for the next twelve months. Two days after his birthday he was off to Hollywood again, to begin filming on the first film in which he was to play a starring role — *Loving You*.

In between the two movies that he made during 1957 (*Loving You* and *Jailhouse Rock*) Elvis returned to Memphis to negotiate the purchase of a mansion on the southern outskirts of the city. He bought Graceland for $100,000, which included the deeds to the Presleys' home on Audubon Drive. He went off on a tour of the midwest and northeast while the house was being redecorated, and moved into what was to become one of the most famous addresses in America in April 1957. He didn't get much chance to enjoy it at first though — by the end of the month he was back in Hollywood starting pre-production work at MGM.

Apart from the record crowds, the hysteria and the snide notices from "adult" critics, the first 1957 tour was notable for the appearance of Elvis's famous gold lame suit. Colonel

Parker had ordered the suit from Nudie Cohen, the Hollywood tailor who specialized in embroidered cowboy suits for country singers who wanted to look flash yet authentic. The gold suit was made of gold thread woven onto a leather lining. The first sight of Elvis in the suit on stage in Chicago caused pandemonium in the audience as several thousand teenagers rushed the stage. After several attempts, around a dozen made it through the police lines and the concert came to an end. Elvis only wore the full suit once more, on the following night in St Louis, though he wore it for the photo that adorned two EPs and an album cover.

Both this tour and the autumn tour of the Pacific northwest were booked by an Australian promoter called Lee Gordon. He was hoping to persuade Colonel Parker that he was capable of handling an Elvis tour to Australia. The promotion certainly went well, though by this time it seemed that Elvis could sell out just about any place on the planet. Parker went along with Gordon, though there may have been good reasons why Parker would never consider a tour outside of North America — principally his own immigrant status.

Elvis was just as hot in Canada as in the States. twenty six and a half thousand fans attended his show in Vancouver, which again came to a premature end when a crowd of teenagers broke through police lines and made for the stage. The musicians turned and ran for the safety of a waiting car. Things were getting more and more out of control.

Posters in 1957 didn't need to tell the audience who Elvis was. Gone was the "RCA's Singing Sensation". Gone also was the listing of any support acts.

Travels in 1957

Elvis's show at the Tupelo Fairgrounds on September 27, 1957, was notable as the first concert played without Scotty Moore and Bill Black. They had resigned in protest after studio time they were promised was withdrawn. They were still on fixed salaries, so releasing records was their only way of earning some extra money off Elvis's reflected glory.

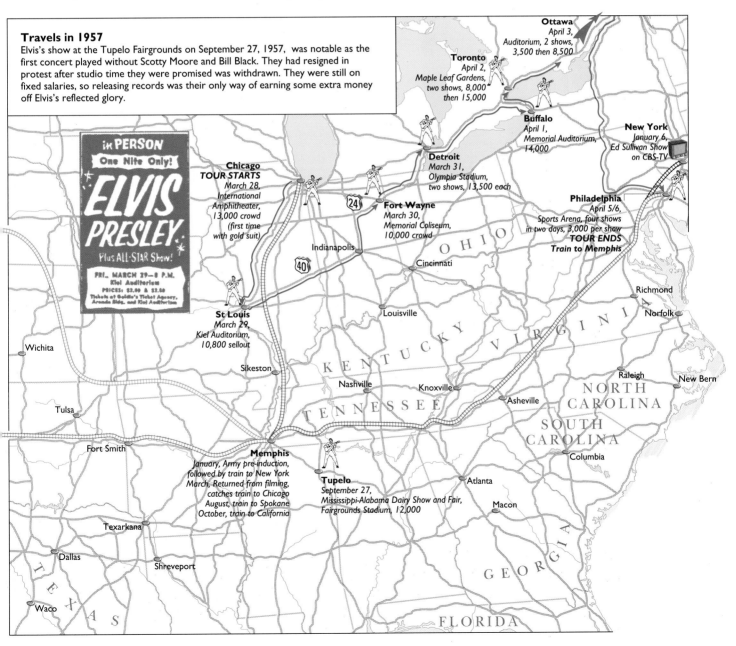

Devil's Music

Middle America bites back

By June 1956, Elvis was too big a phenomenon for the press to ignore. In his early days on the road, his shows had either been unreviewed or covered by a generally enthusiastic reporter with a genuine interest in real music. But now the 'entertainment' correspondents got their turn. These people were generally more used to covering visits by touring orchestras, opera companies or big name crooners to the outposts of America.

Many saw themselves as sophisticated guardians of their towns' cultural standards. They were prudes. Little wonder then that they had trouble coping with Elvis.

"I don't see that any type of music would have a bad influence on people. It's only music." Elvis on juvenile delinquency and rock and roll.

Seattle
"The sound from the audience was like 12,000 girls having their heads shaved at once." John Voorhees, Post-Intelligencer

Tacoma
"He strutted like a duck, his hands dangling loosely in front of him. He went to his knees in an attitude of prayer, taking the slender microphone with him." Don Duncan, Tacoma News-Tribune

"His performance was the most disgusting exhibition this reporter has ever seen. He has a sulky look and his infrequent smile is almost surly. The act was merely variations on a single theme, except that each wiggle was a little more 'low down'." Marjorie Howe, Sioux City Journal

OAHUA
Honolulu
not to scale

"He threw his hips, wobbled his knees, flopped his shoulders then shook and rolled. The more he rolled, the more the audience screamed." Hawaii Lightning News

Oakland

"Presley grabbed the microphone as if it were alive and dragged it around the stage, now petting it, now turning upon it the full vent of his manly wrath. After the last song he slowly edged over to the wings employing the staggering, sulking walk he has made a trademark."

"Gyrations which are simply no more than a male cooch dance complete with bumps and grinds." Glenn Trump, Omaha World Telegraph

Denver

"It's a toss up which is worse, Elvis or his fans. I'd say the edge goes to Elvis." Frances Melrose, Rocky Mountain News

"Would put a burlesque queen to shame. Elvis squirms out his songs." Anne Mary Murphy, Daily Capitol

"He worked himself into an orgiastic rhythm, losing himself to the savage beat. The air raid siren screams of the crowd heightened as Presley's bumps and grinds grew more frantic." Patsy Dinan, Amarillo Daily News

Amarillo

"A hard working stripper who tried anything like it would find herself a guest of the county." Variety

Los Angeles
Long Beach

"Elvis, leaning backwards like an intoxicated seaman with a gale at his heels' while the fans whistled screamed, wept, stomped their feet, jumped up on their seats, ran up and down the aisles and shrieked over and over again 'Ohhh Elvis, Elvis!'." Paul Wallace, Long Beach Press-Telegram

"The gyrating, rotary troubadour was seldom if ever heard by an audience screaming like Zulus every time he moved a muscle. The Pelvis applies more body English to a song than many a baseball pitcher and he has more movements than a well-oiled Swiss watch."

Tucson

"Elvis did about every bump and grind in the book." His movements were *"epileptic"*. Bea Ramirez, Waco News

"He can hardly be classed as just a singer unless one is familiar with the term 'exotic singer', which includes writhing, twitching, squirming and exercising the entire body along with the vocal cords." Shirley Phillips, Arizona Daily Star

The newspapers' reactions to the Elvis Presley live shows in late 1956 and 1957 shouldn't be judged too harshly though. By this time even Elvis and his band were a little mystified about what was happening in front of them, night after night in city after city across America. It seemed as if an Elvis show was simply a license for perfectly ordinary, well brought up girls to lose control of their emotions. Once it started happening, and started getting reported, it was unstoppable. In the end, the only way to stop it was for Elvis to stop playing live shows.

"You couldn't hear Elvis in the front row. Uproar exploded each time he looked as though he might open his mouth. A flash of white teeth from Elvis, a loose-hipped slur of dance steps, a Brando-like gaze from soulful blue eyes, and the floor vibrated from 6,000 stamping feet, whistles shattered the air. He comes across like the midnight express. He kicks, slinks, shimmies and gyrates." Betty Scheibel, San Antonio Light

"Like everything connected to this man, value seems to have no relationship to price. It is an appalling commentary on the taste of his audiences that he performs in such bad taste, for his act as presented in San Antonio was the essence of vulgarity."
"An unholy roller.' 'He got more body English into his songs than a Ubangi witch doctor trying to cure a pestilence." San Antonio News

In addition to the critical newspaper reports Elvis was subject to restraining orders in some cities. A magistrate or police chief would solemnly sit through the matinee to decide whether the evening show should be allowed to go ahead. But when Elvis was prevented from wiggling, the audience went wild just the same.

It seemed you either loved Elvis or you hated him. And if you were young, and particularly if you were female, you loved him. The generation gap was born.

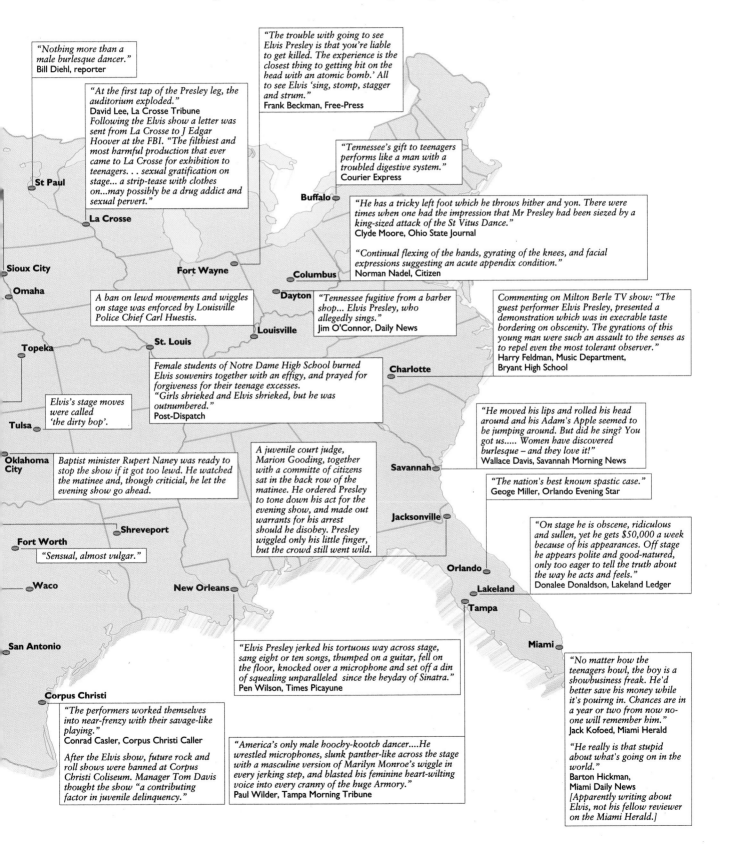

"Nothing more than a male burlesque dancer."
Bill Diehl, reporter

"At the first tap of the Presley leg, the auditorium exploded."
David Lee, La Crosse Tribune
Following the Elvis show a letter was sent from La Crosse to J Edgar Hoover at the FBI. "The filthiest and most harmful production that ever came to La Crosse for exhibition to teenagers. . . sexual gratification on stage... a strip-tease with clothes on...may possibly be a drug addict and sexual pervert."

"The trouble with going to see Elvis Presley is that you're liable to get killed. The experience is the closest thing to getting hit on the head with an atomic bomb.' All to see Elvis 'sing, stomp, stagger and strum."
Frank Beckman, Free-Press

"Tennessee's gift to teenagers performs like a man with a troubled digestive system."
Courier Express

"He has a tricky left foot which he throws hither and yon. There were times when one had the impression that Mr Presley had been siezed by a king-sized attack of the St Vitus Dance."
Clyde Moore, Ohio State Journal

"Continual flexing of the hands, gyrating of the knees, and facial expressions suggesting an acute appendix condition."
Norman Nadel, Citizen

A ban on lewd movements and wiggles on stage was enforced by Louisville Police Chief Carl Huestis.

"Tennessee fugitive from a barber shop... Elvis Presley, who allegedly sings."
Jim O'Connor, Daily News

Commenting on Milton Berle TV show: *"The guest performer Elvis Presley, presented a demonstration which was in execrable taste bordering on obscenity. The gyrations of this young man were such an assault to the senses as to repel even the most tolerant observer."*
Harry Feldman, Music Department, Bryant High School

Female students of Notre Dame High School burned Elvis souvenirs together with an effigy, and prayed for forgiveness for their teenage excesses.
"Girls shrieked and Elvis shrieked, but he was outnumbered."
Post-Dispatch

Elvis's stage moves were called 'the dirty bop'.

"He moved his lips and rolled his head around and his Adam's Apple seemed to be jumping around. But did he sing? You got us..... Women have discovered burlesque – and they love it!"
Wallace Davis, Savannah Morning News

Baptist minister Rupert Naney was ready to stop the show if it got too lewd. He watched the matinee and, though criticial, he let the evening show go ahead.

A juvenile court judge, Marion Gooding, together with a committe of citizens sat in the back row of the matinee. He ordered Presley to tone down his act for the evening show, and made out warrants for his arrest should he disobey. Presley wiggled only his little finger, but the crowd still went wild.

"The nation's best known spastic case."
Geoge Miller, Orlando Evening Star

"On stage he is obscene, ridiculous and sullen, yet he gets $50,000 a week because of his appearances. Off stage he appears polite and good-natured, only too eager to tell the truth about the way he acts and feels."
Donalee Donaldson, Lakeland Ledger

"Sensual, almost vulgar."

"Elvis Presley jerked his tortuous way across stage, sang eight or ten songs, thumped on a guitar, fell on the floor, knocked over a microphone and set off a din of squealing unparalleled since the heyday of Sinatra."
Pen Wilson, Times Picayune

"No matter how the teenagers howl, the boy is a showbusiness freak. He'd better save his money while it's pouirng in. Chances are in a year or two from now no-one will remember him."
Jack Kofoed, Miami Herald

"He really is that stupid about what's going on in the world."
Barton Hickman,
Miami Daily News
[Apparently writing about Elvis, not his fellow reviewer on the Miami Herald.]

"The performers worked themselves into near-frenzy with their savage-like playing."
Conrad Casler, Corpus Christi Caller

After the Elvis show, future rock and roll shows were banned at Corpus Christi Coliseum. Manager Tom Davis thought the show "a contributing factor in juvenile delinquency."

"America's only male hoochy-kootch dancer....He wrestled microphones, slunk panther-like across the stage with a masculine version of Marilyn Monroe's wiggle in every jerking step, and blasted his feminine heart-wilting voice into every cranny of the huge Armory."
Paul Wilder, Tampa Morning Tribune

St Paul
La Crosse
Buffalo
Sioux City
Omaha
Fort Wayne
Columbus
Dayton
Louisville
Topeka
St. Louis
Charlotte
Tulsa
Oklahoma City
Savannah
Shreveport
Jacksonville
Fort Worth
Waco
New Orleans
Orlando
Lakeland
Tampa
San Antonio
Miami
Corpus Christi

'It's All Happened So Fast'

Elvis's America, July 1954 to March 1958

By the time he went into the army in 1958 Elvis had played almost every state in the union. His touring in the early days had been frenetic, picking up shows wherever his manager could arrange them, driving thousands of miles every week to earn a living. As his fame spread, things got more organized. Tours were more sensibly put together. But then the crowds were so big that there were two or three shows a night, and still the distances had to be covered. In the end the crowds got too big and too wild, and the touring stopped. The pattern of Elvis's shows in his great rock and roll years shows how much time he spent playing the South and Texas, before gradually pushing out to the rest of the country. But then television and the movies meant that live shows became unnecessary.

Elvis had a flying start to his career by having a hit record before he'd ever given a professional performance. But, though he produced some classic records during his time at Sun, they were never more than regional hits. In fact each of his five Sun singles followed a rough pattern of selling progressively fewer copies. It was his live shows in Texas, Florida and the South, and the reaction to them, that brought Elvis to the attention of the national music industry.

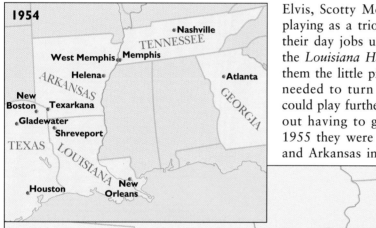

Elvis, Scotty Moore and Bill Black started playing as a trio in July 1954. They all kept their day jobs until they got a contract with the *Louisiana Hayride* in October. That gave them the little piece of financial security they needed to turn pro. That meant that they could play further away from Memphis, without having to get back for work. By early 1955 they were pushing out from Tennessee and Arkansas into east Texas, then way out

1955

1. Booneville
2. Muscle Shoals
3. Hawkins
4. Longview
5. Parkin
6. Gladewater
7. Fort Worth
8. Sweetwater
9. Henderson
10. Greenville

west. They clocked up the miles in Scotty's car with Bill's bass strapped to the roof. Their territory was partly defined by the audience for the *Louisiana Hayride* radio show — Elvis was soon playing on the portion of the show that was relayed through the CBS network to stations throughout Texas and the South. But their manager Bob Neal would also endeavour to get them booked onto shows with big name country stars. A big audience would turn up to see Hank Snow or Slim Whitman or Faron Young, and find a young singer they'd barely heard of was blowing them off the stage. Not all of the audiences liked that, but an awful lot of them did.

Hollywood. In between Elvis played the midwest for the first time, and made his Las Vegas debut.

By 1957 the live shows were becoming unmanageable. Elvis's entry into a city had to be secretly planned and his hotels fortified against over–zealous fans. The fees he could earn from television, the movies and record sales made performing financially unnecessary. In his final year before joining the army he played just a couple of short tours in the Pacific northwest and the northeast taking in cities in Canada, as well as special concerts in Hawaii and Tupelo.

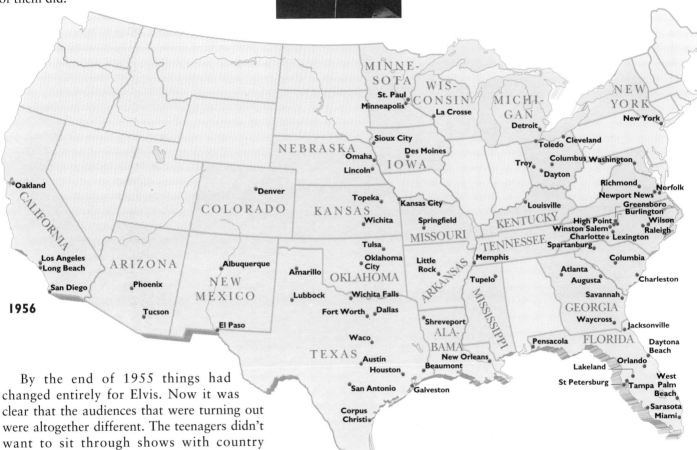

By the end of 1955 things had changed entirely for Elvis. Now it was clear that the audiences that were turning out were altogether different. The teenagers didn't want to sit through shows with country singers, no matter how famous. And in the end they didn't much want support acts of any kind. Elvis was big enough for Colonel Parker to book him on a tour of Virginia and North Carolina in late 1955. He also made brief visits to Cleveland, Indianapolis and Louisville.

In 1956 Elvis became a truly national figure. He kept on playing live shows, but the tours were now arranged around network television shows. Elvis played the east coast a lot in the first few months of the year, in order to be in reach of New York. Shows in California and Arizona were arranged to coincide with television broadcasts from Los Angeles, and the filming of *Love Me Tender* in

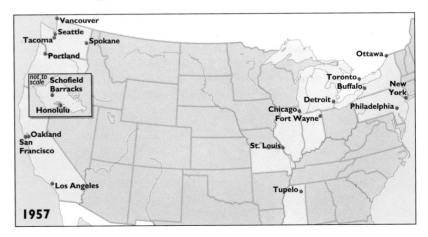

Chronology

January 1956– March 1958

1956

Jan. 1–7	Week of shows from St Louis to Shreveport.
Jan. 10, 11	First RCA recording session takes place in Nashville. 'Heartbreak Hotel', 'I Got A Woman', 'Money Honey', 'I'm Counting On You' and 'I Was The One' taped. First session with DJ Fontana drumming. Floyd Cramer on piano, Chet Atkins rhythm guitar.
Jan. 15–20	Tour of Texas with Hank Snow.
Jan. 27	'Heartbreak Hotel'/'I Was The One' released. First original single on RCA.
Jan. 28	First appearance on national TV on *Stage Show* broadcast live on CBS from New York. The trio play 'Shake, Rattle And Roll' which segues into 'Flip, Flop And Fly', both Big Joe Turner hits, then Ray Charles' 'I Got a Woman'.
Jan. 30, 31	Recording session at RCA building New York City. 'Blue Suede Shoes', 'My Baby Left Me', 'One-Sided Love Affair','So Glad You're Mine', 'I'm Gonna Sit Right Down And Cry' and 'Tutti Frutti' recorded. Scotty, Bill and DJ plus Shorty Long on piano.
Feb. 3	Further recording session at RCA headquarters. 'Lawdy Miss Clawdy' and 'Shake, Rattle And Roll' taped.
Feb. 4	Second TV appearance on 'Stage Show'. Songs performed – 'Baby Let's Play House' and 'Tutti Frutti'.
Feb. 5–10	Tour of Virginia and North Carolina.
Feb. 11	Third TV appearance on Stage Show. Elvis, Scotty and Bill perform 'Blue Suede Shoes' and 'Heartbreak Hotel'.
Feb. 12–16	Continues tour of Virginia and North Carolina.
Feb. 18	Fourth appearance on CBS-TV's *Stage Show*. Perform 'Tutti Frutti' and 'I Was The One'.
Feb. 19–26	Tour of Florida, followed by vacation.
Mar. 13	The album *Elvis Presley* is released, together with an EP and a double EP, both entitled *Elvis Presley*. First EP contains 'Blue Suede Shoes', 'Tutti Frutti', 'I Got A Woman' and 'Just Because'. On the double EP extra tracks are 'I'm Counting On You', 'One-Sided Love Affair', 'I'm Gonna Sit Right Down And Cry' and 'I'll Never Let You Go'.
Mar. 15	Bob Neal's option on his contract as Elvis's manager expires. Elvis now signs a long-term managerial contract with Tom Parker.
Mar. 17	Fifth appearance on 'Stage Show'. Elvis sings 'Blue Suede Shoes' and then his new single 'Heartbreak Hotel' for the first time on national television.
Mar. 18–23	Tour of east coast states.
Mar. 24	Sixth and final appearance on CBS-TV's 'Stage Show'. Performs 'Money Honey' and 'Heartbreak Hotel'.
Apr.	*Heartbreak Hotel* EP released. Title track plus 'I Was The One', 'Money Honey' and 'I Forgot To Remember To Forget'.
Apr. 1	Screen test for Hal Wallis at Paramount Studios, Hollywood. Sings 'Blue Suede Shoes' and acts out scene from 'The Rainmaker'.
Apr. 3	Live television appearance on 'The Milton Berle Show' broadcast by ABC-TV from deck of USS Hancock in San Diego.
Apr. 6	Signs seven-year contract with Paramount Pictures. Initial contract is for three movies at fee of $100,000 rising to $200,000.
Apr. 7	Last 'normal' appearance on Louisiana Hayride.
Apr. 8–13	Tour of Colorado, Texas, New Mexico.
Apr. 14	Plane nearly crashes between Amarillo and Nashville. Recording session in Nashville. 'I Want You, I Need You, I Love You' recorded. Marvin

Hughes plays piano, Chet Atkins also on rhythm guitar.

Apr. 15–21 Tour of Texas and Oklahoma.

Apr. 23–
May 6 Plays New Frontier Hotel, Las Vegas. appears on bill with the Freddy Martin Orchestra. advertized as 'The Atomic Powered singer'

May 'I Want You, I Need You, I Love You'/'My Baby Left Me' released.

May 5 'Heartbreak Hotel' and *Elvis Presley* reach top of the Billboard singles and album charts.

May 11 Elvis buys the first home the Presleys have ever owned, 1034 Audubon Drive, Memphis.

May 13–27 Tour of Midwest.

May 15 Interrupts tour to play Cotton Festival in Memphis.

June 3 Plays Oakland Arena, California

June 5 Second appearance on 'The Milton Berle Show' broadcast live from ABC-TV studios, Los Angeles. Performance of 'Hound Dog', a song he hasn't yet recorded, brings storm of protest from outraged middle America. Also performs 'I Want You , I Need You, I Love You'.

June 6–8 Short tour of southern California and Arizona.

June 22–28 Tour of Georgia and Carolinas.

July 1 Only appearance on NBC-TV's 'Steve Allen Show', broadcast live from New York. Sings 'Hound Dog' dressed in tails to win back mainstream audience.

July 2 Recording session at RCA building in New York. Finished takes of 'Hound Dog', 'Don't Be Cruel' and 'Anyway You Want Me'.

July 4 Benefit concert at Russwood Park Baseball Stadium, Memphis.

July 13 'Hound Dog'/'Don't Be Cruel' released.

July 30 'Hound Dog'/'Don't Be Cruel' sells one million after 18 days.

Aug. 3– 12 Tour of Florida and New Orleans.

Aug. 23 Filming starts on *The Reno Brothers* movie, later changed to *Love Me Tender*, at 20th Century Fox studios, Hollywood.

Aug. 24 Recording session at 20th Century Fox studios for *Love Me Tender* soundtrack. 'Love Me Tender' and 'We're Gonna Move' recorded. Session musicians only used on these takes.

Aug. 31 Seven singles released by RCA, comprising all 12 tracks on the debut LP: 'Blue Suede Shoes'/'Tutti Frutti', 'I Got A Woman'/'I'm Counting On You', 'I'll Never Let You Go'/'I'm Gonna Sit Right Down And Cry (Over You), 'Trying To Get To You'/'I Love You Because', 'Blue Moon'/'Just Because', 'Money Honey'/'One-Sided Love Affair' together with 'Shake Rattle And Roll'/'Lawdy Miss Clawdy'.

Sept. 1–3 Recording session at Radio Recorders studio, Hollywood. Tracks recorded include 'Love Me', 'Ready Teddy', 'Rip It Up', 'Paralyzed', 'Long Tall Sally', 'When My Blue Moon Turns To Gold Again' and 'Old Shep'. Elvis plays piano on 'Old Shep'.

Sept. 4 *Shake Rattle And Roll* (Other tracks: 'I Love You Because', Blue Moon', 'Lawdy Miss Clawdy') and *The Real Elvis* ('Don't Be Cruel', 'I Want You, I Need You, I Love You', 'Hound Dog') EPs released.

Sept. 5 Recording session at 20th Century Fox Studios. 'Poor Boy', and 'Let Me' taped. Studio musicians used.

Sept. 9 First appearance on 'The Ed Sullivan Show' broadcast live from CBS-TV studios in Los Angeles, hosted by Charles Laughton. Highest audience in TV history at the time. Songs Elvis performed: 'Don't Be Cruel', 'Love Me Tender', 'Ready Teddy', 'Hound Dog'.

Sept. 26 Return to Tupelo, performs two shows at Mississippi-Alabama Show 11 years since his first public appearance at the Tupelo Fairgrounds.

Sept. 28 'Love Me Tender'/'Any Way You Want Me' released.

Oct. *Anyway You Want Me* EP released. Title track plus 'I'm Left, You're Right, She's Gone', 'I Don't Care If The Sun Don't Shine', 'Mystery Train'.

Chronology
January 1956–March 1958

Oct. 11–14	Tour of Texas, including opening at Dallas Cotton Bowl, to 26,000 audience.
Oct. 19	*Elvis* LP released, together with *Elvis, Volume 1* EP. EP tracks: 'Rip It Up', 'Love Me', 'When My Blue Moon Turns To Gold', 'Paralyzed'.
Oct. 28	Second appearance on 'The Ed Sullivan Show' broadcast live from New York. Sings 'Don't Be Cruel', 'Love Me Tender', 'Love Me' and 'Hound Dog'.
Oct. 30	Elvis allegedly signs new contract with RCA, enabling his royalty payments to be spread over 20 years.
Nov. 16	The movie *Love Me Tender* premieres at Paramount Theater New York.
Nov. 21	The movie *Love Me Tender* opens in movie theaters nationally. *Love Me Tender* EP, containing title track plus the other songs from the movie, 'Let Me', 'Poor Boy', 'We're Gonna Move', is released.
Nov. 22–25	Tour of Ohio and Kentucky.
Dec.	*Elvis, Volume 2* EP released. Contains 'So Glad You're Mine', 'Old Shep', 'Ready Teddy', 'Anyplace Is Paradise'.
Dec. 4	Elvis meets Carl Perkins, Johnny Cash and Jerry Lee Lewis at Sun Studios, Memphis. Informal recordings later issued (1981) as *The Million Dollar Quartet* album. Tracks taped include 'Peace In The Valley', 'I Shall Not Be Moved' and 'Little Cabin On The Hill'.
Dec. 16	Final show on *Louisiana Hayride* at Shreveport Fairgrounds, 9,000 in attendance.
Dec. 22	Non-singing appearance at the WDIA Goodwill Review, Memphis.
1957	
Jan.	*Strictly Elvis* EP released. Contains 'Long Tall Sally', 'First In Line', 'How Do You Think I Feel', 'How's The World Treating You'
Jan. 4	Army pre-induction physical examination at Kennedy Veterans Hospital, Memphis.
Jan. 6	Third and final appearance on 'The Ed Sullivan Show' live from New York.
Jan. 12,13	Recording session at Radio Recorders studio, Hollywood. Tracks recorded include 'All Shook Up', 'Got A Lot O' Livin' To Do!', 'Peace In The Valley', 'I Believe' and 'Mean Woman Blues'. Gordon Stoker plays piano.
Jan. 15–18, 21, 22	Soundtrack recordings for *Loving You* at Radio Recorders. Tracks later released on record are 'Party', 'Hot Dog' and 'Lonesome Cowboy'.
Jan. 19	'Playing For Keeps'/'Too Much' released. Further recording session at Radio Recorders studio, Hollywood. 'Have I Told You Lately That I Love You', 'Blueberry Hill', 'It Is No Secret' and 'Is It So Strange' taped. Dudley Brooks plays piano.
Jan. 21	Filming starts on *Loving You* at Paramount Studios, Hollywood.
Jan. 24	Recording session at Radio Recorders, Hollywood. '(Let Me Be Your) Teddy Bear' and 'One Night Of Sin' taped.
Feb. 23,24	Recording session at Radio Recorders, Hollywood. 'Loving You', 'One Night', 'When It Rains It Really Pours' among tracks recorded.
Mar. 19	Elvis negotiates the purchase of Graceland, a mansion on the southern outskirts of Memphis for $100,000 including the deeds to his present home in Audubon Drive.
Mar. 22	'All Shook Up'/'That's When Your Heartaches Begin' single and *Peace In The Valley* EP ('Peace In The Valley', 'It Is No Secret', 'I Believe', 'Take My Hand Precious Lord') released.
Mar. 28 – Apr. 6	Tour of Midwest, Northeast

and Canada, first appearance of the gold suit.

Apr. 2 First live show outside the US, as Elvis plays Toronto.

Apr. 10 The Presleys move into Graceland.

Apr. 30 Recording session for soundtrack to *Jailhouse Rock* at Radio Recorders. Tracks later issued on record include 'Jailhouse Rock', '(You're So Square) Baby I Don't Care', on which Elvis plays bass, and 'I Want To Be Free'. Mike Stoller and Dudley Brooks on piano.

May 1 Elvis reports to MGM Studios, Culver City for filming on *Jailhouse Rock*.

June 11 'Teddy Bear'/'Loving You' released.

July 9 The film *Loving You* premieres at the Strand Theater, Memphis, soundtrack LP released.

July 30 *Loving You* opens in movie theaters across the country.

Aug. *Loving You, Volume 1* (Title track plus 'Party', 'Teddy Bear', 'True Love') and *Loving You, Volume 2* ('Lonesome Cowboy', 'Hot Dog', 'Mean Woman Blues', 'Got A Lot O' Livin' To Do') soundtrack EPs released. *Just For You* EP released. Tracks: 'I Need You So', 'Have I Told You Lately That I Love You', 'Blueberry Hill', 'Is It So Strange'.

Aug. 30 – Sept. 2 Tour of Pacific Northwest, including Vancouver.

Sept. 5 - 7 Recording session at Radio Recorders, Hollywood. Tracks include 'Treat Me Nice', 'Don't', 'My Wish Came True', 'Blue Christmas' together with other Christmas songs.

Sept. 21 Scotty Moore and Bill Black resign from Elvis's backing band. While Elvis is earning vast sums of money they still make $100 a week at home or $200 on the road. Their attempt to supplement their income by being allowed recording time at Radio Recorders at the end of a Presley session is refused by Parker, so they quit.

Sept. 24 'Jailhouse Rock'/'Treat Me Nice' released.

Sept. 27 Concert at Tupelo Fairgrounds is Elvis's first without Scotty Moore and Bill Black. Both rejoin him until he goes into the army. Scotty Moore plays occasional recording sessions with Elvis until 1969.

Oct. 10 Movie *Jailhouse Rock* given press premiere.

Oct. 30 *Jailhouse Rock* EP released. Title track plus 'Young And Beautiful', 'I Want To Be Free', 'Don't Leave Me Now', 'Baby, I Don't Care'.

Nov. 8 The film *Jailhouse Rock* opens in movie theaters.

Nov. 10,11 Plays Honolulu Stadium and Schofield Barracks, Hawaii.

Nov. 19 *Elvis' Christmas Album* released together with *Elvis Sings Christmas Songs* EP ('Santa Bring My Baby Back', 'Blue Christmas', 'Santa Claus Is Back In Town', 'I'll Be Home For Christmas'). Reaction is extremely strange, with many radio stations banning the records for being 'in bad taste'.

Dec. 19 Elvis's army draft notice is delivered.

1958

Jan. 7 'Don't'/'I Beg Of You' released.

Jan. 15,16 Soundtrack recording session for *King Creole* at Radio Recorders. Tracks later issued on record include, 'Hard Headed Woman', 'Trouble', 'Crawfish', 'Don't Ask Me Why'.

Jan. 20 Filming starts on *King Creole* at Paramount Studios, Hollywood.

Jan. 23 Continuation of soundtrack recording at Radio Recorders studio, Hollywood. 'King Creole' and 'Young Dreams' recorded.

Feb. 1 Recording session at Radio Recorders, Hollywood. 'Doncha' Think It's Time', 'Wear My Ring Around Your Neck', 'My Wish Came True' and 'Your Cheatin' Heart' taped.

Feb./Mar. Location filming in New Orleans for *King Creole*.

Part Five: DUTY AND EASY MONEY –
THE ARMY AND THE MOVIES
1958–1968

"I learned a lot about people in the Army. I never lived with other people before and had a chance to find out how they think. It sure changed me but I can't tell you off hand how."

"If I were a good actor, I think I would like it a little better, although if I ever break into acting completely I'll still continue singing, I'll still continue making records."

"I never griped. If I didn't like something, nobody knew excepting me."

"I don't believe in Stanislavsky or whatever those methods of acting are called. I have never read Stanislavsky and I don't intend to. I don't believe in drama teachers either. Why should I? The director I work with is my teacher and anything he tells me goes. Why should there be another guy explaining to me what the director wants when I can ask him."

"I was the only child and Mama was always right with me. Maybe she was too good. I suppose because I was an only child I was a little closer. I mean everyone loves their mother but I was an only child and my mother was always with me, all my life, and it wasn't only like losing a mother it was like losing a friend, a companion, someone to talk to."

"Getting back to it wasn't as simple as I thought it'd be."

"[Mom is] my best girl friend, and I bought her and Dad a home in Memphis, where I hope they'll be for a long, long time."

"I don't drink, I don't smoke and I like to go to the movies. Maybe some day I'm gonna have a home and a family of my own and I won't budge from it."

"I've been treated no better nor any worse than any of the other boys, and that's the way I wanted it."

"Well there's nobody that helps you out. They have a director for the scenes, as far as the acting, as far as the singing and all, you're on your own. Nobody tells you how to do that, you have to learn it yourself."

"Am I a rock and roller and balladeer, or a movie actor? I feel I can do both and not let one interfere with the other. I stop thinking of my guitar when I step on a movie stage."

"In some scenes I was pretty natural, in others I was trying to act, and when you start trying to act, you're dead."

"Naturally you can't go places like other people, you can't go to your local theater and things like that. Whenever I want to see a movie, I have the theater manager show it to me after the theater closes up at night. They have a fairground there and I rent the fairground when it closes up sometimes."

"It isn't that I don't like Hollywood. But a man gets lonesome for the things that are familiar to him; his friends and acquaintances. I know I do. I only really feel at home in Memphis."

"If I wasn't sincere I'd just leaf through my work and say 'Gimme my money and I'll get the hell out'."

Introduction

After the two most extraordinary years in the life of any entertainer, Elvis went into retreat. He had, for 30 months, been at the center of a storm of hysteria, popularity and controversy such as America had never seen. For the next ten years he pulled away from contact with the public, and entered a private world surrounded by a small group of companions. He still made records and he certainly made movies — too many of them. But in neither did he show any real commitment, and the results were predictably bad. Between November 1957 and June 1968 he appeared only once on television and did just two live shows — both in 1961.

The hysteria around Elvis was bound to burn itself out sooner or later. Maybe it was better to do something positive to change things, instead of carrying on playing inaudible concerts to bigger and bigger screaming audiences. Elvis went into the army to do his duty to his country, but also because his manager thought it would be a good idea in the long run.

The barren years of the sixties give rise to the greatest speculation about Elvis's relationship with Colonel Parker. When the two joined up in late 1955 Elvis was a rising star, with a huge following in the South, but without a national hit record to his name. Within a few months of signing with Parker he was on national television, was signed to a major record label, had a record sitting on top of Billboard's chart and had signed a seven year contract with Paramount Pictures.

What happened next might have been good for Parker, but was it good for Elvis? It's clear that while Elvis was away in Germany, Parker and Hal Wallis planned out his future movie career for him along with Abe Lastfogel from his music publishers Hill and Range. This would involve a series of light comedies with interludes for singing. The songs from the movies would be issued on soundtrack albums and everyone — RCA, Hill and Range, Paramount Pictures and Colonel Parker — would be happy. For Elvis this meant no serious dramatic roles, and no non-singing parts. To add insult to injury Parker insisted that Elvis did no other recordings apart from his movie soundtracks. There was no point in competing with yourself. RCA was forced to endlessly repackage old material and scour the old studio tapes for material that could be issued as new. The release of second-rate material and awful soundtracks took its toll on Elvis's reputation. In the fifties we know that Elvis took charge of his recording sessions, selecting the material, making the arrangements, and choosing the takes. Parker kept well away. But now the music was subordinated to the movies.

So the question arises, why did Elvis go along with all this? We'll never know the answer. It could be that Elvis felt he owed Parker so much, that he shouldn't interfere. That the Colonel had always known best in the past, and so he must now as well. It could be that after his mother's death he lost interest in his own creative talent. Whatever the reason, Elvis abdicated responsibility for his own artistic output for ten long years.

Duty And Tragedy

Army induction and Gladys Presley's death

Elvis's entry into the army was an event without precedent or parallel. He was at the height of the most popular music career of the century. He was an idol for millions of youngsters all over the world, and he was, in both theirs and their parents eyes, a symbol of youthful freedom and rebellion. Although movie stars had signed up to do their bit for the country in both World Wars, Elvis was in a very different situation. In 1958 America wasn't at war, and avoiding the draft would have been seen as an acceptable choice for Elvis. After all, just through the taxes he paid, he was doing more good for the country out of the army than in it. So why did he go in, and was it his decision?

Elvis was always very dutiful in his statements about the army. He said that he would be proud to serve his country in any way he could, and to pay back some of what the country had given him. He wanted, he said, to be just like any other soldier and do his duty. But those closest to him say that he was dreading the prospect. When he received his official draft notice on December 20, 1957 he was about to start work on his fourth film, *King Creole*, and the first one that had a serious role for him. It also had a high quality director in Michael Curtiz, whose previous work included *Casablanca*, and a starry cast headed by Walter Mathau. Elvis's records had been at Number One on the Billboard chart for half of the preceding year, and his concerts were selling out everywhere. In fact the concerts had become so unmanageable that they'd been drastically reduced. But by 1958 he'd achieved a balance between movies, live shows and recordings. Above all he must have felt on the brink of something big in Hollywood.

On top of all that, Elvis clearly didn't relish spending two years away from his home in Memphis. He had just bought a new house, and surrounded himself with his family and his friends. Graceland was big enough to accommodate everyone that Elvis invited, and he obviously wanted and needed to be with other people at all times. Now he was going to be taken away from this and put with a bunch of guys who he didn't know, and who would very probably resent his success.

His mother Gladys was devastated by the idea of Elvis being taken away from her. Through all the upheavals of the last 22 years, the two of them had stuck together and remained extremely close.

Given all these negatives, the question

remains, why did he go in? Any explanation must center around Tom Parker and the strength of his influence over Elvis and his family. For Elvis it became not so much a matter of "Why am I going in to the army?" as "Why isn't the Colonel doing something to stop me going in?" How much was calcula-

"Where else could a nobody become a somebody so quickly, and in what other nation in the world would such a rich and famous man serve alongside you other draftees without trying to use influences to buy his way out? In my book this is American democracy at its best, the blessed way of life for whose protection you and Elvis have been called upon to contribute twenty-four months of your young lives."
Hy Gardner

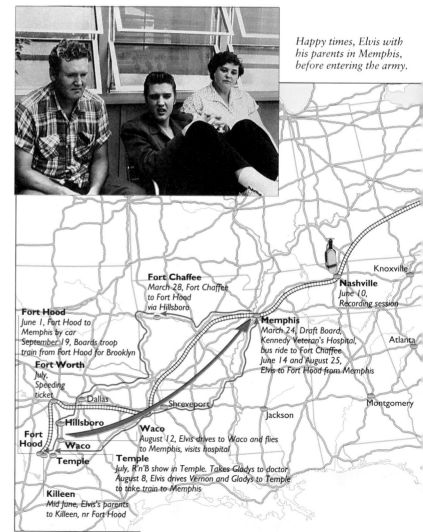

Happy times, Elvis with his parents in Memphis, before entering the army.

Fort Chaffee
March 28, Fort Chaffee to Fort Hood via Hillsboro

Fort Hood
June 1, Fort Hood to Memphis by car
September 19, Boards troop train from Fort Hood for Brooklyn

Fort Worth
July, Speeding ticket

Dallas

Hillsboro

Fort Hood

Waco

Temple

Killeen
Mid June, Elvis's parents to Killeen, nr Fort Hood

Shreveport

Waco
August 12, Elvis drives to Waco and flies to Memphis, visits hospital

Temple
July, R'n'B show in Temple. Takes Gladys to doctor
August 8, Elvis drives Vernon and Gladys to Temple to take train to Memphis

Memphis
March 24, Draft Board, Kennedy Veteran's Hospital, bus ride to Fort Chaffee
June 14 and August 25, Elvis to Fort Hood from Memphis

Jackson

Nashville
June 10, Recording session

Knoxville

Atlanta

Montgomery

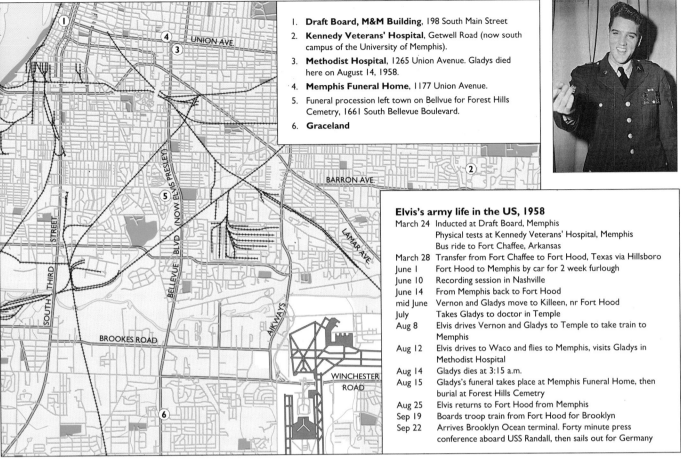

1. **Draft Board, M&M Building**, 198 South Main Street
2. **Kennedy Veterans' Hospital**, Getwell Road (now south campus of the University of Memphis).
3. **Methodist Hospital**, 1265 Union Avenue. Gladys died here on August 14, 1958.
4. **Memphis Funeral Home**, 1177 Union Avenue.
5. Funeral procession left town on Bellvue for Forest Hills Cemetry, 1661 South Bellevue Boulevard.
6. **Graceland**

Elvis's army life in the US, 1958

March 24	Inducted at Draft Board, Memphis
	Physical tests at Kennedy Veterans' Hospital, Memphis
	Bus ride to Fort Chaffee, Arkansas
March 28	Transfer from Fort Chaffee to Fort Hood, Texas via Hillsboro
June 1	Fort Hood to Memphis by car for 2 week furlough
June 10	Recording session in Nashville
June 14	From Memphis back to Fort Hood
mid June	Vernon and Gladys move to Killeen, nr Fort Hood
July	Takes Gladys to doctor in Temple
Aug 8	Elvis drives Vernon and Gladys to Temple to take train to Memphis
Aug 12	Elvis drives to Waco and flies to Memphis, visits Gladys in Methodist Hospital
Aug 14	Gladys dies at 3:15 a.m.
Aug 15	Gladys's funeral takes place at Memphis Funeral Home, then burial at Forest Hills Cemetery
Aug 25	Elvis returns to Fort Hood from Memphis
Sep 19	Boards troop train from Fort Hood for Brooklyn
Sep 22	Arrives Brooklyn Ocean terminal. Forty minute press conference aboard USS Randall, then sails out for Germany

tion on Parker's part, and how much was guesswork, we'll probably never know. In retrospect the gamble of allowing the army to draft Elvis paid off for Parker.

It was, at the time, a publicity sensation, putting Elvis on national news for weeks. But in the long term it moved Elvis's image into the mainstream, where Parker had wanted it to be. He correctly saw that the teenage audience of the fifties would be grown up by the sixties, and would want a different kind of idol. Although Elvis's popularity gradually declined through the sixties, his early audience remained faithful enough to turn out in vast numbers for the concerts in the seventies. This wouldn't have happened for any performer that tried to continually cater for a teenaged audience.

But if the army gave Elvis a chance for enduring popularity, it may have taken away his chance to make good movies. *King Creole* is without doubt his best acting part, but would he have gone on to be a movie star in the mold of his idols Brando and Dean? On the evidence of his future career it seems highly doubtful, but he may have risen above the mediocrity that characterized almost all his sixties films.

The worst tragedy

In June 1958 Vernon and Gladys Presley came to live in a house in Killeen, Texas near Fort Hood, Elvis training camp. In late July Gladys became ill, and Elvis drove her to see a doctor in Temple, Texas. Her condition worsened so that on August 8, Vernon and Gladys took a train back to Memphis. Gladys was admitted to the Methodist hospital in Memphis. Elvis flew from Waco to Memphis on August 12 to visit her. On August 14 she died at the age of only 46. Gladys had suffered from liver problems for some time, though whether she had hepatitis is uncertain. Her death was the most tragic time of Elvis's life. He was distraught and inconsolable for days. Looking around at Graceland and thinking of his fame and all the money he had earned he said with obvious sincerity, that he would give it all just to have his mother back.

Eleven days later Elvis returned to Fort Hood to complete his basic training. It is certainly conceivable that the routine of army life may have helped him to get through the time after Gladys's death. Within a month he was on board the USS Randall off Brooklyn, giving a final press conference before sailing out to army life in Germany.

Just Another Soldier

With the US Army in Germany 1958 to 1960

Elvis arrived in West Germany on Wednesday October 1, 1958, and stayed (except for two brief holidays in Paris) until Wednesday March 2, 1960. He was in Germany as an ordinary soldier: Private 53310761, Company D, 1st Medium Tank Battalion, 32nd Armor, Third Army Division. Yet inevitably, Elvis never lived like an ordinary soldier. The press was with him for his first four days on the base at Friedberg — after they left, he spent only three more nights in barracks before moving into an hotel in nearby Bad Homburg.

For brief periods he went on maneuvers, marches and exercises like his fellow GIs, but most photographs showing Elvis at work were staged specially by army public relations, and for a congenially large proportion of his time, he was off base and at leisure.

As in the first flush of his Memphis fame, he lived in an extraordinarily open way. No long-term accommodation had been arranged in advance, and no security-guards were hired. Elvis hopped nervously in and out of spa hotels he didn't like — and then rented a modest house in a suburban street for the duration of his time in Germany: a house always under siege by fans.

Within days of his arrival, Elvis and his entourage moved out of the oppressively formal Ritter's Park Hotel in Bad Homburg, and in and out of the Hilberts Park Hotel in Bad Nauheim, where another guest was oil sheik Ibn Saud: a man who matched Elvis's penchant for giving away cars by giving out gold watches instead of autographs, but who was his cultural opposite in most other respects. And much richer. The Memphis hillbillies retreated to another Bad Nauheim Hotel, the Grünewald: "a sort of outpatients' hotel for heart-attack victims," Red West called it. Five rooms were rented (Elvis took Number 10), and here they stayed, in great uneasiness, from October 11, until February 3, 1959, when they rented, at an exorbitant price, most of a house at 14 Goethestrasse, Bad Nauheim. The landlady, Frau Pieper, stayed on in the attic, shared their kitchen and insinuated herself into the lives of her extraordinary tenants. Elvis and his entourage remained in the house, virtually open to the public, until the end of his stay in Germany in March 1960.

What other idol would have put up with this? Like the houses he'd lived in with his parents immediately before Graceland, how could anywhere so lacking in privacy have felt

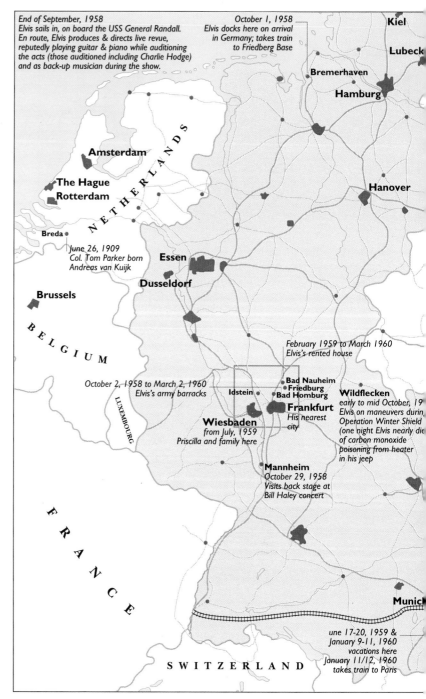

End of September, 1958
Elvis sails in, on board the USS General Randall. En route, Elvis produces & directs live revue, reputedly playing guitar & piano while auditioning the acts (those auditioned including Charlie Hodge) and as back-up musician during the show.

October 1, 1958
Elvis docks here on arrival in Germany; takes train to Friedberg Base

Kiel

Lubeck

Bremerhaven

Hamburg

Amsterdam

The Hague
Rotterdam

NETHERLANDS

Hanover

Breda

June 26, 1909
Col. Tom Parker born
Andreas van Kuijk

Essen

Dusseldorf

Brussels

BELGIUM

February 1959 to March 1960
Elvis's rented house

October 2, 1958 to March 2, 1960
Elvis's army barracks

LUXEMBOURG

Idstein

Bad Nauheim
Friedburg
Bad Homburg

Frankfurt
His nearest
city

Wildflecken
early to mid October, 19
Elvis on maneuvers durin
Operation Winter Shield
(one night Elvis nearly die
of carbon monoxide
poisoning from heater
in his jeep

Wiesbaden
from July, 1959
Priscilla and family here

FRANCE

Mannheim
October 29, 1958
Visits back stage at
Bill Haley concert

Munic

une 17-20, 1959 &
January 9-11, 1960
vacations here
January 11/12, 1960
takes train to Paris

SWITZERLAND

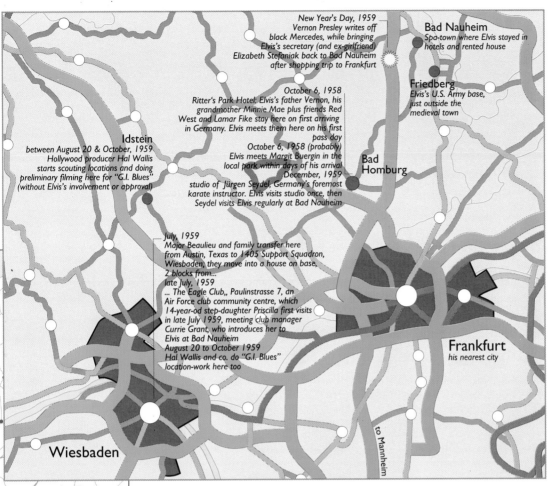

New Year's Day, 1959
Vernon Presley writes off
black Mercedes, while bringing
Elvis's secretary (and ex-girlfriend)
Elizabeth Stefaniak back to Bad Nauheim
after shopping trip to Frankfurt

Bad Nauheim
Spa-town where Elvis stayed in
hotels and rented house

October 6, 1958
Ritter's Park Hotel: Elvis's father Vernon, his
grandmother Minnie Mae plus friends Red
West and Lamar Fike stay here on first arriving
in Germany. Elvis meets them here on his first
pass day
October 6, 1958 (probably)
Elvis meets Margit Buergin in the
local park within days of his arrival
December, 1959
studio of Jürgen Seydel, Germany's foremost
karate instructor. Elvis visits studio once, then
Seydel visits Elvis regularly at Bad Nauheim

Friedberg
Elvis's U.S. Army base,
just outside the
medieval town

Idstein
between August 20 & October, 1959
Hollywood producer Hal Wallis
starts scouting locations and doing
preliminary filming here for "G.I. Blues"
(without Elvis's involvement or approval)

Bad Homburg

July, 1959
Major Beaulieu and family transfer here
from Austin, Texas to 1405 Support Squadron,
Wiesbaden; they move into a house on base,
2 blocks from...
late July, 1959
... The Eagle Club,, Paulinstrasse 7, an
Air Force club community centre, which
14-year-od step-daughter Priscilla first visits
in late July 1959, meeting club manager
Currie Grant, who introduces her to
Elvis at Bad Nauheim
August 20 to October 1959
Hal Wallis and co. do "G.I. Blues"
location-work here too

Frankfurt
his nearest city

to Mannheim

Wiesbaden

By the time he got into the army Elvis was a world-wide, not just an American, phenomenon. His records were selling everywhere, particularly in Western Europe, where teenagers were beginning to experience the affluence of their American equivalents – and buying rock and roll records with their money. Elvis was a household name in West Germany when he arrived, but German youngsters were more reserved than Americans. The crowd of several hundred that greeted him at Bremerhaven were curious rather than hysterical.

EAST GERMANY

Leipzig
November 2, 1959
15 fans jailed for 6 months to
4½ years for shouting"Long live
Elvis Presley!" and anti-régime
slogans
February 17, 1960
Government bans Elvis Presley's
records and films

CZECHOSLOVAKIA

Grafenwöhr

November 3 to
December 20, 1958
1. on maneuvers
2. meets Elizabeth Stefaniak
at army-base movie-house
3. visits her mother & step-father's
house on the base

AUSTRIA

Elvis hadn't wanted to join the army or go to Germany but, accepting these developments, he was just as reluctant to exploit them. Unhappy at the prospect of a film like G.I. Blues, he was hostile to Hal Wallis location-shooting around him in Germany in 1959. Ten years earlier Bad Nauheim had been a location in Howard Hawks's film I Was A Male War Bride, starring Cary Grant.

like a home? Yet Elvis saw no other way, and this ostensible openness betrayed his deep need to stay closed — to everything outside his own insular culture. Just as he would never again leave North America after he left the army, here in exile he never explored, or wanted to, anything beyond the American Southerner milieu of his childhood. The open house, the landlady in the kitchen, the just-folks pokiness of it: this was the narrowness of someone with no curiosity about anything German, or European, or new.

Here was the greatest popular artist of the 20th Century, a man to whom money was no object, in his prime. Free of the Colonel and out in the real world at last, he *wanted* to live with his grandma, his feckless father and a couple of crude, clownish Good Ole Boys who didn't know their Goethestrasse from their Elbe.

Yet while Elvis wanted nothing to change, his time in Germany changed his life dramatically. It was here that he lost his leadership of rock and roll, met his future wife, started taking drugs, and became, as everyone who knew him agrees, a "meaner", more irreversibly lonely figure.

On And Off Base

Elvis in Bad Nauheim and Frankfurt

Elvis's army base was Friedberg Kaserne, also known as Ray Barracks, an ex-SS barracks, outside Friedberg town. The train from Bremerhaven docks brought him inside the gates at 7.30pm, Wednesday October 1, 1958. Elvis was allocated bed 13, hut 3707. After six nights here, he never returned until confined to quarters to convalesce after a hospital stay in October–November 1959. Yet if he slept on base only ten nights in 17 months in Germany, much else happened here in the way of work and pleasure, between his press-conference in the Enlisted Men's Club the morning after his arrival, and that held in the Services Club at 9am, Tuesday March 1, 1960, the day before he flew out of Germany.

Elvis ate Christmas lunch 1958 in the Mess Hall, and in June 1959 performed there for fellow-soldiers with Pim Maas, teenage "Elvis Presley of Holland" competition-winner. Elvis played guitar, Maas piano. They sang 'Baby I Don't Care' and 'Tutti Frutti'. Elvis also frequented the quartermaster's stores, to draw uniforms and weaponry; Headquarters Company's motor stables, to park his jeep; the PX, to buy mini-cigars, gum and Pepsi; and the pharmacy, for "dexies".

A touching moment occurred at the pre-departure press-conference. Elvis was surprised to see Marion Keisker, Sam Phillips's secretary from Sun Records, who had joined the Air Force in 1957 and was now a captain, working for Armed Forces Television. "Marion! In Germany! And an officer! What do I do? Kiss you or salute you?" Marion answered: "In that order!" and hugged him.

Off base, while home became Bad Nauheim, Elvis also made forays into nearby Bad Homburg, where he and his family and friends had first re-united on German soil. Here, in December 1959, Elvis visited the studio of karate teacher Jürgen Seydel, who regularly visited the Presley house thereafter. In Friedberg town, on July 7, 1959, Elvis bought a lawn-mower from Jacob Herrmann's gardening shop: no-one else seemed inclined to sort out the Bad Nauheim garden, through which elvis often escaped persistent fans.

Frankfurt

Frankfurt, twenty miles away, was Elvis's nearest city. Here he visited Bill Haley backstage at Haley's concert on October 23, 1958, and paid visits to a club with a female contortionist. On December 22, 1958, German TV game-show hostess and ex-beauty queen Uschi Siebert presented Elvis with a rare BMW 507 sports car at BMW Gloceckle's showrooms (Elvis didn't realize he was leasing, not buying the car; later there was trouble when he had it repainted) and posed with an Isetta bubble-car. On his way home, with Vernon driving their black Mercedes saloon, they got trapped inside some level-crossing gates as a train scraped by.

Four days later, Elvis attended a "Holiday On Ice" show and met the dancers backstage.

Elvis steps down from the train inside the gates of his US Army Base in Germany, the spartan Friedberg Kaserne, which lies just outside medieval Friedberg town, in lovely countryside. (US Forces have a reputation in Germany for selecting agreeable spots.) Elvis's journey from the dockside at Bremerhaven had taken him through 200 miles of German landscape: his first glimpse of European soil. Someone had painted "Welcome to Germany, Elvis Presley" on the side of one of the carriages. A large crowd of fans was gathered outside the gates.

Bad Nauheim chronology

1. October 7, 1958: Elvis moves his retinue into the Hilberts Park Hotel, Kurstraße 2-4.

2. October 8, 1958: Elvis moves out of Friedberg barracks and checks into the hotel himself (same location as 1).

3. October 11, 1958: moves, with his retinue, to the Hotel Grünewald, 10 Terrassenstraße (Elvis often discusses reincarnation with owner Otto Schmidt).

4. February 3, 1959: moves (with retinue) to rented house at 14 Goethestraße (3000DM per month; landlady Frau Pieper stays in attic & shares kitchen with Elvis's grandmother, Minnie Mae).

5. c. December 23, 1958: meets Elisabeth Stefaniak off train when she arrives to start work as his secretary a couple of days after his return from Grafenwöhr.

6. January 16, 1959: gives blood at local Red Cross center, at Blucherstraße 22, attended by mayor.

7. Early 1959?: takes Margit Buergin to her first nightclub, La Parisienne (not located on map).

8. Early 1959: rents piano (40DM per month) from Kuehlwalter music shop, Reinhardstraße 8.

9. June 17-25, 1959: Frankie Avalon and Cliff Richard visit the house (separately) but Elvis is away, in Munich or Paris.

10. June 26, 1959: returns from Paris.

11. Summer 1959: dates 15-year-old Siegrid Schutz over a three-week period, while she is on holiday in Bad Nauheim with her mother; Elvis meets her at the house, the local park and on the nearby waste-ground where Elvis and friends play football; in January 1960 Siegrid revisits Bad Nauheim and Elvis.

12. September 13, 1959: meets 14-year-old Priscilla Beaulieu, when she is brought to the house by the Wiesbaden Eagle Club show-manager Currie Grant, an Elvis acquaintance.

13. August 20 - October 1959: Hal Wallis and Co. start scouting locations and filming for "G.I. Blues" (without Elvis's involvement or approval) here (and around Frankfurt, Wiesbaden and Idstein). (locations not specified)

14. Late October 1959: to Elvis's displeasure, Hal Wallis visits him at home (in late '59 Col. Parker has fake newspaper delivered to Wallis with headline "Elvis To Re-Enlist"!).

15. November 13, 1959: Elvis puts Monsieur Laurenz, owner/masseur of the de Fleur Clinic, South Africa, into the Rex Hotel, Reinhardstraße 2-4 (M. Laurenz visits Elvis to give him facial and body massages each evening for 2-3 weeks, till Elvis decides he's "a queer" and evicts him).

16. Dr Atta's Surgery, Elvis's dentist, Eleonoren Ring 14.

17. Salon Jean Hemer, Kurstraße 1-3 (Herr Leautzer), Elvis's hairdresser.

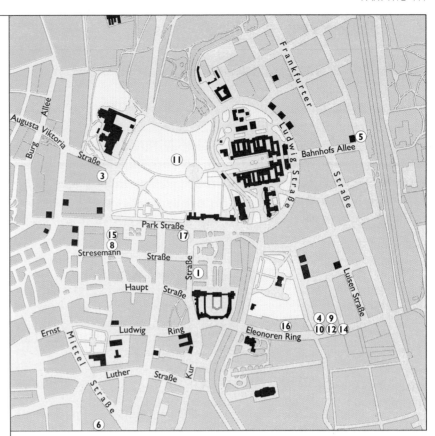

In Spring 1959 he often visited Margit Buergin's parents' home in the city's Eschersheim district, and in May first met Vera Tschechowa, an 18-year-old Munich-based movie starlet well-known for appearances in *Der Arzt von Stalingrad* (*The Doctor From Stalingrad*) and *Noch minder jährig* (*Under Age*). She and Elvis posed with polio victim Stephen Parquett for 'March Of The Dimes' (for 'Confidential' magazine).

Elvis spent the week of June 3–9, 1959, in the Army's 97th Division General Hospital with tonsillitis and a throat infection; Vernon and Dee Stanley visited him to ask if they could marry. Elvis hated the idea but agreed. Gladys had died just 10 months earlier. Elvis was back in hospital, with the same ailments, October 24–28/29, 1959 (and then confined to quarters at Friedberg till November 2).

14 Goetherstraße, Bad Nauheim: Elvis's home in Germany for thirteen months, February 3, 1959, to March 2, 1960 (right). He paid the equivalent of US$800 per month, fourfold the going rate for a modest suburban home. The ground floor comprised side-entrance, vestibule, living-room with kitchen and bathroom off; upstairs were four bedrooms (Elvis's and Vernon's facedback, Minnie Mae's and the room shared by Red West and Lamar Fike faced front) and the staircase to the landlady's attic. Elvis spent hours outside these gates, chatting to fans and signing autographs. By the time he left, he had 2,182 records to take back to the states. He left some books behind, including a 25-cent paperback of 'Cartoons by George Price', given to him by Vernon back in Tupelo, on his 12th Birthday, inscribed "May your birthday be sprinkled throu 'n' through, with Joy and love and good times too. Daddy, 01-05-47."

The US Army were worried that getting Elvis out of Germany would be harder than getting him in. To prevent mob scenes at the dockside, they decided to fly him out.

Elvis last glimpsed Frankfurt on Wednesday, March 2, 1960. He arrived from Friedberg by olive-green bus and entered the US Air Base at 4.45pm. Priscilla was there waiting. (Her own account claims, wrongly, that she and Elvis drove there together by chauffeured car from Friedberg.) Elvis was taken to a Military Air Transport Services C–118 plane. It left the runway at 5pm, heading for… Scotland.

Elvis In Paris

Tracing his footsteps through Europe

Paris was the only foreign city in the world Elvis ever visited voluntarily, outside Canada and Germany. He made two trips to Paris, both for fun, the first in June 1959 and the second just after his 25th birthday in January 1960. "Elvis in Paris"... it's a beguiling prospect, an enticing cultural mix. But only in theory. In fact, disappointingly but predictably, he appears to have done nothing, and gone nowhere, other than the most obvious tourist things in the most obvious places — and precious few even within these narrow limits. Not even a visit to the Louvre, or up the Eiffel Tower. Elvis confined himself to the safest, most unimaginative locations. Even when he sat at a pavement café on the Champs-Elysées, he chose The American Bar.

When Elvis went to Paris in 1959, it was only fifteen years since the city had been occupied by Hitler's troops. The current state of politics was that de Gaulle had become President of France and Khruschev the Soviet premier the previous year. Unlike Elvis, Khruschev famously declared himself shocked by the decadent leg-flashing of the can-can girls when he visited Paris.

Elvis stayed at the Hotel Prince de Galles, where Brando once had boiling water poured in his lap by a waiter. ("The headline for this story," Marlon quipped: "Brando Scalds Balls at Prince de Galles.") Elvis used the hotel on both trips. By the second of these, characteristically, he had a routine worked out. It was a round of nightclubs. He'd start at the Lido, then the Folies-Bergère, Moulin Rouge, Casino de Paris and Carousel, followed by le Ban Tue and 4 O'Clock Club (it opened at 4am). Elvis liked going backstage, was friendly with staff and house-musicians and loved the Lido's (mostly English) Bluebelle Girls. The only quirky place he went was for karate lessons at the shabby Club Yoseikan, to which his German teacher introduced him.

The Folies-Bergère closed down in January

June 1959: while Elvis sits nonchalantly on the Champs-Elysées signing autographs and having a shoeshine, his splendid, critically-underrated rock and roll single 'Big Hunk O' Love' tops the US singles chart, displacing Paul Anka's 'Lonely Boy'. In Britain Elvis's previous single, 'A Fool Such As I' c/w 'I Need Your Love Tonight', ends a four-week run at Number One.

First Paris trip, June 21-25, 1959:
1. Arrives, with Lamar Fike (but not Red West), checking into Hotel Prince de Galles, 33, Avenue Georges V, 8e, holds press-conference at the hotel, same day.
2. Sits at outside table of the American Bar café, 91, Champs-Elysées, (near the Cinema Permanent and the Galerie des Champs-Elysées), 8e.
3. Visits Casino de Paris nightclub, 19, rue de Clichy, 9e.
4. Visits the Lido revue theater, 116, Av. des Champs-Elysées, 8e, and there befriends Nancy Holiday, black singer once famous but whose career is now on the slide; reportedly sings a song on stage and/or plays "Willow Weep For Me" on stage on piano.

Leaves Paris by taxi, June 25, 1959, arriving back in Bad Nauheim next day.

Second Paris trip, January 12-19, 1960:
5. Arrives, again from Munich but by train (hiring whole carriage) with Fike, Charlie Hodge and Rex Mansfield, arriving at le Gare de l'Est (train station); is joined by his German karate instructor Jürgen Seydel for this leg of his trip; again books into the Hotel Prince de Galles on Avenue George V. During his visit Elvis was taken to Murakami Tetsuji, eminent Japanese karate master at his spartan studio at the Club Yoseikan, where he attends 4-day daytime course, starting early mornings.
6. Revisits le Lido.
7. Folies-Bergère, rue Richey.
8. the Moulin Rouge, 82, Boulevard de Clichy (Place Blanche), 11e.
9. Revisits the Casino de Paris.

Returns to Germany in hired black limo.

1993. The Lido still has sixty Bluebelle Girls. The Prince de Galles is still a hotel.

Elvis in Munich

On June 17, 1959, Elvis, Red West and Lamar Fike arrive in Munich by taxi from Bad Nauheim, en route to Paris (except that it isn't en route). Elvis re-acquaints himself with Vera Tschechowa, staying three days at her mother Ada's home in the Obermenzing district. Red and Lamar are thrown out next day, repairing to the Hotel Edelweiss.

Next day Elvis visits the Theater unter den Arkaden to see Vera performing in a play, *The Seducer*. Elvis hires the theater for this performance. They join a friend of Vera's at the Operncafé, and then dine at the opulent Kanne Restaurant on Maximilianstrasse, Munich's main street.

On June 19 Elvis and Vera visit the Bavaria Film Studios during the making of a viking film, and ride a motorboat on Lake Starnberger. That night they visit the Moulin Rouge nightclub, in Munzgasse district. Vera and her friends are embarrassed by Red and Lamar bossing Elvis around, and by their "belching and farting".

Elvis returns to the Moulin Rouge next evening, and stays all night. It may be that Ada Tschechowa has ordered Elvis out of her house by now, though he returns for breakfast. Relations between Elvis and Vera are cooled — he arrives, she complains, with "bits of tinsel everywhere, in his hair and his eyebrows". Elvis and entourage leave that morning, having proved irredeemably vulgar, in the Tschechowas' European eyes.

Seven months later, Elvis repeats his Munich trip in Josef Wehrheim's taxi, arriving about January 9, 1960, again visiting the Moulin Rouge nightclub — but not Vera Tschechowa. He stays two nights (at an unidentified hotel) before going on to Paris, this time by train, on January 11 or 12.

(Above) the Europe Elvis didn't visit. He had to be in West Germany; he spent twelve days in Paris, and an involuntary hour on a runway in Scotland. That was it. Despite his fame, Elvis could probably have got round a good part of Europe without being mobbed as he was in the States. Instead he stuck with what he knew. Did Elvis feel no curiosity about, or openness toward, foreign shores? He had the world at his feet but never saw it.

(Above) Elvis with 18-year-old film starlet Vera Tschechowa — here looking very Audrey Hepburn and gamin — at the Moulin Rouge nightclub, Munich, June 1959. The quiet intimacy of the picture is misleading: there were at least seven other people sitting round the same small table.

"PRESTWICK AIRPORT"
by
William Neill

Here the world's great walked on our common ground,
though we had history before they came:
Wallace once stood upon a nearby mound
to watch the well-stocked barns of Ayr aflame.
When I was young, they called it Orangefield:
Ball and McCudden used to fly from here,
flat western farmland of the fogless bield
long before radar made dark heaven clear.
Now to new fields the flying galleons sail,
tracing their glide-paths over city walls.
Where once the Sleeping Warrior marked the trail,
the ghosts of queueing phantoms haunt the halls.

But here, among the phantoms and the blues,
Elvis touched Scotland once in G.I. shoes.

"*It was here, on the evening of Wednesday, March 2 1960, that Elvis Presley made his one and only visit to Britain... When the DC–7 he was travelling on stopped to refuel at Prestwick, the 25 year old star spent an hour talking to fans, signing autographs, shaking hands and posing for photographs.*

In his olive green uniform, Sergeant Presley charmed all who met him. "This is quite a country," he said. "I must see more of it."

...Then his plane took off into the night.

Despite persistent rumours that he was considering a concert tour, Elvis never set foot on British soil again."

From the Hard Rock Plaque erected at Prestwick International Airport and unveiled by Scotty Moore and D.J. Fontana, 25 October 1993. The airport now has a Graceland Bar.

Back To Normal?

The return to the States and an uncertain future

Elvis Presley flew back in to the United States and to civilian life, on March 3, 1960 in the middle of a snowstorm. He was stranded for two days, along with half of the New York press corps, at McGuire Air Force base in New Jersey, before being able to board the specially chartered train that was to take him to Memphis. If going in to the army had been entering uncharted waters, coming out was just as scary. The world had changed a lot in two years — particularly musically. The demand for Elvis was enormous — his record company, television stations, concert promoters, movie producers all wanted him. But what should he do next?

Elvis lands back on U.S. soil (right) in a snowstorm in the early hours of March 3, 1960 20 months after he left Brooklyn for Germany. As soon as he got out of the Army, Elvis back in uniform in G.I. Blues (middle right) a taste of the movies to come. Before that ABC managed to snap him up for "Frank Sinatra's Welcome Home Party for Elvis Presley" (far right)

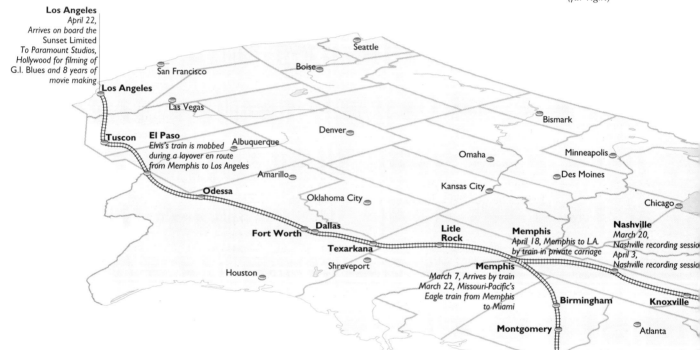

Los Angeles
April 22, Arrives on board the Sunset Limited To Paramount Studios, Hollywood for filming of G.I. Blues and 8 years of movie making

Los Angeles

San Francisco

Seattle

Boise

Las Vegas

Tuscon

El Paso
Elvis's train is mobbed during a layover en route from Memphis to Los Angeles

Albuquerque

Denver

Bismark

Minneapolis

Des Moines

Amarillo

Odessa

Oklahoma City

Kansas City

Omaha

Chicago

Nashville
March 20, Nashville recording session April 3, Nashville recording session

Dallas

Fort Worth

Texarkana

Litle Rock

Memphis
April 18, Memphis to L.A. by train in private carriage

Houston

Shreveport

Memphis
March 7, Arrives by train March 22, Missouri-Pacific's Eagle train from Memphis to Miami

Birmingham

Knoxville

Montgomery

Atlanta

Tallahassee

Jacksonville

Miami
March 26, Recorded Sinatra TV Show in Miami Beach March 29, Returned to Memphis by train

Hollywood

When Elvis went in to the army in early 1958 rock and roll music had reached the pinnacle of its combined creative and commercial potential. The artists who created this new musical form were getting hits with one classic song after another. Chuck Berry, Jerry Lee Lewis, Little Richard and others, as well as Elvis himself were producing music that will live forever.

But over the next couple of years things started to change. The big record companies saw the success of rock and roll and decided that this was the way to make money. Unfortunately, for the most part they had no real understanding of the music, or the reasons for its effect on its young audience. They simply looked at the results and tried to work out the formula. The result was an era of pseudo–rock and roll, sometimes called high school music or doo–wop. At its best it's very good pop, but there wasn't very much of that. More often handsome young men with bland voices to match their looks, sang songs of teenage love over a 4/4 beat — usually with an overladen backing vocal performing behind them. The sad truth was that rock and roll had moved away from the forces that it sprang from and was rapidly disappearing. The music business had killed its own golden goose. On top of that the huge personalities that created the music had either quit the scene, or been forced

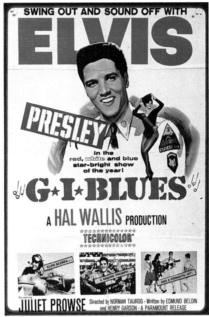

out through scandal. It was to be another four years before British musicians, who had soaked up every note of the classic rock and roll era, brought its energy back to America.

There were a million advance orders for Elvis's first post-army single, even before he'd set foot inside a recording studio. RCA were desperate to get him to record something before he got back into Hollywood, where the

Detroit

Columbus

Buffalo

Pittsburgh

McGuire Air Force Base
March 3, Arrives in snowstorm, 7.40 am. To Fort Dix, next door, for breakfast and 2 hour press conference March 4, Elvis and press corps stranded in Fort Dix by snow

March 5, Boards 'The Tennessean' train for journey to Memphis

Charleston

Asheville

Philadelphia

Charlotte

Richmond

demands of film schedules would take him over. He went to Nashville on March 20 and again on April 3. In these sessions he recorded 'Stuck On You', 'It's Now Or Never' and 'Are You Lonesome Tonight'. Together they give an indication of how Elvis solved the problem of what type of music to sing. He became a ballad singer with a sideline in slightly off-beat numbers sung to a gentle shuffle rhythm. He was aiming for the middle of the road.

In between these sessions Elvis took the train from Memphis to Miami to record a TV special with Frank Sinatra. On the way Parker had arranged that advance notice was given to towns where the train might stop. Elvis greeted increasing crowds from the rear platform of the train. Parker also arranged that 300

After April 1960, the movies became Elvis's life. For the next 8 years he never appeared on television, and gave up live shows after charity concerts in Memphis and Honolulu in early 1961. From now on it was two or three movies a year, every year.

members of Elvis fan clubs were included in the audience for the Sinatra special, to make sure his boy got his fair share of the applause. His host was a difficult figure for Elvis to come to terms with. Sinatra was a sensation with young teenagers ten years before Elvis, though he never achieved the same overwhelming popularity. But Sinatra's career as a singer had faltered and he turned to movie acting. He had appeared in musicals in the 1940s, but then got a dramatic role in *From Here To Eternity* in 1953 after agreeing to a nominal fee. He won an Oscar as Best Supporting Actor, and went on to great acclaim for his starring role in *The Man With The Golden Arm* in 1955. His singing career had revived, and now he was admired in both professions. He must have looked like Elvis's ideal role model.

But in 1957 Sinatra was quoted as saying 'Rock and roll smells phony and false. It is played, sung and written for the most part by cretinous goons. It manages to be the martial music of every sideburned delinquent on the face of the earth.' Nor did this outburst pass Elvis by — it was flung in his face at a pre-concert press conference in Hollywood. He was diplomatic then, but he would have been entitled to be angry. Four years later the two were all smiles — in showbusiness it's sometimes best to have a short memory. The show was broadcast by ABC on May 8.

By that time Elvis had returned to Memphis for a couple of weeks before boarding the Sunset Limited train for Los Angeles on April 18, 1960.

Pleasure Garden

Memphis in the sixties and seventies

On his return from the army in March 1960 Elvis was greeted by a huge crowd in Memphis. While Elvis's wealth enabled him to indulge his every whim — renting movie houses and fairgrounds for parties and buying fleets of cars and motorbikes — his fame made him a prisoner in his mansion. In Hollywood he might have had the company of fellow stars — if he'd wanted it. But in Memphis he was alone at the top of the heap. That was his choice, but it made life that much more unreal.

"After being six or seven hours in the fairgrounds in Memphis on those Dodgems, we were bruised all over, so we gradually got into the painkillers. (Elvis) was high the whole time — and we were most of the time too."
Sonny West on Memphis in the sixties

Although Elvis bought Graceland in 1957, he'd hardly had a chance to live there since. For most of that year he had been filming in Hollywood or on tour, and in March 1958 he had gone into the army. Most significantly, apart from the short vacation after her funeral, he had never been in Graceland without his mother's overwhelming presence in his life. Now, in 1960, he was back in his dream home at the age of 25, a multi-millionaire with the world at his feet.

Elvis remained unchanged by his fame in paradoxical ways that seem to reflect his poor southern upbringing. His origins don't explain why he lived the way he did — after all many movie stars have come from poor families, but have entirely uprooted themselves. But they do help us to understand some of what happened in his extraordinary life. Elvis rented and even bought homes in Hollywood, but he always lived in Memphis.

The 1960s for Elvis consisted of a continual round of movie making with rests back home in Memphis in between, interspersed with trips to Las Vegas and Hawaii for entertainment, and sometimes to Nashville for recording sessions. The movies got to the rate of three a year, but since they only took a few weeks to make, that left a lot of time to fill. When Elvis had originally starting earning serious money in the fifties he had shown generosity to his extended family, just as they had supported Gladys and Vernon through their hard times. Now he gathered his own 'family' around him — a group of friends and associates hired to perform certain duties, but mostly to provide companionship. This group became known as the 'Memphis Mafia', though they were an entirely unsinister bunch. Elvis paid them salaries and bought them cars, and in return received their loyal friendship.

Though each of the Memphis Mafia seems to have written a book about their lives with Elvis, none had more impact than *Elvis — What Happened?*. Published a few weeks before his death the book was principally Red West's response to being sacked by Elvis without explanation after 22 years of loyal service. West, his cousin Sonny and Dave Hebler told how Elvis had changed over the years. They

1.   **Graceland**, 2764 Elvis Presley Boulevard, Whitehaven. Purchased for $100,000. Lived there from March 1957 to his death.

2.   **Blue Light Studio**. Was at Beale and 2nd, now 115 Union Avenue.

3.   **Jim's Barber**. Corner of Beale and Main (as 4).

4.   **Lansky's Clothes Store**, Beale Street.

5.   **Memphian Theater**, 51 South Cooper Street. Now the Playhouse On The Square.

6.   **Fairgrounds Amusement Park**, now Libertyland, 940 Early Maxwell Boulevard.

7.   **Chenault's Drive In**, 1402 Elvis Presley Boulevard (now Helen's Place).

8.   **Loew's State Theater** (Jailhouse Rock premiered Oct 17, 1957, Elvis did not attend)

9.   **Immaculate Conception High School**, 1725 Central Avenue. Priscilla's school.

10. **1266 Dolan Drive** (backs onto Graceland). Vernon and Dee's house. Priscilla was supposed to be under their supervision.

11. **Piccadilly Cafeteria**, Whitehaven Plaza, Elvis Presley Boulevard.

12. **The Gridiron**, 4101 Elvis Presley Boulevard (a few blocks south of Graceland)

13. **Lowell Hayes Jeweller** 4872 Poplar Avenue.

14. **Supercycle**, 624 South Bellevue.

15. **Kang Rhee Institute of Self Defense**, 706 Germantown Parkway (1911 Poplar).

16. **Autorama** (formerly Robertson's Motors), 2950 Airways Boulevard.

17. **Shilling Lincoln-Mercury**, 987 Union Avenue. (south west corner of Union and Pauline).

18. **Madison Cadillac**, 341 Union Avenue.

19. **Goldsmith's Department Store**, 123 Mid-American Mall. Special after hours opening for Elvis and Priscilla

Presley Homes from 1954

20. **2414 Lamar Avenue**. End 1954 to mid 1955. Now the Tiny Tot Nursery School.

21. **1414 Getwell Street**. Mid 1955 to May 11, 1956. Rented.

22. **1034 Audubon Drive**. Purchased April 1956 for $55,000. Moved in May 11. Stayed to March 1957. Neighborhood group asked them to leave.

Elvis found some degree of seclusion at Graceland (right), though there always seemed to be a small crowd at the gates. Elvis showed a distrust of public occasions, and he rarely turned out for awards dinners (below), preferring the company of a small group of friends.

said that he became arrogant and abusive to those around him. More devastatingly it described how Elvis was consuming vast quantities of prescription drugs. The book damaged Elvis's reputation as a wholesome idol, contrasting with the drug-ridden rock music scene around him. But Red West, who was clearly extremely close to Elvis, intended that the book should wake Elvis and his entourage to the risks they were running. The fun times of the sixties — the fairgrounds, the all night movie shows, the special store openings, all looked a little tainted.

In fact, Elvis's behavior, as detailed in the Wests' book, was mild in comparison to the excesses of the rock music scene that was evolving in America. Illicit drugs of every kind were not just available to musicians, but seemed compulsory. Elvis stayed on the right side of the law, but probably damaged himself more than most, by abusing prescription drugs.

Priscilla Beaulieu

Elvis managed to persuade the parents of the 17 year old Priscilla, whom he had met in Germany, to let her come and live in Memphis while she finished school. Ostensibly under the supervision of Vernon and his wife Dee, Priscilla attended the Immaculate Conception School. Elvis continued to date other women at the time, particularly when he was out in Hollywood, so it is unclear what his relationship with Priscilla was. It's a sign of the esteem in which Elvis was held, and the naïveté of the 1960s media, that Priscilla's five-year stay in Graceland before their marriage was never adversely reported at the time. They were married in Las Vegas in 1967, but the marriage lasted less than five years. In early 1972 Priscilla moved out, and in October 1973 Elvis's petition for divorce was finalized. It is clear that losing Priscilla to another man was an enormous blow to Elvis's self-esteem, from which he never really recovered.

The Star Vehicles

Hollywood in the sixties

After *Love Me Tender*, Elvis's 1950s films yielded soundtrack recordings which stood up in their own right. There was no gap between these and the straight-forward Presley singles and LPs. 'Party', 'Got A Lot O' Livin' To Do', 'Mean Woman Blues', 'Loving You'; 'I Want To Be Free', 'Jailhouse Rock', 'Treat Me Nice', 'Don't Leave Me Now', 'King Creole', 'Trouble', 'Don't Ask Me Why', 'As Long As I Have You': whatever weakness one or two may have as songs, the smouldering power intensity Elvis brings to these recordings makes them all utterly authentic, full-blooded Presley records still breathing fire almost forty years on. In the 1960s, this crucial parity between movie-recordings and real ones was discarded. As the movies grew flimsier, their songs grew mimsier. Like the films themselves, the soundtrack records grew embarrassingly weak. They'd lost all connection with Elvis's musical roots. His 1960s movies meant that Elvis spent the decade visibly and audibly throwing away his credibility.

The whole enterprise bitterly disappointed millions of fans. It stole over us gradually. We began by skating over the weaknesses of these plots, the gooey bits, the risible fun-time sequences, the anaemic, sexless on-screen romances. We forgave *G.I. Blues*. We didn't know it would be the first of a gridlock of such "star vehicles" (vehicles less and less roadworthy) which would try to pull us into the cinema several times a year for the next eight years.

We'd just got Elvis back from the army, and he'd given us the great studio album *Elvis Is Back*, in which it was obvious from tracks like his magnificent 'Reconsider Baby' — a classical reinvention of a classical blues origi-nal — that he'd been bursting to get back to recording the music of his roots. We'd been open to 'It's Now Or Never'. We were even disarmed by 'Wooden heart', and some of the other *G.I Blues* tracks weren't bad — but what was this? How could we be having to say, of the uniquely magnificent *Elvis Presley, for God's sake*, that his work "wasn't bad"?!

Reassurance followed. First came the authentic gospel album *His Hand In Mine* (never mind the religion, the voice was mag-nificent) and then the movies *Flaming Star* and *Wild In The Country*, which both so empha-sised Elvis the actor that they hardly included songs at all. We mainly demurred at Elvis' "Wild" character's implausible self-righteous-ness toward Tuesday Weld, whose "bad girl" was extremely sexy.

In the late 1961 came *Blue Hawaii* — and such was the fervour Elvis still generated that there were lines around the block at cinemas all across the western world on the film's release. When Elvis made his tantalisingly-delayed entrance in the movie (his plane lands, we wait, the door opens, we wait, Elvis finally emerges) there were screams in the cinemas as if he'd appeared before us in real life!

Truly, the film was awful, and he was beginning to sound, as John Lennon offended us by remarking in 1963, like Bing Crosby. It was the beginning of the end. This was not what had convulsed America. This was not what had sent Elvis Presley to the top of the pop, country and R&B charts repeatedly and sensationally and made him the biggest star in the universe. Yet this was what was on offer, and as the formula became more and more cynically applied, the movies' production-val-ues got transparently cheaper and cheaper.

So did those of the soundtrack albums. The LP *It Happened At The World's Fair* served notice relatively early that technical shoddiness was going to get through too. Recorded at MGM's own sound studio in August 1962, the telling gruesomeness of songs like 'Cotton Candy Land' and 'I'm Falling In Love Tonight' was compounded by their thin, hissy vocal sound. It is audibly cheap. Whereas producers like Sam Phillips had worked miracles with the minimum of equipment and a lot of loving care, MGM and RCA with all their millions didn't seem to care at all. That kind of production incompe-tence had never been associated with the pre-army Elvis. From now on it would be par for the course.

(Far right) On the Paramount set with direc-tor Norman Taurog, pro-ducer Hal B. Wallis and Juliet Prowse during the making of G.I. Blues, (1960). Taurog would go on to direct eight other Elvis films. Wallis had already produced Loving You *and* King Creole, *the latter in partnership with the far more distinguished director Michael Curtiz. It was a partnership which had created one of Hollywood's all-time greatest movies: the incom-parable* Casablanca, 1942, *starring Bogart and Ingrid Bergman. It was certainly incomparable to G.I. Blues.*

(Below) Elvis in Charro, *one of Elvis's last Hollywood movies, and unusual for the amount of location-work involved. Elvis spent several weeks filming in and around Apache Junction, thirty miles outside Phoenix, Arizona in July–August 1968. The film was also unusual in having inciden-tal music by Hugo Montenegro, who was enjoying a million-selling hit that year with the theme from Clint Eastwood's spaghetti-west-ern* The Good The Bad And The Ugly. *Again, no comparison, unfortunately for Elvis.*

1. **Paramount Studios**. Elvis was contracted to Paramount, who contracted him out to other studios for many pictures. His Paramount movies were shot in the studio with a few location shots.

2. **Twentieth Century Fox Studios**. *Love Me Tender, Flaming Star, Wild In The Country* were all produced by Fox and partly filmed at their Hollywood studio.

3. **Radio Recorders**, Santa Monica Boulevard. The studio for Elvis's earliest Hollywood recordings. He continued to use the studio for some recordings in the 1960s.

4. **RCA Studios**, 6263 Sunset Boulevard. Elvis recorded here from April 1960 onwards.

5. **565 Perugia Way**, Bel Air. This was the house that Elvis rented for much of the 1960s. The Beatles met him here on August 27, 1965. Two months previously Elvis hit Number One in Britain for the first time in 3 years with 'Crying In The Chapel'.

6. **1059 Bellagio Road**, Bel Air. Another Hollywood home that Elvis rented.

7. **10550 Rocca Place**, Bel Air. Another rented home.

8. **1174 Hillcrest Rd**. The first house that Elvis bought in Los Angeles.

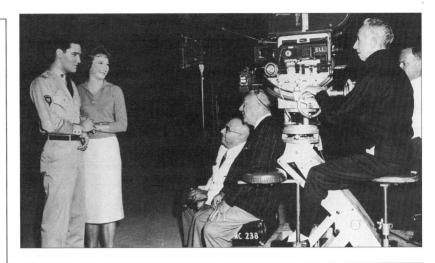

9. **MGM Studios**, Culver City. *Jailhouse Rock, It Happened At The World's Fair, Kissin' Cousins, Viva Las Vegas, Girl Happy, Harum Scarum, Spinout, Double Trouble, Stay Away Joe, Speedway, Live A Little, Love A Little, The Trouble with Girls, Elvis, That's The Way It Is* and *Elvis On Tour* were all produced by MGM, with most being shot at the Culver City studios.

10. **NBC Studios**, 3000 West Almaeda Avenue, Burbank. The 1968 TV special "Elvis" was shot at these studios.

11. **144 Monovale**, Holmby Hills. Elvis stayed here during his divorce proceedings.

12. **Long Beach Recreation Park**. The fairgrounds were a favourite haunt of Elvis and his friends in their early stays in Hollywood.

13. **United Artists**. *Follow That Dream, Kid Galahad, Frankie And Johnny, Clambake* were produced by United Artists and mostly filmed at their studio.

14. **Universal Studios**. *Change of Habit*, Elvis's last Hollywood film was shot here and on location in downtown Los Angeles in 1969

16. **Long Beach Municipal Auditorium**. Played concert June 7, 1956.

17. **Inglewood Form**. Sell-out concert, May 11, 1974.

18. **Anaheim Convention Center**. Two concerts, April 23/24, 1973.

19. **Long Beach Arena**. Concerts November 14/15, 1972.

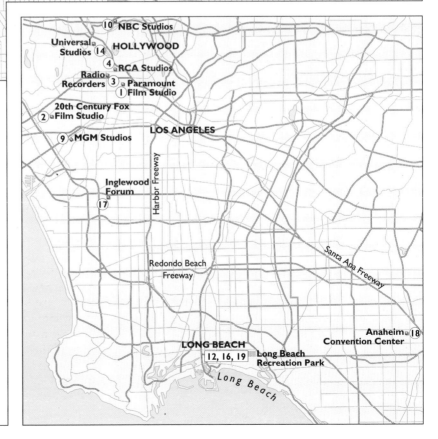

The Hollywood System

Movie locations from California to Florida

Hal Wallis and Colonel Parker had cooked up the 1960s Elvis movie formula between them. The contempt and cynicism which motivated these two old men, and its celluloid results, are delineated brilliantly in Albert Goldman's *Elvis* biography. The one effective section of this otherwise shoddy, malevolent book is the chapter called 'About Face!' in which Goldman details with passionate relish the machinery Wallis and Parker set going.

What he doesn't pin down is the cold tale of falling receipts and record–sales that was the inevitable result. This too makes interesting reading: for even in their own crude commercial terms, it was deeply foolish to wring Elvis through this tenth-rate movie mangle.

Elvis's 1950s movies were mega-successful. *Love Me Tender* grossed $1 million in three days, its title song Elvis's fourth US Number One hit single of 1956. *Loving You* was the 7th highest grossing film of 1957, its title song also a millon-selling Number One single coupled with the film-song 'Teddy Bear'. The LP and EP also topped the charts. *Jailhouse Rock* grossed $4 million in its first seven weeks on release, yielding another Number One single and EP; *King Creole* gave him yet another Number One record, a Number One EP for 23 weeks and a Number Two LP.

Not so in the early 1960s. The early rising dollar-curve flattened out, then plummeted. *G.I. Blues* briefly hit the Number Two grossing spot and yielded a Number One LP and Elvis's longest charting record, 111 weeks. The *Blue Hawaii* LP was Number One for twenty weeks; the film grossed $2 million in under two months; 'Can't Help Falling In Love' was Elvis's 29th gold record.

Encouraged by movie-songs, however, a record as toothless as 'Good Luck Charm' was now considered good enough to be an Elvis single. It was his last Number One until the movie-making stopped. The *Follow That Dream* EP peaked at Number 15, *Kid Galahad's* at 30.

And so it went. 'One Broken Heart For Sale' (*It Happened At The World's Fair*), didn't make the Top 10. The film was 1963's 55th grossing movie. *Kissin' Cousins*, made that year, had tellingly low production costs ($800, 000). The title song of 1964's 'Viva Las Vegas' peaked at Number 29, the EP man-

> *"I think that if he'd ever done a serious role and been directed properly, he could have been quite marvellous."*
> Dennis Hopper

Hawaii
Blue Hawaii, 1961
Girls! Girls! Girls!, 1962
Paradise Hawaiian Style, 1966

WASHINGTON
Seattle
It Happened At The World's Fair

NEVADA

St Helena and the Napa Valley
Wild In The Country, 1961

Las Vegas
Viva Las Vegas, 1964,
(Tropicana and Flamingo Hotels,
University of Nevada Gymnasium)
Elvis, That's The Way It Is, 1970
(International Hotel)

CALIFORNIA

Thousand Oaks, California
Roustabout, 1964
San Fernando Valley, California
Flaming Star, 1960

Henderson, Nevada
Viva Las Vegas, 1964

ARIZONA

Big Bear Lake, California
Kissin' Cousins, 1964
Idyllwild, California
Kid Galahad, 1962

Los Angeles

Sedona and Cottonwood, Arizona
Stay Away Joe, 1968

Phoenix, Arizona
Elvis, That's The Way It Is, 1970
(Veterans Memorial Stadium)

Apache Junction and Superstition Mountains
Charro!, 1969

Los Angeles,
Spinout, 1966
\(Ascot Motor Racing, Dodger Stadium)
Clambake, 1967 (Los Angeles beaches)
Live A Little, Love A Little, 1968 (Downtown streets, Hollywood-
Citizen-News offices)
Change Of Habit, 1969 (Fifth and Main Streets)

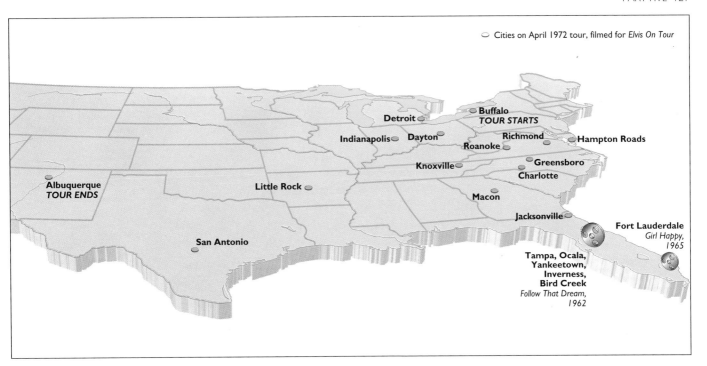

○ Cities on April 1972 tour, filmed for *Elvis On Tour*

Detroit
Buffalo
TOUR STARTS
Indianapolis Dayton
Richmond
Roanoke
Hampton Roads
Knoxville
Greensboro
Charlotte
Albuquerque
TOUR ENDS
Little Rock
Macon
Jacksonville
Fort Lauderdale
Girl Happy,
1965
San Antonio
Tampa, Ocala,
Yankeetown,
Inverness,
Bird Creek
Follow That Dream,
1962

aging Number 92 for one week. In an odd blip, the *Roustabout* LP topped the charts in the first week of 1965 — his last Number One album until 1973. That summer while the Beatles reigned, the Beach Boys quit the beach for complex *Pet Sounds* and Dylan re-energized rock with 'Like A Rolling Stone', Elvis was reduced to 'Queenie Wahine's Papaya' in *Paradise Hawaiian style*. His 1966 movies grossed $2.5, $2 and $1.7 million; the best he could do in 1967 was $1.95 million for *Easy Come, Easy Go*, nine months after release. *Charro*, 68th-biggest film of 1969, grossed $1.5 million. The profit must have been nil. Look back at *Jailhouse Rock*: $4 million in seven weeks.

And there's no point weighing the relative merits of *Clambake* and *Harum Scarum*. Boredom and shame are the only possible critical responses. All through the 1960s we were loosening up, discovering the complexities of sexuality, constructing the alternative society, questioning the integrity of Uncle Sam and unjust war... and Elvis, who had earned our loyalty by the instinctive, far-reaching questioning of society wrapped up in his music, his clothes, his street-cool insolence: here he was making movies that imposed on us a nightmare pre-Elvis America. What Elvis became in the 1960s was a formative disillusionment for many people. Except for Colonel Parker, and possibly the CIA, no one wanted life to have taken this turn.

No wonder that when the Beatles landed in America there were placards reading 'Elvis Is Dead — Long Live Ringo'.

Right: Laurel Goodwin and Elvis during the making of Girls! Girls! Girls!, *1962, caught in a far more surreally comic, human moment than any in the film. Elvis's other co-star was the lovely Stella Stevens, who'd been in TV series 77 Sunset Strip and went on to movie-roles in* The Nutty Professor, It's A Mad Mad Mad Mad World *and* Ballad Of Cable Hogue.
Below: A scene from Viva Las Vegas (Love In Las Vegas *in Britain), with Elvis nearly as old in spirit as the couple sitting behind him.*

Fantasy Islands

Elvis's Hawaii

When Elvis went to Hollywood in 1960 he entered an unreal world. He was now entirely separated from the millions of people who had bought his records, seen his shows and watched him on television in the 1950s. He was to stay that way for the next 8 years. Although only a handful of his movies were actually set in Hawaii, the islands became the archetypal setting for an Elvis film. And because his films were all that was seen of him, Elvis's public image was set against a background of palm trees, white beaches, summer sun and girls in swimsuits. In his movies Elvis was living out the fantasy of the American male. But it didn't take long for all this to bore first his audience, then Elvis himself.

Elvis first arrived in Hawaii in November 1957 to play the last two shows before he went into the army in March 1958. The shows that Elvis played in Hawaii often had a special significance. In 1957 he played two shows at the Honolulu Stadium on November 10, then played to 10,000 servicemen, servicewomen, family and friends at the Schofield Barracks Post Bowl. These were Elvis's last shows for more than two years.

The only live shows that Elvis played between November 1957 and his Las Vegas opening in July 1969, were one in Memphis, and one more, yet again in Hawaii. This show was at the Bloch Arena in Honolulu on March 25, 1961, in aid of a memorial to the USS Arizona which had been sunk at Pearl Harbor. Elvis's plane was greeted at Honolulu Airport by 3,000 fans. At the concert he played a mixture of old and new material to 6,000 fans,

including 'One Night' and 'All Shook Up' as well as 'It's Now Or Never' and 'I Need Your Love Tonight'. He closed the show, as he had done in the fifties with a lengthy rendition of 'Hound Dog'.

In audience terms, Elvis's biggest show of them all was played in Hawaii. In January 1973 *Elvis: Aloha From Hawaii* was broadcast via satellite to a worldwide audience of over one billion.

"Blue Hawaii restores Elvis Presley to his natural screen element — romantic, non-cerebral film musical."
Variety on *Blue Hawaii*

"Elvis is given a plethora of songs whether or no they fit smoothly into the action, but handles his role capably enough."
Variety on *Girls! Girls! Girls!*

Elvis's Hawaii

▒	U.S. Naval Reservation
░	Honolulu International Airport
Hanolei Bay	movie location
Honolulu (1973)	concert venue (date)
□	hotels where Elvis regularly stayed

Elvis played concerts at: Honolulu Stadium and Schofield Barracks (1957), Bloch Arena (1961), Honolulu International Center (1972) and the live "Aloha From Hawaii" broadcast in 1973). Blue Hawaii was filmed on location at Waikiki Beach, Honolulu Airport, Ala Mona Park, Kauai Airport and Lydgate Park. Girls! Girls! Girls! includes shots from Ala Wai Yacht Harbor, Kewalo Basin and Milolii on Hawaii's Kona coast. Paradise Hawaiian Style, filmed in 1965 and released in 1966, uses locations from Polynesian Cultural Center on Oahu, Hanauma Bay, Hanalei Bay Resort on Kuai and at the Sheraton Hotel on Maui.

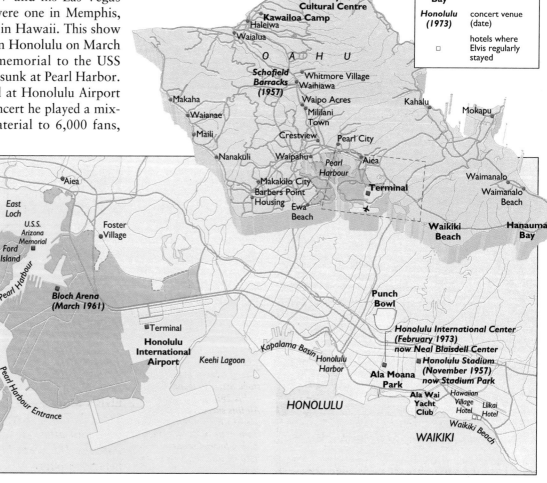

Map labels: Hanalai, KAUAI, Lihue, NIIHAU, HAWAIIAN ISLANDS, OAHU, Honolulu, MOLOKAI, Hoolehua, Kalaupapa, Kapalua, Kahului, Lanai City, Kahului, Hana, LANAI, MAUI, Hawi, Waimea, Kailua-Kona, Hilo, HAWAII, Milolii

Elvis is pictured with two of the most important men in his movie career, Hal Wallis, producer (right) and Norman Taurog, director. Wallis also negotiated the film deals with Colonel Parker on behalf of Paramount.

In March 1961, even as Elvis was playing his last concert for eight years, camera crews from Paramount Pictures were on the islands of Oahu and Kauai, searching out and filming background locations for Elvis's new movie *Blue Hawaii*. This was to be the film that set the pattern for the next decade. Coming hard on the heels of the financial failure of *Flaming Star*, the success of *Blue Hawaii* and its mega-selling soundtrack album convinced Tom Parker and his Hollywood cronies that this was the way for Elvis to go. Not that Parker needed convincing — he'd been in favor of bland vehicles with breaks for occasional songs all along. If Elvis had succeeded as a dramatic actor that might have made him a more independent figure.

So, over the next seven years Elvis made frequent trips out to Hawaii to make a succession of ever-more absurd movies. In *Blue Hawaii* Elvis played Chad Gates, employed as a guide by a Hawaiian tourist agency. He escorts a group of schoolgirls around the islands, together with their chaperone, and, as

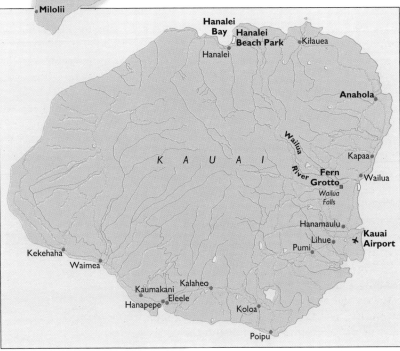

Map labels: Hanalei Bay, Hanalei Beach Park, Kilauea, Hanalei, Anahola, Wailua River, Kapaa, Fern Grotto, Wailua, Wailua Falls, KAUAI, Hanamaulu, Kauai Airport, Lihue, Pumi, Kekehaha, Waimea, Kaumakani, Kalaheo, Eleele, Hanapepe, Koloa, Poipu

THE WORLD'S LUSHEST PARADISE OF SONG

ELVIS PRESLEY RIDES THE CREST OF THE WAVE IN BLUE HAWAII

A HAL WALLIS PRODUCTION

TECHNICOLOR® AND IN PANAVISION®

14 TERRIFIC SONGS!

JOAN BLACKMAN · ANGELA LANSBURY · NANCY WALTERS   DIRECTED BY NORMAN TAUROG · SCREENPLAY HAL KAN

The movie Blue Hawaii was released in November 1961, and managed to be the 18th biggest grossing film that year, taking $2 million in the first two months. The soundtrack album was one of Elvis's most successful ever, staying for twenty weeks at the top of the Billboard chart. The single 'Can't Help Falling In Love', taken from the album and latterly a favorite in Elvis's stage act, also went gold — his 29th single to do so. All this success effectively sealed Elvis's movie fate — from now on he was stuck with a formula that became progressively more stale.

they say, complications arise. Everything is sorted out in the end though, and Chad gets to marry his girlfriend played by Joan Blackman to the strains of 'The Hawaiian Wedding Song'. In the late fifties a new type of film had emerged. These 'beach movies' portrayed young white Americans having fun in the sun. They ran out of steam fairly quickly. Elvis unfortunately carried on the tradition single–handed, and *Blue Hawaii* was even originally titled *Hawaiian Beach Boy*.

Girls! Girls! Girls! continued the Hawaii theme in 1962, this time with Elvis as a charter boat pilot and part-time night club singer. The film is notable only for one of Elvis's better songs of the time — 'Return To Sender'. The transportation motif was taken up again after an interval of four years, in *Paradise Hawaiian Style*, with Elvis playing a helicopter pilot.

Chronology

March 1958–June 1968

1958

Mar. 24	Elvis reports to draft board in Memphis. After a physical he travels to Fort Chaffee, Arkansas by army bus.
Mar. 25	GI haircut is administered by James Peterson.
Mar. 28	Leaves Fort Chaffee, Arkansas for Fort Hood, Texas for basic training.
Apr. 1	'Wear My Ring Around Your Neck'/'Don'tcha Think It's Time' is released.
June 1	Start of two week leave. Drives from Fort Hood to Memphis.
June 10	'Hard Headed Woman'/ 'Don't Ask Me Why' released. Last single on 78 format. Recording session in Nashville. 'A Fool Such As I', 'I Need Your Love Tonight', 'A Big Hunk O' Love', 'Ain't That Loving You Baby' and 'I Got Stung' recorded.
June 14	Returns to Fort Hood.
June	Vernon and Gladys move to rented house in Killeen near Fort Hood. Elvis moves in with them.
July 2	The movie *King Creole* goes on general release across the country.
Late July	Gladys falls ill, Elvis takes her to a doctor in Temple.
Aug.	*King Creole* LP released.
Aug. 8	Elvis drives Vernon and Gladys to Temple to take train to Memphis.
Aug. 12	Elvis drives to Waco and flies to Memphis. Visits his mother in the hospital
Aug. 14	Gladys dies at 3:15am. Vernon is with her, Elvis is at Graceland.
Aug. 15	Gladys's funeral in Memphis. She is buried at Forest Hill Cemetery.
Aug. 16	Elvis attends the funeral of Red West's father.
Aug. 25	Returns to army duty at Fort Hood from Memphis.
Sept. 19	Boards troop train from Fort Hood for Brooklyn.
Sept. 22	Arrives Brooklyn Ocean Terminal. 40 minute press conference aboard USS Randall, then sails out.
Oct.	*King Creole, Volume 1* and *King Creole, Volume 2* EPs released.
Oct. 1	Arrives at Bremerhaven, West Germany. Train from there to Friedberg.
Oct.	Vernon, Minnie Mae (Elvis's grandmother), Red West and Lamar Fike arrive at Ritter's Park Hotel, Bad Homburg.
Oct. 7–10	Elvis moves, with his family and friends, into Hilberts Park Hotel, Bad Nauheim.
Oct. 11	Elvis, together with family and friends moves into Hotel Grunewald, Bad Nauheim.
Oct. 21	'One Night'/'I Got Stung' is released.
Oct. 23	Goes to Bill Haley concert in Mannheim, West Germany.
Nov. 3	Transfer to Grafenwohr for tank maneuvers. Meets and dates Elizabeth Stefaniak, the 18-year-old German-born step-daughter of a fellow soldier.
Nov. 27	Promoted to Private First Class.
Dec. 20	Unit returns to Friedberg.
Dec. 23	Elizabeth Stefaniak comes along to be Elvis's secretary.

1959

Jan. 8	Elvis is interviewed by Transatlantic phone on his 24th birthday on *American Bandstand*.

Feb. 3	Elvis and his entourage move into a rented house at 14 Goehestrasse, Bad Nauheim.
Feb. 9	*For LP Fans Only* is released.
Mar.	*Elvis Sails* EP, containing recordings of two press conferences, released.
Mar. 10	'A Fool Such As I'/'I Need Your Love Tonight' released.
Apr.	*A Touch Of Gold* EP is released.
June 1	Elvis is promoted to Specialist Fourth Class.
June 17	Travels to Munich at start of two-week leave. Stays with German actress Vera Tschechowa, and her parents.
June 19	Travels on to Paris with various companions.
June 26	Returns from Paris to Friedberg.
June	'A Big Hunk O' Love'/'My Wish Came True' released.
September	*A Date With Elvis* LP released.
Sept. 13	Priscilla Beaulieu, 14-year-old stepdaughter of an Air Force Captain, is introduced to Elvis in Bad Nauheim.
Oct.	Unit is transferred to Wildflecken for maneuvers.
Oct.	*A Touch Of Gold, Volume 2* EP released.
Oct. 24	Elvis taken back to Frankfurt for hospital treatment of recurrent tonsilitis.
Oct. 29	Discharge from hospital.
Nov. 2	Elvis fans are jailed in East Germany for shouting anti-Government slogans and 'Long Live Elvis Presley'.
Dec.	*50,000,000 Elvis Fans Can't Be Wrong* LP released.

1960

Jan. 20	Elvis is promoted to Sergeant.
Feb.	*A Touch Of Gold, Volume 3* EP released.
Feb. 17	The Government of East Germany bans Elvis records and movies.

Mar. 1	Press conference at Friedberg Army Base. Elvis talks about his Army experiences.
Mar. 2	Elvis boards military transport plane at Frankfurt Airport. Stops for brief refuelling at Prestwick Airport, Scotland.
Mar. 3	Lands at McGuire Air Force base, New Jersey, and transfers to nearby Fort Dix. Two-hour press conference.
Mar. 5	Boards train for trip to Memphis.
Mar. 7	Arrives in Memphis to be greeted by thousands of fans.
Mar. 8	Elvis gives a press conference in his office in an outbuilding at Graceland.
Mar. 20	First post-army recording session in RCA's new studio in Nashville.
Mar. 23	'Stuck On You'/'Fame And Fortune' rush-released.
Mar. 26	Records Timex TV special in Miami with Frank Sinatra hosting.
Apr. 3	Recording session in Nashville to complete album. Tracks included 'Are You Lonesome Tonight?', 'It's Now Or Never' and 'Fever'.
Apr. 20	Arrives in Hollywood after two-day train journey from Memphis.
Late Apr.	*Elvis Is Back* LP released.
Apr. 26	Filming starts at Paramount on *G.I. Blues*.
Apr. 27	First recording session at RCA Hollywood studios. Tracks for the movie *G.I. Blues*.
May 6	Recording session at RCA Hollywood studios.
May 8	Timex/Frank Sinatra TV special is broadcast by ABC.
July 3	Vernon Presley marries Dee Stanley in Huntsville, Alabama. Elvis does not attend.
July	'It's Now Or Never'/'A Mess Of Blues' released.

Chronology

March 1958–June 1968

Aug. 12	Recording session at RCA Hollywood for tracks for *Flaming Star* movie.
Aug. 16	Filming starts on *Flaming Star* at Twentieth Century Fox and on location.
Oct.	*G.I. Blues* soundtrack album released.
Oct. 30	Recording session in Nashville for *His Hand In Mine* gospel album, plus 'Crying In The Chapel'
Nov.	'Are You Lonesome Tonight?'/'I Gotta Know' released.
Nov. 7	Recording session at RCA Hollywood for movie *Wild In The Country*.
Nov. 10	Filming starts for *Wild In The Country* on location in Napa Valley, California.
Nov. 23	*G.I. Blues* movie released across the country.
Dec.	*His Hand In Mine* LP released.
Dec. 8	Priscilla Beaulieu starts vacation at Graceland.
Dec. 20	*Flaming Star* movie goes on general release.
1961	
Jan. 18	Elvis signs five year movie contract with Hal Wallis.
Feb. 5	'Surrender'/'Lonely Man' released.
Feb. 25	'Elvis Presley Day' in Tennessee. After charity lunch at the Claridge Hotel, Memphis, Elvis gives two shows in the Ellis Auditorium.
Mar. 12	Recording session in Nashville for album *Something For Everybody*.
Mar. 21–23	Recording session at Radio Recorders, Hollywod for soundtrack to *Blue Hawaii*.
Mar. 25	Arrives Honolulu Airport. Plays show at Bloch Arena in aid of USS Arizona

	memorial appeal.
Mar. 27	Filming starts on *Blue Hawaii*.
Apr.	*Elvis By Request, Flaming Star* Compact EP released.
May	'I Feel So Bad'/'Wild In The Country' released.
June	*Something For Everybody* album released.
June 22	*Wild In The Country* goes on general release.
June 25	Recording session in Nashville for *Pot Luck* album.
July 5	Recording session in Nashville for *Follow That Dream* movie soundtrack.
July	Filming starts on *Follow That Dream* at United Artists studios, Hollywood, then moves to Florida for location shooting.
Aug.	'(Marie's The Name Of) His Latest Flame'/'Little Sister' is released.
Oct.	*Blue Hawaii* soundtrack album released.
Oct. 15	Recording session in Nashville.
Oct. 26	Recording session for *Kid Galahad* soundtrack at Radio Recorders studio, Hollywood.
Nov.	Filming starts on *Kid Galahad* in Hollywood and at Idyllwild, California.
Nov.	'Rock-A-Hula Baby'/'Can't Help Falling In Love' released.
Nov. 22	*Blue Hawaii* movie opens across the country.
1962	
Feb.	'Good Luck Charm'/'Anything That's Part Of You' released.
Mar. 18	Recording session in Nashville for *Pot Luck* album.
Mar. 20	Filming begins on *Girls! Girls! Girls!* movie in Hollywood.

Mar. 26	Recording session at Radio Recorders for soundtrack to *Girls! Girls! Girls!*
Apr. 7	Elvis travels to Hawaii for location filming of *Girls! Girls! Girls!*
May	*Follow That Dream* EP released.
May 23	*Follow That Dream* opens in movie theaters.
June	*Pot Luck* LP released.
July	'She's Not You'/'Just Tell Her Jim Said Hello' released.
Aug. 27	Filming starts at MGM studios, Culver City for *It Happened At The World's Fair*. Location shots were done in Seattle.
Aug. 29	*Kid Galahad* opens in theaters.
End Aug.	Recording session at MGM studios for *It Happened At The World's Fair* soundtrack.
Sept.	*Kid Galahad* EP released.
Sept. 4–17	Filming in Seattle for *It Happened At The World's Fair*.
Oct.	'Return To Sender'/'Where Do You Come From' released.
End Oct.	Priscilla Beaulieu moves to Graceland.
Nov. 21	*Girls! Girls! Girls!* opens across the country. Soundtrack album released in November.

1963

Jan. 22, 23	Recording session at Radio Recorders Hollywood for soundtrack to *Fun In Acapulco*.
Jan. 28	Filming starts on *Fun In Acapulco* at Paramount Studios, Hollywood.
Late Jan.	'One Broken Heart For Sale'/'They Remind Me Too Much Of You' released.
Apr. 10	*It Happened At The World's Fair* opens on general release, the movie soundtrack is also released in April.
May 26–28	Recording session in Nashville.

June	'(You're The) Devil In Disguise'/'Please Don't Drag That String Around' released.
July 7–11	Recording sessions at Radio Recorders in Hollywood for soundtrack to *Viva Las Vegas*.
July 15–27	Filming on location in Las Vegas.
Aug.	*Elvis' Golden Records, Volume 3* LP released.
Oct.	'Bossa Nova Baby'/'Witchcraft' released.
Oct. 3	Recording session in Nashville for *Kissin' Cousins* soundtrack.
Oct.	*Kissin' Cousins* filmed in 16 days in Hollywood and Bear Lake, California.
Nov. 27	*Fun In Acapulco* opens across the country. Soundtrack album released.

1964

Jan. 12	Recording session in Nashville.
Feb.	'Kissin' Cousins'/'It Hurts Me' released.
Feb. 9	Beatles appear on *The Ed Sullivan Show*, breaking Elvis's 1956 audience record. Elvis sends a congratulatory telegram.
Feb. 24	Recording session at Radio Recorders, Hollywood for *Roustabout* soundtrack.
Mar. 6	*Kissin' Cousins* opens in theaters, soundtrack album is released in April.
Mar. 9	Filming starts on *Roustabout* in Hollywood and on location in California.
Apr.	'Kiss Me Quick'/'Suspicion' released.
Apr.	'Viva Las Vegas'/'What'd I Say' released.
June 5	Filming starts on *Girl Happy*.
June 16	Recording session at Radio Recorders, Hollywood for soundtrack to *Girl Happy*.
June 17	*Viva Las Vegas* opens in movie theaters.
July	*Viva Las Vegas* EP released.

Chronology
March 1958–June 1968

July	'Such A Night'/'Never Ending' released.
mid July	Location shooting in Florida for *Girl Happy*.
Sept.	'Ain't That Loving You Baby'/'Ask Me' released.
Oct. 12	Filming starts on *Tickle Me* at Allied Artists, Hollywood.
Nov. 11	*Roustabout* movie opens in movie houses. Soundtrack album released this month.

1965

Feb. 24	Recording session for *Harum Scarum* soundtrack in Nashville.
Mar.	'Do The Clam'/'You'll Be Gone' released.
Mar. 15	Filming starts on *Harum Scarum*. Shot in 18 days at Goldwyn studios, Culver City.
Apr.	'Crying In The Chapel'/'I Believe In The Man In The Sky' released. A-side had been recorded in 1960.
Apr. 7	*Girl Happy* opens in movie theaters, soundtrack album is released in April.
May 13	Recording session at United Artists studio Hollywood for *Frankie And Johnny* soundtrack.
May 24	Filming starts on *Frankie And Johnny*.
June	'It Feels So Right'/'(Such An) Easy Question' released.
July 7	*Tickle Me* movie opens, soundtrack EP released in July.
Aug.	*Elvis For Everyone* LP released and 'I'm Yours'/'Long Lonely Highway' released.
Aug. 2	Recording session for soundtrack to *Paradise Hawaiian Style*.
Aug. 5–17	Location filming in Hawaii for *Paradise Hawaiian Style*.
Aug. 27	Beatles pay a visit to Elvis at his home on Perugia Way, Bel Air.
Sept.	Elvis's contract with RCA is extended for another ten years.
Oct. 21	Bill Black, Elvis's original bass player, dies in Memphis.
Nov.	'Puppet On A String'/'Wooden Heart' released.
Nov. 24	*Harum Scarum* opens in movie theaters, soundtrack LP released in November.
Dec. 27	'Tell Me Why'/'Blue River' released.

1966

Jan.	'Blue Christmas'/'Santa Claus Is Back In Town' released.
Feb. 21	Overdubbing session at MGM studios for soundtrack to *Spinout*. Filming for the movie takes place over the next few weeks on location in LA and at MGM studio.
Feb.	'Joshua Fit The Battle'/'Known Only To Him' and 'Milky White Way'/'Swing Down Sweet Chariot' released.
Mar.	'Frankie And Johnny'/'Please Don't Stop Loving Me' released.
Mar. 30	*Frankie And Johnny* opens in movie theaters, soundtrack album released in April.
May 25–28	Recording session at RCA's Nashville Studio B, mainly for *How Great Thou Art* LP. First session with Felton Jarvis producing.
June	'Love Letters'/'Come What May' released.
June 10	Recording session in Nashville.
June 26	Recording session at MGM, Culver City for *Double Trouble* soundtrack.

July 6	*Paradise Hawaiian Style* goes on general release in movie theaters. Sound track album released.
July 11	Filming starts on *Double Trouble* at MGM.
Sept.	'Spinout'/'All That I Am' released.
Sept. 12	Filming starts on *Easy Come, Easy Go* at Paramount studios.
Sept. 28	Recording session.
Nov. 23	*Spinout* movie goes on general release together with soundtrack album.
Nov. 25	'If Every Day Was Like Christmas'/'How Would You Like To Be' released.
1967	
Jan. 6	'Indescribably Blue'/'Fools Fall In Love' released.
Feb. 9	Elvis buys Circle G Ranch at Walls, Mississippi south of Memphis.
Feb. 21	Recording session in Nashville for *Clambake* soundtrack.
Mar. 8	*How Great Thou Art* album released.
Mar. 10	Filming starts on *Clambake*, but then is delayed 3 weeks due to Elvis's head injury.
Mar. 20	Recording session in Nashville. Only one song ('Suppose') which was never released.
Mar. 22	*Easy Come, Easy Go* opens in movie theaters.
Mar. 24	*Easy Come, Easy Go* soundtrack EP released. Fails to make any Billboard chart.
Apr. 5	*Double Trouble* opens in movie theaters.
May	'Long Legged Girl (With The Short Dress On)'/'That's Someone You'll Never Forget' released.
May 1	Elvis Presley and Priscilla Beaulieu are married at the Aladdin Hotel, Las Vegas.
May 29	Second wedding ceremony staged at Graceland for Memphis friends.
June	*Double Trouble* soundtrack

	album released.
June 19	Recording session at MGM studios for *Speedway* soundtrack.
June 26	Filming starts on *Speedway*.
Aug.	'There's Always Me'/'Judy' released.
Sept. 10–12	Recording session at RCA Studio B in Nashville.
Oct.	'Big Boss Man'/'You Don't Know Me' released.
Oct. 2	Recording session in Nashville.
Oct. 9	Filming starts on *Stay Away Joe* at MGM, Culver City then on location in Arizona.
Nov. 19	*Clambake* soundtrack album released, movie opens three days later.
1968	
Jan.	'Guitar Man'/'High Heel Sneakers' released.
Jan. 15,17	Recording session in Nashville.
Feb. 1	Lisa Marie Presley born in Baptist Memorial Hospital, Memphis.
Feb. 17	*Elvis' Gold Records, Volume 4* album released.
Mar. 8	*Stay Away Joe* goes on general release in movie theaters.
Mar. 9	'US Male'/'Stay Away Joe' released.
Mar. 11	Filming starts on *Live A Little, Love A Little* at MGM, Culver City. Recording session for soundtrack at Goldwyn studios.
Apr. 13	'We Call On Him'/'You'll Never Walk Alone' released.
May	'Your Time Hasn'§t Come Yet Baby'/'Let Yourself Go' released.
June 12	*Speedway* goes on general release together with soundtrack album.

Part Six: ESCAPING THE SYSTEM – THE COMEBACK YEARS 1968–1974

"I came out [of the Army] and made a picture called *GI Blues* where I thought I was still in the army. I made more movies. It kind of got into a routine and a rut and I kind of wanted to come back and work live in front of people again."

"One cannot write too highly concerning this album — it scores 11 out of 10! Everything about it displays the kind of sublimity which had been missing for almost a decade."
Roy Carr on *From Elvis In Memphis*

"Elvis sauntered to center stage, grabbed the microphone from its stand, hit a pose from the fifties — legs braced, knees snapping almost imperceptibly — and before he could begin the show, the audience stopped him cold. Just as he was about to begin his first song the audience hit him with a roar. He looked. All 2,000 people were on their feet, pounding their hands together and whistling."
Jerry Hopkins on Las Vegas, 1969

"Supernatural, his own resurrection."
Rolling Stone on Las Vegas, 1969

"I got tired of singing to the guys I beat up in motion pictures."

"People can buy your records and hear you sing, and they don't have to hear you come out to hear you sing. You have to put on a show to draw a crowd. You have to give them a show, something to talk about."

"I know right away which songs are right for me."

"Very much in command of the whole scene."
Variety on Las Vegas, 1969

"I can cut fifteen songs on a session. Me and the boys sometimes get together late at night and it's late morning when we call it a day."

Introduction

By the summer of 1968 Elvis's career had reached its lowest point. While the American music scene was full of creativity and experimentation, he was stuck in a cultural backwater of mediocre movies with, even worse, appalling songs. Where once he had been the touchstone for all other musicians, he was now an irrelevant curiosity. He hadn't had a single in the Top Ten of the Billboard chart since 'Crying In The Chapel' in 1965 (a record that had actually been recorded in 1960), with no prospect that he ever would again. Whereas his fellow rock and rollers had eventually won a new generation of fans by sticking to the spirit of the music, Elvis had frittered away his talent on middle-of-the-road garbage aimed at pleasing everyone, while pleasing no-one. To turn this situation around, and to reveal Elvis as a consummate musician with a vast legacy of music, and a real future, would take a miracle. Fortunately one was about to happen, in the unlikely shape of a television program.

In truth this was Elvis's second comeback, and the third time he had used television to set out his stall. In 1956 his live TV appearances on *Stage Show*, *The Milton Berle Show* and *The Ed Sullivan Show* had catapulted him into national and worldwide fame. On his return from the army in 1960 he turned to television again — this time on the *Timex Frank Sinatra Special* — to relaunch his career. And now, at the lowest point in his career, it was to be a television program that presented a new Elvis to the world.

This time Elvis really did get lucky. The 1968 NBC Special was a triumph of presentation, engineered by a team of young music enthusiasts led by producer Steve Binder. They brilliantly echoed Elvis's great days of the fifties, while also pointing the way to a musical future. Elvis quickly became re-enthused by the music he was singing, and by the music around him. At that time American music was a ferment of creativity which Elvis seemed to see for the first time. After the TV special he quickly organized a recording session, but one unlike any he had done in the past ten years. He went into the American Studios in his hometown of Memphis, well away from the dead hand of Hollywood and the influence of RCA's Nashville set-up. He hired a whole new set of musicians and produced his most important work for eleven years. Elvis was back.

The choice of Las Vegas to launch his live career seems inevitable only in retrospect. His return to live performance was a triumph. But was Las Vegas the best choice for Elvis, and whose choice was it? Was there any other way to go? Would Elvis have been happy to go back on the road with just a rock and roll band? Whatever the answers, Elvis's Las Vegas comeback set the tone for all his future shows.

The King Is Back!

The making of the TV special in

On December 3, 1968 NBC broadcast one of the most famous television programs in the history of American entertainment. In the process Elvis Presley, whose career had become close to a laughing stock, was resurrected as the King of rock and roll and put on the path to a fresh and vital phase in his career. In one of the greatest revivals the music world has ever seen, Elvis escaped from the seemingly inevitable downward spiral of increasingly awful movies and banal soundtrack albums that he had produced for the better part of 8 years. For just about the only time since 1955 Elvis briefly escaped from Colonel Parker's dead hand, and was put to work with people with fresh ideas and the ability to carry them out. Elvis's return to the real world of music was awaited with fascination by millions. The result was a revelation for Elvis himself, for the music business, for RCA, for his fans and for rest of the world.

The Singer Special was one of a series sponsored by the sewing machine company and made by NBC. The show's young production team were so inexperienced that they didn't put it up for any broadcasting awards — though it's likely it would have swept the board. The show was re–broadcast in 1969 and a longer 90–minute version was shown after Elvis's death.

The idea for the NBC Singer TV Special show may have originally come from Colonel Parker. For several years he had been peddling an edited tape of Elvis's Christmas songs, with a few spoken greetings in between, to radio stations, as The Elvis Presley Christmas Show. It occurred to him that this might go well on television, so he put out some feelers to NBC. But why did he wait until 1968? It may be that by that time the returns on Elvis's movies were diminishing so fast that any new contract would show a forced reduction in Elvis's fees — Elvis's contract with Paramount was due for renewal in 1968. It could be that Elvis himself was becoming more vocal about his unhappiness with the movies.

Whatever the reason, NBC agreed to a deal with Parker, and then set about hiring some people to put the hour–long show together. Bob Finkel, the man who was responsible for the show, needed a producer who could get the best out of Elvis, who would be able to talk the same musical language. He chose 23–year–old Steve Binder, an independent producer who was well–known inside the television and music industries for the T.A.M.I. show. Binder wasn't entirely knocked out at the idea of doing the show. In fact he decided early on that if he wasn't going to be able to do it the way he wanted, then he wouldn't do it at all. His first conversation with Parker confirmed all his fears about the project – Parker talked continually about Christmas songs and Christmas messages — whereas his first conversation with Elvis fired his determination to do the show. Binder made numerous

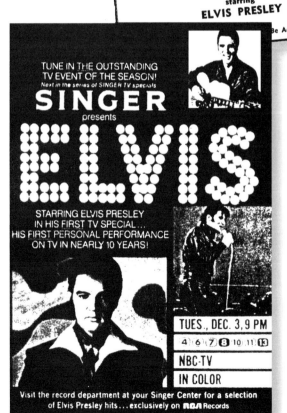

Elvis and TV
Elvis was one of the first entertainers to become a national star on television, in 1956. But he didn't appear on TV for eight years, before the NBC special made him a star all over again.

suggestions to Elvis and Parker about how he thought the show might work. Once Parker was out of the way Elvis agreed to everything with enthusiasm. Binder said later that to work with Elvis was "In my career, the easiest ... he always gave one hundred and ten percent."

The program was shot in June at NBC's studios in Burbank, California. As soon as rehearsals got under way the dressing rooms were converted into a mini–apartment, so that Elvis and some friends could stay there. It seems that Elvis's principal soulmate at this time was Charlie Hodge, a close friend and fellow musician who played a significant role in the special. The program itself consisted of three segments — a 'biogra-

CLOSE-UP

ELVIS
9:00 ❹ ⑳

SPECIAL COLOR Surrounded by musicians and adoring fans, Elvis Presley headlines his first TV special.

The fans are up and screaming as Elvis rocks through a nostalgic medley of his hits: "Heartbreak Hotel," "Hound Dog," "All Shook Up," "Can't Help Falling in Love with You," "Jailhouse Rock" and "Love Me Tender." He also sings "Memories" and his seasonal hit "Blue Christmas."

The Blossoms vocal group and dancer-choreographer Claude Thompson open a gospel medley with "Sometimes I Feel like a Motherless Child," and Elvis joins them for "Where Could I Go but to the Lord?" "Up Above My Head" and "Saved!"

A rocking production number stars Elvis as a traveling musician (singing "Guitar Man") who leaves a dull job ("Nothingsville") for an amusement park ("Big Boss Man") and modest night-club success ("Trouble"). Finale: "If I Can Dream," written for Elvis by vocal arranger Earl Brown. (60 min.)

"I only knew Elvis for a very short window, and in the window that I knew him there were no drugs, there was no temperament, there was just this terrifically nice guy who was just so enthusiastic and so easy. If anything I'd have liked a little more confrontation, but he was just so anxious to do it and to stretch. The last day I saw Elvis he said 'Steve, I'm never gonna sing another song I don't believe in, I'm never gonna make another picture I don't believe in.' I said 'Elvis I hear you, but I'm not so sure you're strong enough to live up to that' ... It was kind of an omen of what was to come."
Steve Binder, producer NBC TV special

The black leather suit that Elvis wore for the "rock and roll" segment of the show is as famous as his gold lamé suit from 1957 and his white jumpsuits of the 1970s. It was specially designed to give the audience an echo of the great days of the fifties — though Elvis never wore leather back then. Its principal effect was to contrast this new Elvis with the increasingly unappealing Hawaiian-shirted figure of his movies.

phy in song' featuring the song 'Guitar Man', a gospel sequence, and an informal jam session. The latter was the most innovative section. Binder brought in Scotty Moore and DJ Fontana from Elvis's original band, Charlie Hodge also sat in. The idea was to get Elvis back to his roots, for the musicians to talk informally and for the music to arise spontaneously. As a musical piece it was only partly successful, but it showed an entirely new side of Elvis to the public.

The show's finale was a matter of some dispute between Parker and Binder. Parker wanted a Christmas song, or at least a schmaltzy standard. Binder wanted something

relevant to the real world, to put Elvis back in contact with the music that was being played in America at that time. The argument was settled by Earl Brown writing 'If I Can Dream' the night before the sequence had to be shot.

The TV special was also a new musical direction for Elvis. He himself was frustrated by the music that he had been creating with RCA for the past six or seven years. Colonel Parker had ruled that there should be no albums apart from movie soundtracks, and RCA had been reduced to re–issuing old material to get round that. For the TV special the musical arranger came up with a kind of orchestral rock and soul that Elvis was to follow for his most successful music of the late sixties.

After the special Elvis was to head for Memphis and record with the musicians that knew how to create the sound he wanted. They had of course been there all the time, but Elvis was only now beginning to wake up to what had been going on around him.

In January and February 1969 he went into the American Studios in Memphis — the first time he had recorded in his home town since he left Sun in 1955. The result was the albums *From Elvis In Memphis* and *From Memphis To Vegas/From Vegas To Memphis,* including the singles 'In The Ghetto' and 'Suspicious Minds'. They not only sold millions of copies, they restored Elvis Presley's reputation as a master of his art.

The soundtrack of the TV special was issued as an album a week before the program was aired. It reached Number 8 on the Billboard Album Chart, making it Elvis's first Top Ten LP for three years, and stayed on the chart for thirty two weeks.

Viva Las Vegas

The first live shows for 8 years, July 1969; Elvis's Las Vegas

It's worth remembering the worldwide excitement that accompanied Elvis's decision to return to live performance. It was headline news in almost every country in the world. After the success of the TV special, could Elvis, the greatest performer the world had ever seen, produce his old magic on stage? Elvis was fired up to go back on the road — to do some real touring, for the first time since the 1950s. The part of the TV Special he liked best had been the black-leather session: this had been the real stuff. It was the part the audience liked best too: the intimate part, revealing a fit, handsome, still-young Elvis Presley with his alert sense of humor and his rock and roll spirit refreshingly intact. The part he liked less was the big-production stuff. He knew it was over-produced, too showbiz. So there he was, eager to go back out there, to take risks, to retrieve his faith in his real artistic self. He wanted to tour with a stripped-down band, four or five people. Wouldn't it have been great?

"Like a jug of corn liquor at a champagne party... (the audience looked at Elvis) as if he were a clinical experiment." Newsweek on Elvis in Las Vegas, 1956.

The Colonel, of course, had other, seedier ideas. He'd put Elvis on in Las Vegas back in 1956. Big mistake. Now he determined to put him on there again. In other words, Parker wanted to make the legendary, godlike king of rock music stage his live come-back in the place in America most dedicated to the pre-Elvis world of crooners and phoney variety routines, where over-thirties people came for the gambling, not the music, and where they'd been eating their dinners, clinking the cutlery and waving to the waiters during Elvis's act. This is what he wanted to do to the greatest white blues singer, the most musically potent performer in history.

Clearly there was no humiliation Colonel Parker wouldn't foist upon Elvis. As usual, he was wrong even by his own lights of commercial greed. By the end of the 1960s rock groups were making millions of dollars from albums and from live appearances in stadiums and outdoor festivals. Rock had transformed the record business into *big* business. Elvis's movie-soundtrack albums were being outsold by dozens of people — many of whom Colonel Parker had never heard of. He was the one living in the past, not those who believed that Elvis could go out there and join them. Of course he couldn't do it with the Blue Moon Boys — but he could have hired the contemporary equivalent — a band, which would have been wholly in tune with his roots and his genius and would have kept him in touch with both. The respect for Elvis among young American and British musicians was strong enough for him to have got more or less any band he wanted to back him. And

he'd just made a wholly credible album: his material didn't need to be only the old hits.

For Parker, rock and roll was still a nine-day wonder and a small-time earner, despite all the evidence of Elvis's own 1950s career and lots of other people's 1960s careers. Yet again he wanted Elvis to turn his back on all this and become a hapless and awkward force-fit in an already exhausted showbiz-routine world. The eternal mystery is why Elvis tolerated this. Why *was* he always the hapless one, "poor Elvis, stuck with this terrible shit"? Why didn't this grown man drop Parker and take charge of his own life?

The deal was done, and a very bad deal it was too. Instead of being out on the road with a storm of brilliant, hot, authentic music, Elvis was reduced to copying the vulgar, lowest-common-dominator mediocrity of the Tom Jones floorshow, backed by an orchestra like an elephant.

As the Jerry Hopkins review (right) shows, Elvis was applauded just for being there. He would have been a success anywhere, but Las Vegas was such a low target to aim for. He could have done so much better. The first show was such a "success" that Colonel Parker at once revised the deal he'd done. Instead of four weeks at $100,000 per week, Elvis was now signed at $125,000 a week for two months a year *for five years*. It was ludicrous. Elvis was in chains once again, and the International, grossing this figure many times over, was making a large profit out of a show-room that was normally a loss-leader for the gambling tables. It was a double humiliation: a financial joke and an artistic horror-story.

"Elvis sauntered onto center stage, grabbed the microphone from its stand, hit a pose from the fifties — legs braced, knees snapping almost imperceptibly — and before he could begin the show, the audience stopped him cold. Just as he was about to begin his first song the audience hit him with a roar. He looked. All 2,000 people were on their feet, pounding their hands together and whistling." Jerry Hopkins on the first Las Vegas opening, 1969.

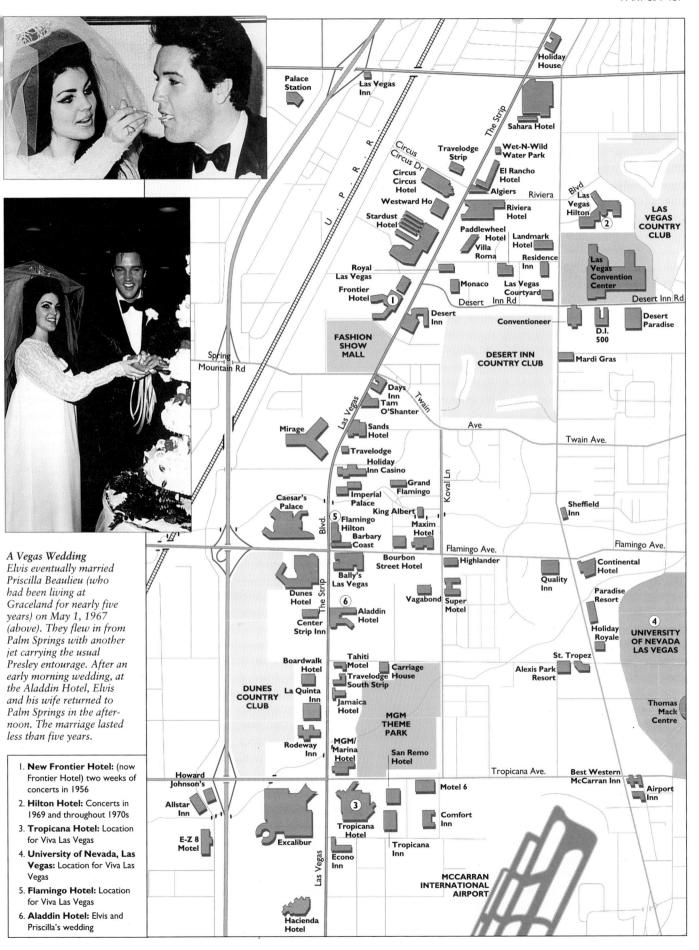

A Vegas Wedding
Elvis eventually married Priscilla Beaulieu (who had been living at Graceland for nearly five years) on May 1, 1967 (above). They flew in from Palm Springs with another jet carrying the usual Presley entourage. After an early morning wedding, at the Aladdin Hotel, Elvis and his wife returned to Palm Springs in the afternoon. The marriage lasted less than five years.

1. **New Frontier Hotel:** (now Frontier Hotel) two weeks of concerts in 1956

2. **Hilton Hotel:** Concerts in 1969 and throughout 1970s

3. **Tropicana Hotel:** Location for Viva Las Vegas

4. **University of Nevada, Las Vegas:** Location for Viva Las Vegas

5. **Flamingo Hotel:** Location for Viva Las Vegas

6. **Aladdin Hotel:** Elvis and Priscilla's wedding

Holiday House
Las Vegas Inn
Palace Station
The Strip
Sahara Hotel
Circus Circus Dr
Travelodge Strip
Wet-N-Wild Water Park
Circus Circus Hotel
El Rancho Hotel
Algiers
Riviera
Blvd
Las Vegas Hilton
LAS VEGAS COUNTRY CLUB
Westward Ho
Riviera Hotel
Stardust Hotel
Paddlewheel Hotel
Villa Roma
Landmark Hotel
Residence Inn
Las Vegas Convention Center
Royal Las Vegas
Monaco
Las Vegas Courtyard Inn Rd
Desert
Desert Inn Rd
Frontier Hotel
①
Desert Inn
Conventioneer
Desert Paradise
FASHION SHOW MALL
D.I. 500
Mardi Gras
Spring Mountain Rd
DESERT INN COUNTRY CLUB
Days Inn Tam O'Shanter
Twain
Las Vegas
Ave.
Twain Ave.
Mirage
Sands Hotel
Travelodge
Holiday Inn Casino
Koval Ln
Grand Flamingo
Sheffield Inn
Caesar's Palace
Imperial Palace
King Albert
⑤ Flamingo Hilton
Maxim Hotel
Flamingo Ave.
Flamingo Ave.
Barbary Coast
Bourbon Street Hotel
Highlander
Continental Hotel
Blvd
Bally's Las Vegas
Quality Inn
Paradise Resort
Dunes Hotel
The Strip
⑥
Vagabond
Super Motel
④ UNIVERSITY OF NEVADA LAS VEGAS
Aladdin Hotel
Holiday Royale
Center Strip Inn
St. Tropez
Thomas Mack Centre
Boardwalk Hotel
Tahiti Motel
Carriage House
Alexis Park Resort
DUNES COUNTRY CLUB
La Quinta Inn
Travelodge South Strip
Jamaica Hotel
MGM THEME PARK
Rodeway Inn
MGM/ Marina Hotel
San Remo Hotel
Tropicana Ave.
Best Western McCarran Inn
Airport Inn
Howard Johnson's
Motel 6
Allstar Inn
③
Comfort Inn
E-Z 8 Motel
Excalibur
Tropicana Hotel
Tropicana Inn
Las Vegas
Econo Inn
MCCARRAN INTERNATIONAL AIRPORT
Hacienda Hotel

The Roadshow Begins

1969, 1970, 1971 tours

Was the 1969 Las Vegas comeback to be a route into performing live on tour, or was Elvis going to turn into a cabaret performer — strictly for after dinner entertainment. In January 1970 he went back toVegas for another month's worth of shows, and then decided to test the waters out there in the big wide world. He took his travelling circus to Houston, Texas on February 27 for a scheduled six concerts in three days. These were to be his first live shows in a real auditorium (if the Astrodome can be described that way) for eight years. He'd had a lot of practice in Las Vegas but the Houston shows were a different ball-game. For one thing he would be playing in front of over 30,000 people every night.

Elvis seemed set right in 1970. He had followed his NBC TV special with a dramatic return to form in the recording studio. After one excellent album and two mega-selling singles ('In The Ghetto' and 'Suspicious Minds'), November 1969 saw the release of *From Memphis To Vegas/From Vegas To Memphis*, the first half being recorded live in Las Vegas in August 1969. This gave his fans some idea of what they could expect from an Elvis live show, should he ever get around to playing their part of the country. It was a potent mixture of rock and roll hits and his strong contemporary material. In fact this same material was to form the basis of his stage show for the next seven years, and of numerous live albums

that recycled the same titles. But for now it was fresh and exciting. Elvis's return wasn't just a television and Vegas illusion. He was back with a vengeance.

The Houston concerts didn't prove much, except that the Astrodome's acoustics were atrocious, and that there was a huge audience out there for Elvis shows. Given the schedules of the later years, when touring almost became an obsession, Elvis took things fairly easily to start with. At this time he may have felt the need to concentrate more on recording, while things were going so well. If he'd stuck to the kind of pattern he had in 1970 he might have been better off in the long run – in later years the quality of his records again

One of the more bizarre episodes in Elvis's life happened in December 1970. On December 19 he took a plane to Washington DC, then another to Los Angeles. There he picked up Jerry Schilling, and Senator George Murphy. The three returned to Washington, where on Monday they managed to arrange a visit to the FBI Bureau of Narcotics and Dangerous Drugs, and then to the White House. By this time Red West had arrived and he, Elvis and Schilling called on President Nixon. Elvis asked for a badge validating him as a federal narcotics officer, and Nixon arranged for one to be brought over. Elvis hugged the President and returned to Memphis.

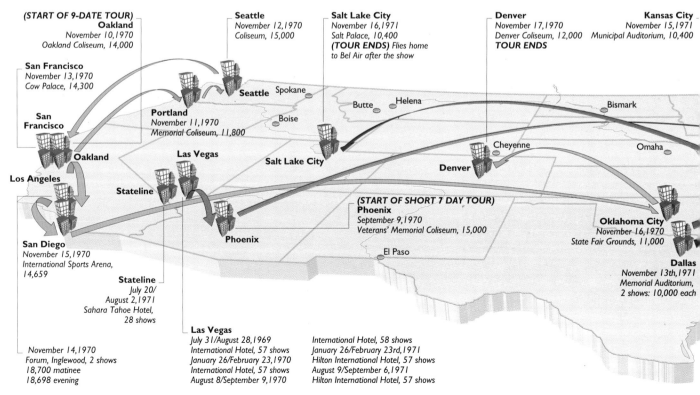

(START OF 9-DATE TOUR)
Oakland
November 10,1970
Oakland Coliseum, 14,000

Seattle
November 12,1970
Coliseum, 15,000

Salt Lake City
November 16,1971
Salt Palace, 10,400
(TOUR ENDS) *Flies home to Bel Air after the show*

Denver
November 17,1970
Denver Coliseum, 12,000
TOUR ENDS

Kansas City
November 15,1971
Municipal Auditorium, 10,400

San Francisco
November 13,1970
Cow Palace, 14,300

Portland
November 11,1970
Memorial Coliseum, 11,800

San Francisco

Seattle Spokane

Butte Helena

Bismark

Los Angeles

Oakland

Las Vegas

Salt Lake City

Boise

Cheyenne

Omaha

Denver

Stateline

(START OF SHORT 7 DAY TOUR)
Phoenix
September 9,1970
Veterans' Memorial Coliseum, 15,000

El Paso

Oklahoma City
November 16,1970
State Fair Grounds, 11,000

San Diego
November 15,1970
International Sports Arena, 14,659

Phoenix

Dallas
November 13th,1971
Memorial Auditorium, 2 shows: 10,000 each

Stateline
July 20/ August 2,1971
Sahara Tahoe Hotel, 28 shows

November 14,1970
Forum, Inglewood, 2 shows
18,700 matinee
18,698 evening

Las Vegas
July 31/August 28,1969
International Hotel, 57 shows
January 26/February 23,1970
International Hotel, 57 shows
August 8/September 9,1970

International Hotel, 58 shows
January 26/February 23rd,1971
Hilton International Hotel, 57 shows
August 9/September 6,1971
Hilton International Hotel, 57 shows

White jumpsuits
For his first comeback shows at Las Vegas, Elvis actually wore a fairly conventional black two-piece suit. The change to white jumpsuits launched the careers of a thousand Elvis impersonators, while giving him at least a distinctive image. The theatricality this leant to Elvis's shows was welcome when it worked, though in later years things seemed to get a little out of hand, what with capes, scepters, insignia and the rest. Also a lithe 35 year-old carried the costume off rather better than a tired, overweight 40 year-old.

slipped, and touring was the only way of keeping the money coming in. Ironically when he was at his best he toured less than when he was physically depleted.

He went back to Las Vegas for a third season in the summer of 1970, then embarked on his first real tour since 1957, a week-long swing from Phoenix to Mobile. His earlier fear of flying was forgotten on the seventies tours. It had become possible to get anywhere from anywhere else by the next day by private jet. The seventies tours didn't need to be based in one particular region of the country. Although this might reduce flying time, once

Elvis had his own plane he seemed to want to spend as much time in it as possible. Occasionally Elvis flew back to Memphis to spend the night after a show, and often didn't get to stay in a town at all. While this was undoubtedly convenient, it didn't help his state of mind to be entirely insulated from the world around him over the next seven years. He went to more cities in America than almost anyone else, but saw only airports, limousines, hotel rooms and the insides of concert halls.

Unfortunately the undermining of Elvis's return to form began almost immediately. First RCA released another compilation on their low-priced Camden label. Entitled *Let's Be Friends* (April 1970) it contained tracks and leftovers from three of Elvis's last movies (a world he'd gladly put behind him, shame his record company couldn't do the same), together with some out-takes from the American Studios sessions. Elvis might have wondered what was the point of striving for excellence, when his second rate material was happily pumped out as well. This was followed in November 1970 by *Almost In Love* which followed the same formula. In between RCA launched a lavish 4–album boxed set *Worldwide Gold Award Hits, Volume 1*. While nicely packaged it did immediately give the new Elvis competition from his own back catalogue. In June 1970 the live album procession began with *On Stage — February 1970*, an album of covers of other people's songs performed at Las Vegas. Coming only seven months after the live *From Memphis To Vegas* it was a sign of things to come.

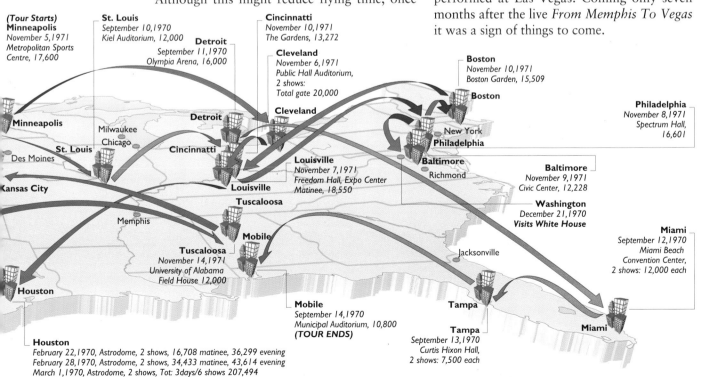

(Tour Starts)
Minneapolis
November 5,1971
Metropolitan Sports Centre, 17,600

St. Louis
September 10,1970
Kiel Auditorium, 12,000

Detroit
September 11,1970
Olympia Arena, 16,000

Cincinnatti
November 10,1971
The Gardens, 13,272

Cleveland
November 6,1971
Public Hall Auditorium,
2 shows:
Total gate 20,000

Boston
November 10,1971
Boston Garden, 15,509

Philadelphia
November 8,1971
Spectrum Hall,
16,601

Louisville
November 7,1971
Freedom Hall, Expo Center
Matinee, 18,550

Baltimore
November 9,1971
Civic Center, 12,228

Washington
December 21,1970
Visits White House

Miami
September 12,1970
Miami Beach
Convention Center,
2 shows: 12,000 each

Tuscaloosa
November 14,1971
University of Alabama
Field House 12,000

Mobile
September 14,1970
Municipal Auditorium, 10,800
(TOUR ENDS)

Tampa
September 13,1970
Curtis Hixon Hall,
2 shows: 7,500 each

Houston
February 22,1970, Astrodome, 2 shows, 16,708 matinee, 36,299 evening
February 28,1970, Astrodome, 2 shows, 34,433 matinee, 43,614 evening
March 1,1970, Astrodome, 2 shows, Tot: 3days/6 shows 207,494
November 11,1971, Hofheinz Pavilion, 12,000

Minneapolis
Milwaukee
Chicago
St. Louis
Des Moines
Kansas City
Detroit
Cincinnatti
Cleveland
New York
Philadelphia
Boston
Baltimore
Richmond
Memphis
Louisville
Tuscaloosa
Mobile
Jacksonville
Tampa
Miami
Houston

Live At Madison Square Garden

The New York shows and the 1972 Tours

Apart from his 1956 TV shows, Elvis had never played live in New York City before 1972. Now he decided to take the town by storm. He was booked in to play four shows in three days at New York's premier music venue, Madison Square Garden. Any doubts about his appeal in the Big Apple were quickly dispelled — all four shows sold out within a day of tickets going on sale. RCA also hatched a plan to record the concerts, mix an album, press and release it all within two weeks. It was good hype, but the musical results were patchy. In addition most of the tracks were already available in live versions. The Presley fans were being milked for yet more of their cash.

The 1972 Tours

April 5, Buffalo to April 19, Albuquerque

June 9, New York to June 20th, Tulsa

November 8, Lubbock to November 18, Honolulu

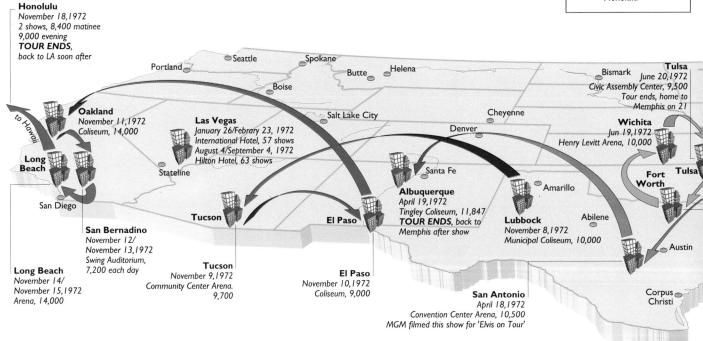

Honolulu
November 18,1972
2 shows, 8,400 matinee
9,000 evening
TOUR ENDS,
back to LA soon after

to Hawaii

Portland
Seattle
Spokane
Butte
Helena
Boise

Oakland
November 11,1972
Coliseum, 14,000

Las Vegas
January 26/Febrary 23, 1972
International Hotel, 57 shows
August 4/September 4, 1972
Hilton Hotel, 63 shows

Salt Lake City

Cheyenne

Denver

Tulsa
Bismark
Tulsa
June 20,1972
Civic Assembly Center, 9,500
Tour ends, home to
Memphis on 21

Wichita
Jun 19,1972
Henry Levitt Arena, 10,000

Long Beach

Stateline

Santa Fe

Albuquerque
April 19,1972
Tingley Coliseum, 11,847
TOUR ENDS, back to
Memphis after show

Amarillo

Lubbock
November 8,1972
Municipal Coliseum, 10,000

Abilene

Fort Worth

Tulsa

San Diego

Tucson

El Paso

San Bernadino
November 12/
November 13,1972
Swing Auditorium,
7,200 each day

Tucson
November 9,1972
Community Center Arena.
9,700

El Paso
November 10,1972
Coliseum, 9,000

Austin

Long Beach
November 14/
November 15,1972
Arena, 14,000

San Antonio
April 18,1972
Convention Center Arena, 10,500
MGM filmed this show for 'Elvis on Tour'

Corpus
Christi

The four New York concerts were attended by anyone and everyone in the east coast music world. There was a feeling that Elvis had somehow been forgiven by the younger generation of musicians. They had grown up with his music and worshipped him in the fifties, and been saddened by his decline into mediocrity in the sixties. Now he was back at the top. John Lennon, George Harrison and Bob Dylan all came along.

Elvis's concert performances showed their usual variability, and the self–imposed time schedule didn't allow RCA to select the best from the four shows. He played evening shows on June 9, 10 and 11, with a matinee performance on Saturday 10. The album *Elvis As Recorded At Madison Square Garden* was

taken only from the evening show on the 10th. The only tracks on it that hadn't been issued as live recordings previously were 'Never Been To Spain' and 'For The Good Times'.

Earlier in the year Elvis had ended a run of mediocre singles with the release of a live version of Micky Newberry's 'American Trilogy'. The song ties together three emotive traditional songs into a quasi–religious anthem. It had been a staple part of Elvis's stage shows for a few months before it was released. Although the backing in the middle part of the single sounds both leaden and overblown, there's no doubting the strength and conviction of the performance. The song was a great hit with live audiences and was expected to do some

"This time out is the best yet for Presley. His format is taut, he pays attention to his songs and his audience, the karate exercises are quite vigorous and his ringside kissing technique is like a dozen midway attractions, rolled into one."
Variety on Las Vegas opening, February 1972

serious business on the charts. But in the event 'American Trilogy' reached only 66 on the Billboard Hot 100. Reasons suggested for this failure include the play length and the recent success of Newberry's own version. Nevertheless it remains a puzzle as to why one of his most popular songs was a flop. Thankfully Elvis's most convincing single for some time came in August 1972. 'Burning Love' was written by Dennis Linde, who also overdubbed a guitar line. A lively rocker with a real drive behind it, the single gave Elvis his biggest hit since 1969, reaching Number 2 on the Billboard chart.

Elvis was the first performer to sell out Madison Square Garden for four successive concerts. Total takings were $730,000 from an overall crowd of 80,000. Before the first show Elvis held a news conference at the New York Hilton (right).

Indianapolis
April 12, 1972
Fair Ground's Coliseum, 11,000

Fort Wayne
June 12, 1972
Memorial Coliseum,

Dayton
April 7, 1972
University of Dayton Arena, 13,788

Chicago
June 16, 1972
Chicago Stadium, 22,000
June 17, 1972
22,000 matinee
20,000 evening

Buffalo
April 5, 1972
Memorial Auditorium, 17,340
First tour, Elvis travels in his Lear Jet

Detroit
April 6, 1972
Olympia Stadium, 16,216

Milwaukee
June 14/June 15, 1972
Auditorium Arena, 10,500 then 11,000

New York
June 9/June 11, 1972
Madison Square Garden
First performer to sell out 4 straight gigs at MSG
Four concerts in 3 days, total 80,000

Duluth

St. Paul

nes

as

Milwaukee

Chicago

St. Louis

Evansville

Fort Wayne

Detroit

Dayton

Indianapolis

Knoxville

Memphis

Boston

New York

Richmond

Roanoke

Greensboro

Charlotte

Macon

Hampton Roads
April 9, 1972
Coliseum
11,000 matinee, 10,650 evening

Richmond
April 10, 1972
Coliseum, 11,500

Greensboro
April 14, 1972
Coliseum, 16,300

Charlotte
April 13, 1972
Coliseum, 12,000

Jacksonville
April 16, 1972
Veterans Memorial Coliseum
2 shows, 9,258 then 9,500

Little Rock
April 17, 1972
T H Barton Coliseum, 10,000

Tuscaloosa

Monroe

Jackson

Montgomery

Mobile

Lake Charles

Baton Rouge

Houston

New Orleans

Lakeland

Tampa

Miami

ort Worth
ne 18, 1972
arrant County
onvention Center Arena,
4,122 record for venue

Evansville
June 13, 1972
Robert's Memorial Stadium, 11,500

Knoxville
April 8, 1972
University of Tennessee, Stokley Athletics Center, 2 shows 10,550 matinee 13,300 evening

Macon
April 15, 1972
Coliseum combined total, 23,000

Roanoke
April 11, 1972
Civic Center Coliseum, 13,788

The documentary 'Elvis On Tour' went on release on November 1, 1972. It won the Golden Globe award for Best Documentary of 1972. Variety called it "A bright entertaining pop music documentary." But the Hollywood Report said it was "little more than an ambitious public relations tract."

Elvis On Tour

In 1972 Elvis's touring schedule stepped up a gear. During the year he undertook three major tours, as well as playing two stints at Las Vegas. The April 1972 tour was filmed for the movie *Elvis On Tour*. Although the camera crews followed him throughout the tour from Buffalo to Albuquerque, the concert at San Antonio on April 18th formed the basis for the film.

Later in the year Elvis returned to Hawaii for the first time in 11 years and in preparation for his forthcoming live TV broadcast. In the interval he had become a big star in Japan. It is reported that 3,000 Japanese fans came over to Honolulu in chartered aircraft for the concert at the International Center.

Separate lives

This was the year that Elvis's internal world was dramatically changed by his formal separation from Priscilla. Though they remained friends, the fact that she left him was an enormous blow to his self image. Elvis announced publicly in January that Priscilla was moving to her own apartment with Lisa Marie, and in February she left.

In July 1972 Elvis met Linda Thompson at a movie show in Memphis. She was to remain a constant companion until 1976, though during this time Elvis was occasionally dating other women. Much of the material Elvis recorded in his later years seems to relate to his difficulties in coming to terms with his divorce from Priscilla.

One Billion Tune In

The Hawaii TV Special and the 1973 Tours

By 1973 Elvis had played his way around most of the major cities in the United States. Ever since his return to live touring in 1970, there had been rumours and expectations that he might play abroad. Fans in Britain and the rest of Europe, Australia and Japan had been faithful to him for many years. And for many years they kept up the pressure to try to get him to play concerts in their countries. The Colonel's answer to this was to arrange a television show that would be broadcast all over the world simultaneously, via the new wonders of satellite transmission. The result was one of the biggest audiences in world television history — and a failure to satisfy Elvis's overseas fans.

The *Aloha From Hawaii Via Satellite* special was filmed in the Honolulu International Convention Center in front of 5,500 fans. A dress rehearsal on the previous evening had also played before a full audience. Although the show might have seemed to have global pretensions, it was principally aimed at opening a new market for Elvis and Elvis products in the Far East. The show was broadcast live at 12.30a.m. to catch the peak television slot in Japan. Elvis Presley Week had been declared in Tokyo in the build up to the program, where it gained around 40 per cent of

viewers. The Philippines, South Vietnam, Thailand, South Korea, Hong Kong and Australia all joined in, to give an audience of over a billion.

In Europe some networks showed an edited version of the show the next day, but fans in Britain didn't get to see the program at all. After the show was over Elvis played a few more songs to an empty auditorium, just for the cameras. Most of these were included in an extended version of the show which was eventually seen on American television in April.

The double album *Elvis — Aloha From Hawaii Via Satellite* was rush-released by RCA on February 14, in much the same way as the previous year's *Live At*

Elvis's reputation as a recording artist might have been even higher if his record company had come up with some sort of strategy for the development of his career. In a sense he was almost too successful for his own good. Despite their success with Elvis RCA failed to sign up any other significant rock and roll singers. They were enormously dependent on Elvis product and so they got what they could from it. Perhaps the most frustrating aspect for the Elvis fan, was the constant issuing of third rate or recycled Elvis tracks on RCA's budget label Camden. It wasn't all RCA's fault of course. In the sixties Colonel Parker had forbidden Elvis to record anything but movie soundtracks, in order not to compete with them. RCA had to go back to the old sessions to find things to put out. In addition Elvis often recorded without conviction, leaving them without a good version of a song. But this may have been a product of their earlier strategy, where anything would do as long as it had his name on it.

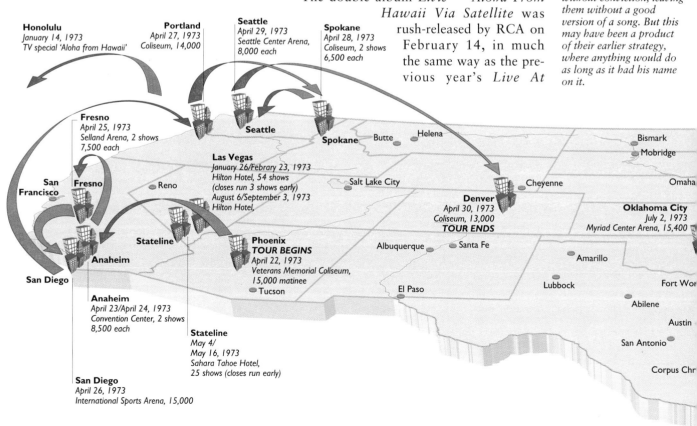

Honolulu
January 14, 1973
TV special 'Aloha from Hawaii'

Portland
April 27, 1973
Coliseum, 14,000

Seattle
April 29, 1973
Seattle Center Arena,
8,000 each

Spokane
April 28, 1973
Coliseum, 2 shows
6,500 each

Fresno
April 25, 1973
Selland Arena, 2 shows
7,500 each

Las Vegas
January 26/Febrary 23, 1973
Hilton Hotel, 54 shows
(closes run 3 shows early)
August 6/September 3, 1973
Hilton Hotel,

Denver
April 30, 1973
Coliseum, 13,000
TOUR ENDS

Oklahoma City
July 2, 1973
Myriad Center Arena, 15,400

Phoenix
TOUR BEGINS
April 22, 1973
Veterans Memorial Coliseum,
15,000 matinee

Anaheim
April 23/April 24, 1973
Convention Center, 2 shows
8,500 each

Stateline
May 4/
May 16, 1973
Sahara Tahoe Hotel,
25 shows (closes run early)

San Diego
April 26, 1973
International Sports Arena, 15,000

Honolulu · San Francisco · Fresno · Reno · Seattle · Spokane · Butte · Helena · Bismark · Mobridge · Salt Lake City · Cheyenne · Omaha · Stateline · Anaheim · Albuquerque · Santa Fe · Amarillo · San Diego · Tucson · El Paso · Lubbock · Fort Wor · Abilene · Austin · San Antonio · Corpus Chr

The original TV special on January 14, 1973 was to benefit the Kui Lee Cancer Fund. The longer version transmitted on American television in April 1973 was sponsored by the 'Chicken-Of-The-Sea Tuna Company. Their company logo appeared on a limited number of albums — now collector's items.

One Elvis peculiarity that surfaced in 1973 was a short version of the Bob Dylan song 'Don't Think Twice, It's All Right' on the album Elvis. It was part of a between-takes jam session that found its way onto the finished album. The full 8-minute rendition was released years later, showing Elvis in much better form than on the dull 'official' tracks on the LP.

Madison Square Garden. This was Elvis's sixth live LP in four years, with most tracks having appeared before both in live and studio versions. Despite all this, the album went to the top of the Billboard chart and eventually sold 2 million copies. *The Aloha From Hawaii* special could have been some kind of thank you to all his fans. But during the performance he seemed edgy, while his physical trappings were a sign of his increasing loss of a sense of reality. Though some songs stand out, most are not treated with the conviction they deserve. The Elvis capes and insignia verged on a Liberace parody. It was an omen of things to come.

Elvis abroad

Various promoters had been eager to get Elvis to tour outside America since 1956. The promoter of his 1957 tours hoped to persuade Colonel Parker that if he could handle an Elvis tour in the States, he'd be able to take him to Australia. In England there were constant rumours of impending Presley visits throughout his career. One report speculated that Elvis had been booked to perform in a glass box in the center of London's Wembley Stadium. The sides of the box would magnify the image of the singer, so that the crowds in the stadium would be able to see him clearly! Presumably the occupants of the box would have been fried if the sun had shone. Thankfully that idea never got further than a newspaper report.

It's now generally accepted that Elvis didn't tour outside the US (apart from a very few Canadian dates) because Colonel Parker was an illegal immigrant from Holland. He would have been exposed if he had applied for a passport. As Parker liked to check out all of Elvis's venues (if only to look as if he was doing something for his money) this rings true. But Elvis never showed any great interest in going to other parts of the world in any case. He was presumably free to go where he wanted to for his vacations, and he had the wealth to travel all over the world. Instead he went to Las Vegas, Hawaii or Palm Springs. If it hadn't been for the army he would never have left North America — even *Fun In Acapulco* was filmed in Hollywood!

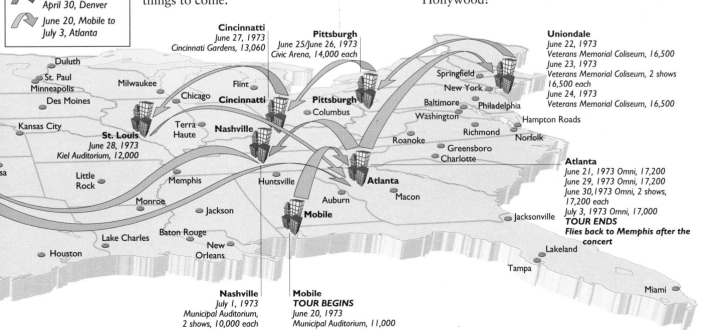

Never Ending Demand

The 1974 Tours

Elvis had nothing left to prove in his live concerts and it was beginning to show. In fact over the period of the seventies his performances had always been variable. His much-publicized weight problems also fluctuated dramatically — in later years he was often thinner than he was in 1972. But overall he was losing his health and his ability to perform well. In 1974, after years of cleaning up with less than adequate albums and singles, his records started once again to fail to sell. Now he had to keep touring to finance his extravagant life style — the money wasn't coming in from anywhere else.

The Presley fans continued to turn out for the concerts. Every venue he played was close to capacity, although he was playing some for the second or third time. New material was introduced into his stage act, but people seeing him for the first time wanted to hear the old songs too, so they were endlessly recycled. Elvis played around 800 shows from 1970 to 1977, mostly with the same band, in venues that all looked and sounded much the same. It was hard to keep a sense of spontaneous excitement.

It was decided that one of Elvis's appearances in his home town should be recorded for yet another live album. He hadn't performed a live show in Memphis since the 1961 charity events. So the March 20 show at the Mid-South Coliseum was taped and duly issued as *Recorded Live On Stage in Memphis*. The album was marketed as the record of a tri-

"Despite the thickening around the middle and rather puffy countenance, Presley is the center of attention for femmes who squeal, writhe and grab for his neck scarves whenever he cruises ringside. Certainly the extra poundage doesn't interfere with his familiar type of belting or mooing ballads."
Variety on Elvis's 1974 Las Vegas shows

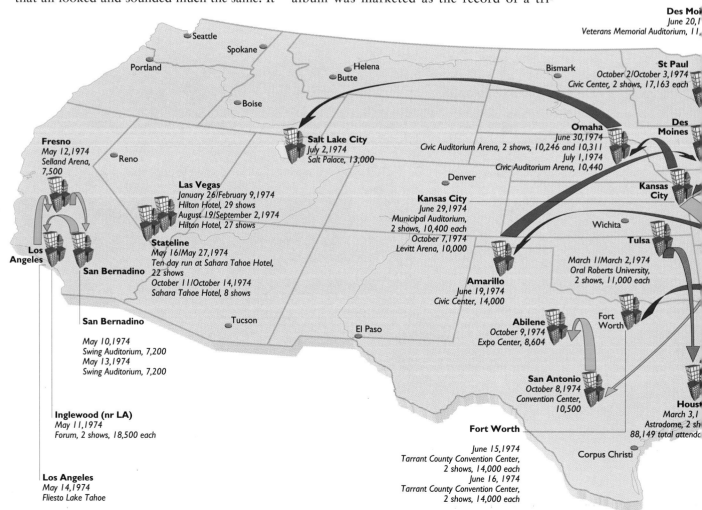

Des Moi
June 20, 1
Veterans Memorial Auditorium, 11,

St Paul
October 2/October 3, 1974
Civic Center, 2 shows, 17,163 each

Des Moines

Omaha
June 30, 1974
Civic Auditorium Arena, 2 shows, 10,246 and 10,311
July 1, 1974
Civic Auditorium Arena, 10,440

Kansas City

Fresno
May 12, 1974
Selland Arena, 7,500

Salt Lake City
July 2, 1974
Salt Palace, 13,000

Denver

Kansas City
June 29, 1974
Municipal Auditorium, 2 shows, 10,400 each
October 7, 1974
Levitt Arena, 10,000

Wichita

Las Vegas
January 26/February 9, 1974
Hilton Hotel, 29 shows
August 19/September 2, 1974
Hilton Hotel, 27 shows

Tulsa

Los Angeles

San Bernadino

Stateline
May 16/May 27, 1974
Ten-day run at Sahara Tahoe Hotel,
22 shows
October 11/October 14, 1974
Sahara Tahoe Hotel, 8 shows

March 1/March 2, 1974
Oral Roberts University,
2 shows, 11,000 each

Amarillo
June 19, 1974
Civic Center, 14,000

Fort Worth

San Bernadino

May 10, 1974
Swing Auditorium, 7,200
May 13, 1974
Swing Auditorium, 7,200

Tucson

El Paso

Abilene
October 9, 1974
Expo Center, 8,604

San Antonio
October 8, 1974
Convention Center,
10,500

Houst
March 3, 1
Astrodome, 2 sh
88,149 total attend

Inglewood (nr LA)
May 11, 1974
Forum, 2 shows, 18,500 each

Fort Worth

June 15, 1974
Tarrant County Convention Center,
2 shows, 14,000 each
June 16, 1974
Tarrant County Convention Center,
2 shows, 14,000 each

Corpus Christi

Los Angeles
May 14, 1974
Fliesto Lake Tahoe

As in the previous year with 'Burning Love' Elvis managed to show that he could still produce exhilarating music when he tried. This time it was 'Promised Land' a Chuck Berry song from 1964. Elvis actually recorded it at Stax studios in Memphis at the end of 1973, for release in October 1974. The song is one of Berry's greatest, and Elvis's treatment is excellent. Unfortunately he did all too few rock and rollers in his last years.

umphant homecoming. But, being a live show, Elvis was obliged to play a good selection of his old material, which was then put on the album. This time the LP failed to have the sales impact of the *Madison Square Garden* and *Aloha From Hawaii* recordings. RCA's Felton Jarvis decided to drop the live format for albums, until Elvis's repertoire changed dramatically.

In their 1982 book *Elvis: The Illustrated Record*, Roy Carr and Mick Farren argue that some of Elvis's later poor performances can be put down to his intense dislike of being recorded live. He would deliberately skip through any new songs that he decided to perform, and insert snippets of irrelevant monologue into others, occasionally deliberately messing up what were otherwise strong performances of some songs, so that they couldn't be used by RCA. If true, this bizarre farce was not only an insult to his paying audience, it was also unnecessary — RCA had already decided they'd milked the live format for everything they were ever going to get. Within a couple of years, Elvis would add to their headaches by refusing to go into studios as well.

Detroit
September 29,1974
Olympia Stadium matinee,
17,105
October 4,1974
Olympia Stadium matinee,
17,105

Dayton
October 6,1974
Dayton Arena, 2 shows,
13,500 each

Indianapolis
October 5,1974
Expo Center,
2 shows,
14,000 each

Columbus
June 25,1974
St John's Arena, 14,000

South Bend
September 30,1974
Notre Dame Athletic &
nvention Center, 12,301
October 1,1974
Notre Dame Athletic &
nvention Center, 12,301

Cleveland
June 21,1974
Convention Center
Public Hall, 10,000

Baltimore

September 27/
September 28,1974
Fieldhouse,
College Park,
Maryland University,
2 shows, 15,000 each

Niagara Falls
June 24,1974
International Convention
Center, 2 shows,
13,113 each

Niagara Falls

Milwaukee
June 28,1974
waukee Arena,
11,800

Detroit
Indianapolis

South Bend

Cleveland
Columbus

Dayton

Philadelphia
Baltimore

Providence **Providence**
June 22,1974
Civic Center Auditorium,
2 shows, 13,113 each

Philadelphia
June 23,1974
Spectrum, 2 shows, 40,000 total

Bloomington
June 27,1974
Indiana University
Assembly Hall, 16,000

Louisville

Roanoke
March 10,1974
Civic Center,
10,640

Hampton Roads
March 11,1974
Coliseum, 10, 957

Richmond
March 12,1974
Coliseum, 11,791

Louisville
June 26,1974
Freedom Hall,
20,000

Richmond
Greensboro

Memphis

Murfreesboro

Knoxville

Greensboro
March 13,1974
Coliseum, 16,200

Richmond
March 18,1974
Coliseum, 11,791

nsas

Auburn
March 5,1974
University Memorial
Coliseum, 13,239

Charlotte
March 9,1974
Coliseum, 2 shows,
11,960 each

Murfreesboro
March 14,1974
Middle Tennessee
State University, 12,500
March 19,1974
Middle Tennessee
State University,
12,500

Montgomery
March 5,1974
Garrett Coliseum, 11,328

Monroe
March 4,1974
Center, 8,000
March 7,1974
Center, 8,000

Baton Rouge

New Orleans

Jacksonville

Lakeland

Tampa

Miami

March 1, Tulsa to March 20, Memphis

May 10, San Bernadino to May 13, San Bernadino

June 15, Fort Worth to July 2, Salt Lake City

September 27, Baltimore to October 9, Abilene

Memphis
March 16/March 17,1974
Mid-South Coliseum,
2 shows per day, 12,300 each
March 20,1974
Mid-South Coliseum, 12,300
(Recorded for live LP)

Baton Rouge
June 17,1974
University of Louisiana
Assembly Center, 15,000
June 18,1974
University of Louisiana
Assembly Center, 15,000

Knoxville
March 15,1974
University of
Tennessee
Stokley Athletic Center,
2 shows, 13,305 each

Chronology

June1968–October 1974

1968

June	Rehearsals for NBC Singer special begin at NBC-TV studios, Burbank California.
June 25	Press conference for television editors concerning forthcoming TV special.
June 27–30	Filming of *Elvis* TV special at Burbank.
July 22	Location filming begins for *Charro* in Arizona, followed by studio shots in Hollywood.
Sep. 15	'Almost In Love'/'A Little Less Conversation' released.
Oct. 14	Recording session at MGM studios for soundtrack to *The Trouble With Girls*.
Oct. 15	'If I Can Dream'/'Edge Of Reality' released.
Oct. 23	*Live A Little, Love A Little* opens at movie theaters.
Oct. 28	*The Trouble With Girls* starts filming in Hollywood.
Nov. 25	Soundtrack album to the TV special *Elvis* is released.
Dec. 3	Singer NBC TV Special *Elvis* is broadcast.

1969

Jan. 13–16	Recording session at American Studios, Memphis.
Jan. 20–24	Continuation of recording session.
Feb. 17–24	Further recordings at American Studios. These three sessions produced tracks for Elvis's acclaimed comeback albums *From Elvis In Memphis* and *From Vegas to Memphis*.
Mar.	'Memories'/'Charro' released.
Mar. 5	Recording session at Universal studios, Hollywood for soundtrack to *Change Of Habit*.
Mar./Apr.	Filming *Change Of Habit* in Hollywood and Los Angeles.
Mar. 13	*Charro* released into movie theaters.
Apr. 15	'In The Ghetto'/'Any Day Now' released.
June	*From Elvis In Memphis* album and 'Clean Up Your Own Backyard'/'The Fair Is Moving On' released.
July 31	Elvis returns to live performing at the International Hotel, Las Vegas.
Aug. 17	NBC-TV special re-broadcast.
Aug. 22–26	Las Vegas shows taped and tracks used in live portion of forthcoming album.
Aug. 28	Finishes Las Vegas run of concerts.
Sept.	'Suspicious Minds'/'You'll Think Of Me' released.
Sept. 3	*The Trouble With Girls* opens in movie theaters.
Nov. 10	*Change Of Habit* goes on general release in movie theaters.
Nov. 16	*From Memphis To Vegas/From Vegas To Memphis* double album released.
Nov.	'Don't Cry Daddy'/'Rubberneckin' released.

1970

Jan. 26	Elvis opens at the

International Hotel, Las Vegas for a month-long series of shows.

Feb.　'Kentucky Rain'/'My Little Friend' released.

Feb. 27–Mar. 1　Elvis plays a total of six shows at the Houston Astrodome, his first outside Las Vegas for nine years.

May　'The Wonder Of You'/'Mama Liked The Roses' released.

June　*On Stage–Feb. 1970* album released.

June 4–9　Recording session at RCA Studio B in Nashville.

July　'I've Lost You'/'The Next Step Is Love' released.

Aug.　*Elvis: Worldwide Gold Hits, Volume 1* four-album set released.

Aug. 10　Opens at Las Vegas International Hotel, plays until September 7.

Sept. 9　Starts first tour since 1957 with concert at the Veterans' Memorial Coliseum in Phoenix, Arizona.

Sept. 14　Tour ends in Mobile, Alabama.

Sept. 22　Recording session in Nashville.

Oct.　'You Don't Have To Say You Love Me'/'Patch It Up' released.

Nov. 11　The documentary film *Elvis–That's the Way It Is* opens in movie theaters. The accompanying album is released in the same month. Elvis starts a tour in Portland, Oregeon.

Nov. 17　Tour ends in Denver.

Dec.　'There Goes My Everything'/'I Really Don't Want To Know' released.

Dec. 21　After flying from Memphis to Washington, then to Los Angeles to pick up Jerry Schilling,

then back to Washington, Elvis meets President Nixon at the White House. The President presents Elvis with a narcotics officer badge.

1971

Jan.　*Elvis Country* album released.

Jan. 26　Opens at Las Vegas for month-long engagement.

Mar.　'Rags To Riches'/'Where Do They Go Lord' released.

Mar. 15　Recording session in Nashville.

May　'Only Believe'/'Life' released.

May 15–21　Recording session in Nashville.

June　*Love Letters From Elvis* LP released.

June 8,9　Recording session for *He Touched Me* album.

July　'I'm Leavin''/'Heart Of Rome' released.

July 20　Opens at the High Sierra Room in the Sahara Tahoe Hotel, Stateline, Nevada for two weeks.

Aug.　*Elvis: The Other Sides, Worldwide Gold Award Hits, Volume 2* four-album set released.

Aug. 9–Sep. 6　Plays International Hotel, Las Vegas.

Oct.　'It's Only Love'/'The Sound Of Your Cry' released.

Nov. 5　Starts tour in Minneapolis.

Nov. 19　*Elvis Sings The Wonderful World Of Christmas* album and 'Merry Christmas Baby'/'O Come All Ye Faithful' single released.

1972

Jan.　'Until It's Time For You To Go'/'We Can Make the Morning' released.

Chronology

June 1968–October 1974

Jan. 8	Elvis informally announces that Priscilla is moving out with Lisa Marie.
Jan. 19	South Bellevue Boulevard in Memphis is officially renamed Elvis Presley Boulevard.
Jan. 26	Opening night of Las Vegas run (to February 23).
Feb.	*Elvis Now* LP released.
Feb. 17	Las Vegas show is taped, including take of 'An American Trilogy' to be released as a single in April.
Feb. 23	Priscilla moves out with Lisa Marie.
Mar. 27,28	First recording session at RCA Hollywood studios. Session is filmed for *Elvis On Tour*.
Mar.	'He Touched Me'/'Bosom Of Abraham' released.
Apr. 5	Tour starts in Buffalo.
Apr.	*He Touched Me* album and 'An American Trilogy'/'The First Time Ever I Saw Your Face' released.
Apr. 19	Tour ends in Albuquerque.
June 9–11	Press conference in New York Hilton, followed by total of four shows at Madison Square Garden.
June 12	Tour continues with concert in Fort Wayne, Indiana.
June 19	*Elvis As Recorded At Madison Square Garden* album released.
June 20	Tour ends in Tulsa, Oklahoma.
July 27	Elvis and Priscilla formally separate.
Aug.	'Burning Love'/'It's A

	Matter Of Time' released.
Aug. 4	Las Vegas run of shows starts (to September 4)
Aug. 18	Elvis's lawyer files divorce petition in court in Santa Monica.
Nov.	'Separate Ways'/'Always On My Mind' released.
Nov. 1	The documentary movie *Elvis On Tour* goes on general release.
Nov. 8	Tour starts in Lubbock, Texas.
Nov. 19	Tour ends in Honolulu.
1973	
Jan.	*Separate Ways* LP released.
Jan. 14	Live television broadcast of 'Elvis: Aloha From Hawaii' from International Center, Honolulu to Asia and Australia.
Jan. 26	Start of run of shows at Las Vegas Hilton (to February 23).
Feb.	*Elvis : Aloha From Hawaii Via Satellite* double album released.
Mar. 1	Signs new seven-year contract with RCA. Includes RCA buying royalty rights on all of Elvis's catalog to date for $5 million.
Apr.	'Steamroller Blues'/'The Fool' released.
Apr. 4	Extended version of 'Elvis: Aloha From Hawaii' TV special broacast by NBC.
Apr. 22	Tour starts in Phoenix, Arizona.
Apr. 30	Tour ends in Denver.
May 4	Start of run of shows at Sahara Tahoe Hotel, Stateline, Nevada (to May 17)

June 20	Tour starts in Mobile, Alabama.
July 3	Tour ends in Atlanta.
July 14	*Elvis* album (also known as the Fool album) released.
July 21–24	Recording session at Stax studios Memphis.
Aug. 6	Summer shows at Las Vegas start (to September 3).
Sept.	At Elvis's home in Palm Springs female companion overdoses on Hycodan cough syrup. She is rushed to hospital and suffers no permanent damage.
Sept.	'Raised On Rock'/'For Old Times Sake' released.
Sept. 24	Recording session at Elvis's home in Palm Springs.
Oct. 9	Elvis and Priscilla agree divorce settlement at Santa Monica Superior Court. Both are present.
Oct. 15	Elvis is rushed to Baptist Memorial Hospital in Memphis with pneumonia and pleurisy. In addition he is later reported to have had an enlarged colon and a form of hepatitis.
Nov.	*Raised On Rock* album released.
Dec. 10–15	Recording session at Stax studios, Memphis.

1974

Jan.	*Elvis – A Legendary Performer, Volume 1* album released.
Jan. 26	Las Vegas Hilton run of shows starts (to February 9)
Feb.	'I've Got A Thing About You Baby'/'Take Good Care Of Her' released.
Mar.	The album *Good Times* is released.
Mar. 1	Tour starts in Tulsa, Oklahoma.

Mar. 20	Tour ends in Memphis, where the show is recorded for a live album.
May 10–13	Short tour starts and ends in San Bernadino.
May 16	Start of run at Sahara Tahoe Hotel (to May 27).
May	'If You Talk In Your Sleep'/'Help Me' released.
June 15	Tour starts in Fort Worth.
July 2	Tour ends in Salt Lake City.
July	*Elvis Recorded Live On Stage In Memphis* album released.
Aug. 19	Opens run at Las Vegas Hilton (to September 2).
Sept. 27	Starts tour in Baltimore.
Oct. 9	Tour ends in Abilene, Texas.
Oct. 11	Starts run at Sahara Tahoe Hotel (to October 14).
Oct.	'Promised Land'/'It's Midnight' and the album *Having Fun With Elvis On Stage* released.

Part Seven: DECAY AND DEATH 1975–1977

"When I don't do a good job, I know it and I'm blue as hell. You'll pardon my language, but I mean it."

"As long as there's a public, as long as you're pleasing the people, it'd be foolish to quit."

"Let's face the facts. Anybody in the public eye, their life is not as private anymore. Everything you do, the public knows about it and that's how it's always been and that's how it always will be."

"I'm always travelling around the country, working in a different city every day."

"Retirement? I'll never quit as long as I'm doing OK."

"I want to entertain people. That's my whole life, to my last breath. I don't ever want to stop singing."

"If I hit them all I can retire and not feel that I short-changed anybody. Physically I'm not well enough to keep doing this."

"I appreciate their wanting to see me and their loyalty. I intend to continue to perform as long as I am able and for as long as they want me. I really love singing for my fans. It's my life. I want them to be excited and to go away saying 'Man! Wow!'."

"It's ironic, but it appears that history is repeating itself. My career is again as hectic as it was in the fifties. The people mob every arena. It's frightening. Somehow it doesn't seem normal. I'm grateful for their loyalty but it's scary. I wonder what's next."

"Elvis had the arteries of an 80-year old man. His body was just worn out. His arteries and veins were terribly corroded. An autopsy usually takes 24 hours. Usually, any vital organs that are removed for study are returned and put into a bag and dropped into the coffin before burial. But not in Elvis's case. His brain, his liver, his kidneys and all the rest have been left out for tests here."
A Baptist Memorial Hospital Nurse
August 1977, quoted in *Rolling Stone* no. 248, September 22, 1977

Introduction

Elvis began to show signs of serious physical distress in 1975. He had cancelled odd concerts in the past, but in August 1975 he was flown to the hospital in Memphis mid-way through a season of shows in Las Vegas. In common with other episodes of illness in Elvis's life, this one is surrounded by a certain air of mystery. Exhaustion, influenza, hypertension, disease of the colon, irregular heartbeat — all were cited in official and unofficial statements in Elvis's final years. It's natural that anyone giving themselves the punishing schedule of touring that Elvis did should have the odd breakdown. But it's now clear that for many years he had been taking large amounts of prescription drugs, and that these were a direct or indirect cause of his illnesses, and death.

Life had been irretrievably strange for Elvis Presley since he became just about the most famous person in America at the age of 21. He paid all the usual prices of fame. He was unable to go anywhere without being stared at or photographed, a constant posse of fans camped outside his door, everyone he met had to be scrutinized for their real motives, and even his closest friends deferred to him in everything. Little wonder that he had trouble living a 'normal' internal life, when his external one was so abnormal.

According to long-time friend and companion Red West, Elvis was first introduced to drugs during his time in the Army. In common with many performers he found it hard to 'come down' after a show. In the fifties he would often drive all night after a concert to work the adrenaline out of his system, before sleeping all day, and then starting again. By the time the seventies tours came he was taking pills to calm himself down, but then he might need some to give him the lift to get through a show, and then some others to get to sleep. It's hard to know the amounts he was taking at any one time, but it's certain that Dr. Nichopoulos would order large quantities before each tour, and that, despite claims to the contrary, these were intended primarily for Elvis.

Elvis's behavior became unpredictable as the years wore on. This may have been due to the drugs, but was surely connected with the continuing difficulties of living such an abnormal life. The end of his marriage to Priscilla was a bitter blow from which he never fully recovered. And in 1976 Linda Thompson, the woman who had been beside him since Priscilla left, also pulled out. A few months earlier he had sacked Red West the man who had been with him ever since the Sun Records and Louisiana Hayride days. Despite the constant crowd at Graceland, for the last few months of his life he must have felt a little lonely.

It's common to assume that because Elvis's death was so tragic, his life was full of misery and loneliness. It seems more likely that he got a lot of pleasure out of life. He certainly drew enormous enjoyment from music — both listening and performing, and he loved to be surrounded by people. Graceland was for many years a happy place for Elvis, his family and his friends. If he had gone outside its walls and into the real world more often he might have served himself better. But if he was trapped by extraordinary fame, he did enjoy some of the pleasures as well as the costs.

Illness and Exhaustion

The 1975 Tours

Although Elvis's physical condition had been less than perfect for sometime, he had almost always managed to fulfil his engagements. But now, as he turned 40, the long history of drug-taking, combined with the sheer exhaustion of his continual performances, took its toll. On a flight from Memphis to Las Vegas in August, Elvis complained of difficulty with his breathing. The plane landed at Dallas, where he rested. He went on to Vegas, but on August 21 Elvis flew back to Memphis with his physician Dr Nichopoulos, and entered the Baptist Memorial Hospital.

"He looks healthy and sounds good. Once he gets on stage he carries the singing load and minimizes the patter, a wise departure from several previous visits." Variety on the March 1975 Las Vegas opening

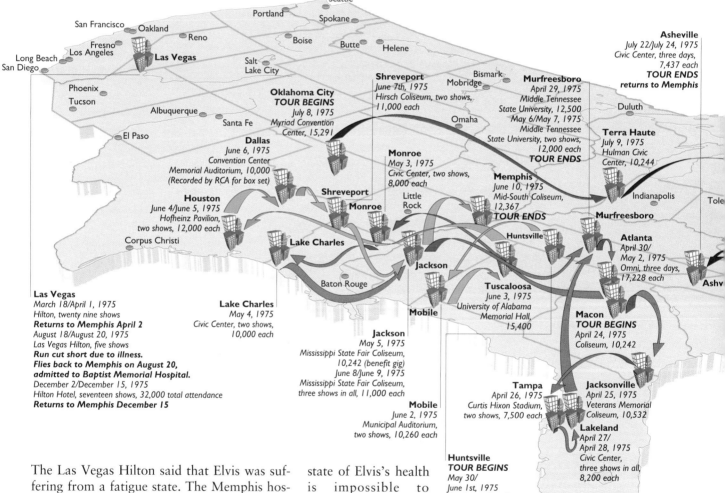

Asheville
July 22/July 24, 1975
Civic Center, three days,
7,437 each
TOUR ENDS
returns to Memphis

Oklahoma City
TOUR BEGINS
July 8, 1975
Myriad Convention
Center, 15,291

Shreveport
June 7th, 1975
Hirsch Coliseum, two shows,
11,000 each

Murfreesboro
April 29, 1975
Middle Tennessee
State University, 12,500
May 6/May 7, 1975
Middle Tennessee
State University, two shows,
12,000 each
TOUR ENDS

Terra Haute
July 9, 1975
Hulman Civic
Center, 10,244

Dallas
June 6, 1975
Convention Center
Memorial Auditorium, 10,000
(Recorded by RCA for box set)

Monroe
May 3, 1975
Civic Center, two shows,
8,000 each

Memphis
June 10, 1975
Mid-South Coliseum,
12,367
TOUR ENDS

Houston
June 4/June 5, 1975
Hofheinz Pavilion,
two shows, 12,000 each

Shreveport
Monroe

Murfreesboro

Huntsville

Atlanta
April 30/
May 2, 1975
Omni, three days,
17,228 each

Lake Charles

Jackson

Tuscaloosa
June 3, 1975
University of Alabama
Memorial Hall,
15,400

Las Vegas
March 18/April 1, 1975
Hilton, twenty nine shows
Returns to Memphis April 2
August 18/August 20, 1975
Las Vegas Hilton, five shows
Run cut short due to illness.
Flies back to Memphis on August 20,
admitted to Baptist Memorial Hospital.
December 2/December 15, 1975
Hilton Hotel, seventeen shows, 32,000 total attendance
Returns to Memphis December 15

Lake Charles
May 4, 1975
Civic Center, two shows,
10,000 each

Mobile

Jackson
May 5, 1975
Mississippi State Fair Coliseum,
10,242 (benefit gig)
June 8/June 9, 1975
Mississippi State Fair Coliseum,
three shows in all, 11,000 each

Macon
TOUR BEGINS
April 24, 1975
Coliseum, 10,242

Tampa
April 26, 1975
Curtis Hixon Stadium,
two shows, 7,500 each

Jacksonville
April 25, 1975
Veterans Memorial
Coliseum, 10,532

Mobile
June 2, 1975
Municipal Auditorium,
two shows, 10,260 each

Lakeland
April 27/
April 28, 1975
Civic Center,
three shows in all,
8,200 each

Huntsville
TOUR BEGINS
May 30/
June 1st, 1975
Von Braun Civic Center,
five shows in all,
8,000 each

The Las Vegas Hilton said that Elvis was suffering from a fatigue state. The Memphis hospital said he was admitted for treatment of fatigue and for tests. Later reports suggest that he suffered from hypertension and from an impacted colon. He stayed in the hospital until September 5, and two nurses were then assigned to take care of him in Graceland. During the time he was in the hospital, Elvis's father Vernon suffered a serious heart attack and was admitted to the same institution.

Dr Nichopoulos declared that exhaustion was Elvis's main problem, and that he would be fit again in three to five months. The real state of Elvis's health is impossible to determine, but there is little doubt that he was taking prodigious quantities of prescription drugs. (During the year his step-brother and aide Rick Stanley was arrested in Memphis for passing a forged prescription for Demerol. Elvis posted his bail.) One effect of the drugs was to make his behaviour erratic and sometimes dangerous.

On July 22 after a concert in Asheville in North Carolina Elvis was watching television in his hotel suite. Something on the TV upset

Charleston
July 11/July 12, 1975
Civic Center, three shows in all,
8,400 each

Niagara Falls
July 13, 1975
International Convention Center,
two shows, 11,500 each

New Haven
July 16/July 17, 1975
Veterans Memorial Coliseum,
two shows, 10,000 each

Richfield
July 10, 1975
Cleveland Coliseum, 21,000
July 18, 1975
Cleveland Coliseum, 21,000

Springfield
July 14/July 15, 1975
Civic Center Arena,
9,000
New Haven

Bangor

Baltimore
Philadelphia

Uniondale

Richmond

Hampton
Roads

Greensboro
July 21, 1975
Coliseum, 16,300

Norfolk
July 20, 1975
two shows, 21,000

Uniondale
July 19, 1975
Nassau Coliseum, two shows,
16,500 each

April 24, Macon
to May 7,
Murfreesboro

May 30,
Huntsville to June
10, Memphis

July 8, Oklahoma
City to July 24,
Asheville

prompt Elvis to get some money back from somewhere — he put two of his other three planes up for sale in September. From now on he went everywhere in the Lisa Marie.

In spite of his difficulties this year, Elvis went out on a typically record–breaking note. He was booked to play a special New Year's Eve concert at the city stadium in Pontiac, Michigan. Over 62,000 fans turned out for the party, which set a world record attendance figure for one show.

On the recording front, 1975 marked the last time Elvis ever went into a studio (from now on he would lay down vocal and some other tracks in Graceland only). It also saw his last Top 20 single in his lifetime — 'My Boy'. In an increasingly desperate strategy RCA coupled together Elvis's two latest hit singles with a bunch of tracks recorded back in 1973 at the Stage Studios in Memphis. Apart from the title track, the resulting *Promised Land* album is a disappointment. Even worse was 1974's *Having Fun With Elvis On Stage* — a true lesson in how to humiliate your most valuable artist. The fact that Elvis's reputation has, after all, survived such trash is a tribute to the man's talent and the extraordinary loyalty of his fans. Yet again Elvis managed one great single in the year. 'T–R–O–U–B–L–E' was another solid rock and roller. Unfortunately it didn't make higher than Number 45 on the Billboard chart, which might explain why Elvis returned to ballads.

him, so he pulled out a pistol and shot it. The bullet ricocheted and struck Dr Nichopoulos in the chest, just an inch or two from the heart. Luckily for him, the bullet was nearly spent. During shows in Ashville Elvis gave away three diamond rings worth over $40,000 in total, and gave his guitar to a member of the audience.

Back in Memphis his extravagance continued unabated. On January 17 he bought eleven Cadillacs to give to friends, and on July 27 he bought fourteen, including a gold and white which he gave to a teller at a local bank when he heard it was her birthday.

In addition Elvis had at last managed to purchase his dream airplane — a Convair 880 jet which he named the 'Lisa Marie'. The plane cost $1.2 million, and Elvis spent a further $1 million refurbishing the interior. The plane had its maiden flight from Memphis to Nashville on November 27. The purchase did

Shrinking World

January–August 1976

In 1976, the penultimate year of his life, Elvis played more concerts than any other year, apart from 1955. In addition to playing 71 concerts in 40 cities during the first eight months of the year, he recorded a new album, *From Elvis Presley Boulevard, Memphis*, and saw the release of *Elvis — A Legendary Performer, Volume 2*. Of more long-term significance was the release of the album *The Sun Sessions* in April 1976. The re-release in album form of his first recordings, made in Memphis 20 years previously, was to restore Presley's reputation as one of the key musical innovators of the twentieth century.

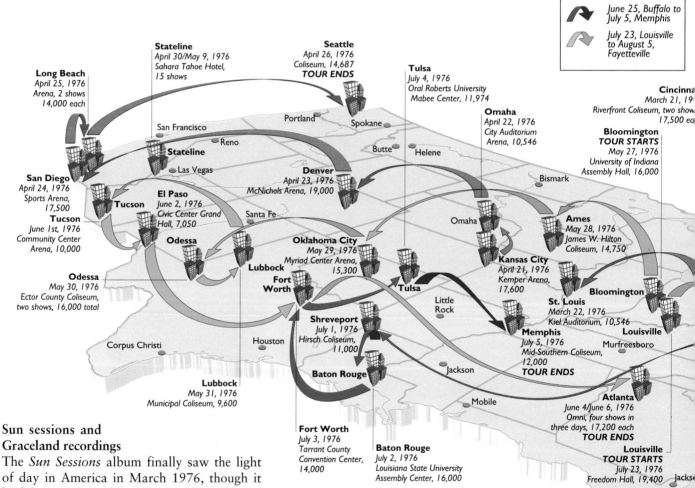

TOURS 1976

March 17, Johnson City to March 22, St Louis
April 21, Kansas City to April 26, Seattle

May 27, Bloomington to June 6, Atlanta

June 25, Buffalo to July 5, Memphis

July 23, Louisville to August 5, Fayetteville

Sun sessions and Graceland recordings

The *Sun Sessions* album finally saw the light of day in America in March 1976, though it had been released in Britain the previous August. The British division of RCA had been hassling for some time to get an album containing Presley's work for Sun, to satisfy the intense British interest in early rock and roll. At this time the creative energies that had produced so much extraordinary popular music in the sixties seemed to have run their course. Music in America and elsewhere was either vapid chart-based pop, or pretentious art-house rock. But, as in the fifties, young musicians were looking elsewhere for inspiration.

And they found it in rock and roll — a musical form that had been parodied, commercialized, toned down and ridiculed, but remained what it had always been — vibrant and liberating. The result of this re-discovery became apparent with the explosion of punk and new wave, which gave popular music a much-needed shot in the arm, in an echo of Presley's deeds in 1956.

True to form RCA originally vetoed the idea of an album of Presley's Sun recordings,

During 1976 Elvis's physical well-being became a matter of growing concern to his entourage and to his fans. But no-one seems to have been willing or able to convince him that some drastic action was needed. The relentless touring schedule increased, but Elvis was seeing less of the world than ever. He was whisked from private plane to limousine to concert hall to hotel suite. And every one of them looked much the same. He never saw the inside of a recording studio after 1975, preferring to lay down vocal tracks inside the walls of Graceland. His world was shrinking, and nobody seemed able to do anything about it.

and then eventually released it as *The Elvis Presley Sun Collection*, as the launch album for their RCA Starcall budget series. The reverse of the album contained ads for other artists in the series, and no notes on the recordings. This is how the most important set of recordings made in the second half of the twentieth century were re-issued to a general audience. It is a sign of how far the understanding of Presley's music has improved that such a travesty is now unthinkable. Thankfully the album was almost immediately repackaged as *The Sun Sessions* with full sleeve notes.

In January 1976 RCA released *Elvis — A Legendary Performer, Volume 2*. This hodge-podge contained out-takes ranging from 1955's Harbor Lights, through Hollywood soundtracks to some more leftovers from the 1968 TV special. RCA's policy of dribbling out material which must have been lying together in their vaults seems cynical and ultimately damaging to the reputation of their most important artist.

Meanwhile, Elvis spent the early part of February 1976 recording at home in Graceland. His depressed physical and mental state meant that he refused to work in recording studios. The vocal tracks for *From Elvis Presley Boulevard, Memphis, Tennessee* were recorded in the jungle room in Graceland. Despite recent success with some rock and rollers (Promised Land, TROUBLE) Presley returned to slow songs for this album. The titles of the tracks alone give strong clues to his mental disposition at the time — 'Hurt', 'Never Again', 'Bitter They Are', 'Love Coming Down'. The resulting vocal performance is as tortured as any he ever gave.

Roanoke
August 2, 1976
Civic Center, 10,598

Largo
June 26, 1976
Capitol Center, two shows,
40,000 total

Rochester
July 26, 1976
Community War Memorial
Auditorium, 10,000

Charleston
July 24, 1976
: Center, two shows,
8,500 each

Richmond
June 29, 1976
Coliseum, 11,900

Syracuse
July 25, 1976
Onondaga War Memorial Auditorium, 8,500
July 27, 1976
Onondaga War Memorial Auditorium, 8,500

Buffalo
June 25, 1976
Memorial
Auditorium,
17,500

Hartford
July 28, 1976
Civic Center, 12,314

Springfield
July 29, 1976
Civic Center, 10,000

Detroit

cinnati

Charleston

Buffalo

Rochester

Syracuse

Hartford

Springfield

Bangor

Roanoke

**New
Haven**

Providence

Providence
June 26, 1976
Civic Center, 2 shows,
13,500 each

Johnson
City

Greensboro

Largo

Philadelphia

Charlotte
March 20, 1976
Coliseum, two shows,
12,000 each

Richmond

**Hampton
Roads**

Philadelphia
June 28, 1976
Spectrum, 19,000

Newhaven
July 30, 1976
Veterans Memorial
Auditorium, 9,600

Fayetteville

Greensboro
June 30, 1976
Coliseum, 16,000

Fayettteville
August 3/August 5, 1976
Cumberland County Memorial
Auditorium, three shows in
three days, 7,000 each
TOUR ENDS

Hampton Roads
July 31/August 1, 1976
Hampton Coliseum,
two shows 11,000 each

Johnson City
TOUR STARTS
March 17/March 19, 1976
Freedom Hall, 3 shows,
7,000 each

"I only really feel at home in Memphis at my own Graceland mansion. A man gets lonesome for the things that are familiar to him. I know I do."

Another vast stadium in another city for another concert. This one happens to be the Mid-South Coliseum in Presley's home town of Memphis. It's located in the same park as the Fairgrounds, where the Presley entourage often rode the roller-coasters all night.

A Lonely Life

September to December 1976

There were conflicting signals from Elvis during the last part of his penultimate year. On the one hand he was touring as frantically as ever. In fact more than ever — 1976 was to be his busiest year for live shows in 21 years. His weight is reported to have come down to the point where he was wearing jumpsuits made in 1972, but hadn't fitted him since! But despite that, there were signs that thing's were going badly in other ways. He continued to refuse to work in recording studios. The reports that he was in poor health and was behaving strangely were born out by the decision of his long-time companion Linda Thompson to leave him. In July he sacked his oldest friend Red West. Now he really was all alone.

August 27, San Antonio to September 8, Pine Bluff

October 14, Chicago to October 27, Carbondale

November 24, Reno to November 30, Anaheim

December 27, Wichita Falls to December 31, Pittsburgh

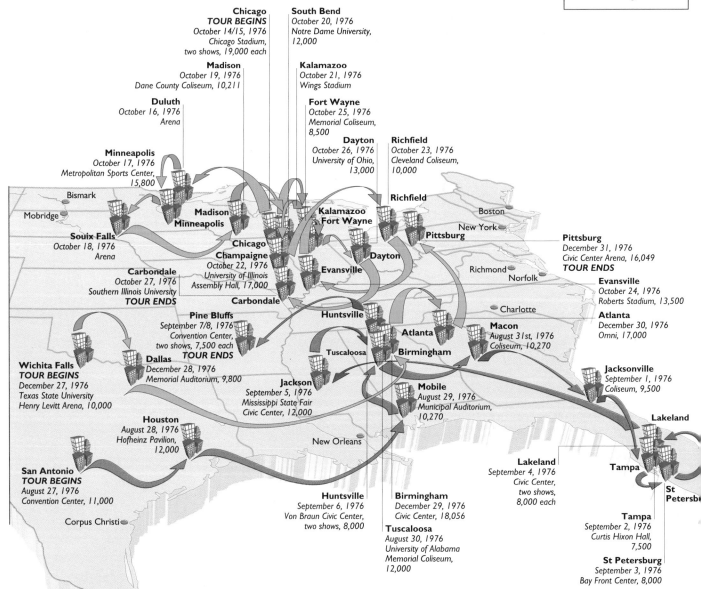

Chicago
TOUR BEGINS
October 14/15, 1976
Chicago Stadium,
two shows, 19,000 each

South Bend
October 20, 1976
Notre Dame University,
12,000

Madison
October 19, 1976
Dane County Coliseum, 10,211

Kalamazoo
October 21, 1976
Wings Stadium

Duluth
October 16, 1976
Arena

Fort Wayne
October 25, 1976
Memorial Coliseum,
8,500

Minneapolis
October 17, 1976
Metropolitan Sports Center,
15,800

Dayton
October 26, 1976
University of Ohio,
13,000

Richfield
October 23, 1976
Cleveland Coliseum,
10,000

Bismark

Mobridge

Minneapolis

Boston

New York

Souix Falls
October 18, 1976
Arena

Madison

Kalamazoo
Fort Wayne

Richfield

Pittsburg

Pittsburg
December 31, 1976
Civic Center Arena, 16,049
TOUR ENDS

Chicago
Champaigne
October 22, 1976
University of Illinois
Assembly Hall, 17,000

Dayton

Richmond

Norfolk

Evansville

Carbondale
October 27, 1976
Southern Illinois University
TOUR ENDS

Evansville
October 24, 1976
Roberts Stadium, 13,500

Carbondale

Huntsville

Charlotte

Atlanta
December 30, 1976
Omni, 17,000

Pine Bluffs
September 7/8, 1976
Convention Center,
two shows, 7,500 each
TOUR ENDS

Atlanta

Macon
August 31st, 1976
Coliseum, 10,270

Wichita Falls
TOUR BEGINS
December 27, 1976
Texas State University
Henry Levitt Arena, 10,000

Dallas
December 28, 1976
Memorial Auditorium, 9,800

Tuscaloosa

Birmingham

Jacksonville
September 1, 1976
Coliseum, 9,500

Jackson
September 5, 1976
Mississippi State Fair
Civic Center, 12,000

Mobile
August 29, 1976
Municipal Auditorium,
10,270

Lakeland

Houston
August 28, 1976
Hofheinz Pavilion,
12,000

New Orleans

Lakeland
September 4, 1976
Civic Center,
two shows,
8,000 each

Tampa

San Antonio
TOUR BEGINS
August 27, 1976
Convention Center, 11,000

St Petersb

Corpus Christi

Huntsville
September 6, 1976
Von Braun Civic Center,
two shows, 8,000

Birmingham
December 29, 1976
Civic Center, 18,056

Tampa
September 2, 1976
Curtis Hixon Hall,
7,500

Tuscaloosa
August 30, 1976
University of Alabama
Memorial Coliseum,
12,000

St Petersburg
September 3, 1976
Bay Front Center, 8,000

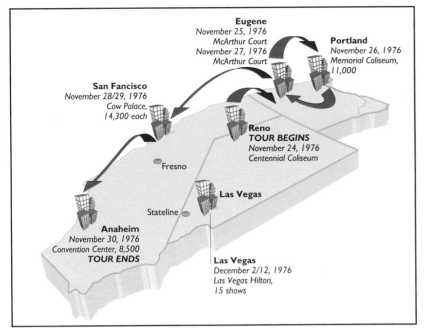

Although Elvis was thinner than he had been for some time, it seems that the battle to keep his weight down took its toll in other ways. Perhaps the loss of the stabilizing influence of long-term friends made things worse. He had always been able to do more or less what he wanted, but now there was no one to stop him taking this to extremes.

All of Elvis's new recorded material released in 1976 and 1977 was either taped at Graceland or taken from earlier live performances. Sessions at Graceland in February and October gave two singles 'Moody Blue' and 'Way Down', and material for the album *Moody Blue*. Neither single did much business, leaving Elvis without a Top Ten hit for the last five years of his life, but the album reached Number 3 following Elvis's death in August 1977.

Though Elvis almost certainly didn't know much about it, a peculiar event happened at the gates of Graceland in the early hours of November 23, 1976. Elvis had first met Jerry Lee Lewis at the Sun studios in Memphis in December 1956 — the 'Million Dollar Quartet' occasion. Being two of the biggest personalities in the music world, and sharing the same origins and the same town, it seems likely that they met up from time to time. On the night in question Jerry Lee has said that he was invited over to Graceland by Elvis. Other versions suggest that Jerry Lee had heard a lot of rumours about Elvis going down the tubes and decided to go over and

Jerry Lee Lewis has always lived his life in public, and seems to have got frustrated by Elvis's seclusion, perhaps tinged with a little jealousy over Elvis always being called "The King of Rock and Roll". "I don't call myself the King' Jerry Lee has said 'I'm simply the best." The document below is the Record of Arrest of Jerry Lee outside Graceland.

sort things out for him. The fact that he crashed into the gate of Graceland drunk and in possession of a loaded .38 Derringer pistol dissuaded the guards from letting him in. A patrol car arrived shortly after and took Mr Lewis away. It seems unlikely that Jerry Lee would have been able to save Elvis — he himself had absorbed enough drugs and liquor to kill most men. But the lives and careers of these two residents of Memphis provide a fascinating contrast, as well as some of the greatest music ever performed.

The Last Journey

Live shows January to August, 1977

On the surface things seemed fairly well on track for Elvis. During 1977 he took time for a couple of vacations in Palm Springs and Hawaii. He had gotten his weight down, and there were a string of sold-out tours to take him through the year. CBS was going to film one of the concerts for another TV special. In his personal life he had found a new companion, and he was enjoying making records at his home studio in Graceland. But this all masked a harsher reality. Before each tour Elvis was being prescribed large quantities of stimulants and tranquilizers. He refused to attend a recording session in Nashville. He was hospitalized half-way through his second tour, and his output of new music had declined to zero.

By early 1977 RCA was desperate to get more recorded output from Elvis. Apart from a few tracks recorded at Graceland in February and October 1976, there was nothing in the can. Once again they were forced to repackage old live material, this time as the *Welcome To My World* album, while pretending that they weren't. Later in the year they supplemented the Graceland sessions with overdubbed live material to fill out the album *Moody Blue*.

On January 22, Elvis's record producer Felton Jarvis, managed to persuade him to come over to Nashville, where a recording session had been set up at the Creative Workshop studios. Elvis had not been inside a proper recording studio for nearly two years. Elvis duly booked in to the Sheraton Hotel — and stayed there. Jarvis brought over demo tapes and Elvis listened. The musicians in the studio busied themselves by laying down

rhythm tracks and vocal backings for the songs recorded at Graceland. After three days Elvis got on a plane and returned to Memphis.

One week later Jarvis tried again. This time a make-shift studio was set up in the racquet-ball court behind Graceland. Musicians and singers were brought in and put up in a near-by motel. Everyone waited. After three days Elvis said he had a sore throat and everyone went home. Given his obvious appetite and enthusiasm for performing live, it's difficult to know exactly why Elvis developed such a strong antipathy to recording. He may have been so disappointed with the records that were released under his name that he wanted to somehow punish RCA. But there was no way of doing that without harming himself. He wanted to go on playing concerts, but to do that without turning into just another revival act, meant that he had to produce new material occasionally.

The old tried and tested formula of the TV special was wheeled out in June 1977. But rather than making the effort to do something creative and different, as in 1968, CBS and RCA opted to simply record and film some live shows, and splice them together. In fairness to them, in Elvis's current state of mind it didn't seem likely they were going to get anything else out of him. The shows at Omaha, Lincoln and Rapid City in late June were recorded, with the bulk of the program coming from the last show. 'Elvis In Concert' was broadcast on October 3, 1977.

The strains of touring

On March 31, halfway through a concert in Baton Rouge, Elvis left and was flown back to Memphis. He was hospitalized for intestinal flu and fatigue. He was discharged after five

Tempe
TOUR STARTS
March 23, 1977
Arizona State University,
14,047
Santa

Tucson

Lubbock

Abilene
March 27, 1977
Taylor County Coliseum,
7,500

Austin
March 28, 1977
Municipal Auditorium,
6,000

Corpus Christi

Alexandria
March 29/30, 1977
Rapids Palace Coliseum,
two shows, 15,000 each
Remainder of tour cancelled

"Presley was heavy-lidded and appeared to most observers to be weak and tired.... paunchy and apparently pained. ...Anaemic singing, bewildered patter and awkward stage movements."
Variety on May 29 show in Baltimore

"Physically I'm not well enough to keep doing this."
Elvis in 1976

days and was back touring within another two weeks. On May 29 a concert in Baltimore was held up for 30 minutes while Elvis received treatment backstage. Not surprisingly he looked tired. It's clear in hindsight that the relentless touring was taking a huge physical toll, which in the end contributed to his death.

Nobody seems to have had the strength of purpose to advise him, or the power to tell him, to have a real rest. A couple of years off might have made all the difference. But he wasn't listening to anyone else in any case.

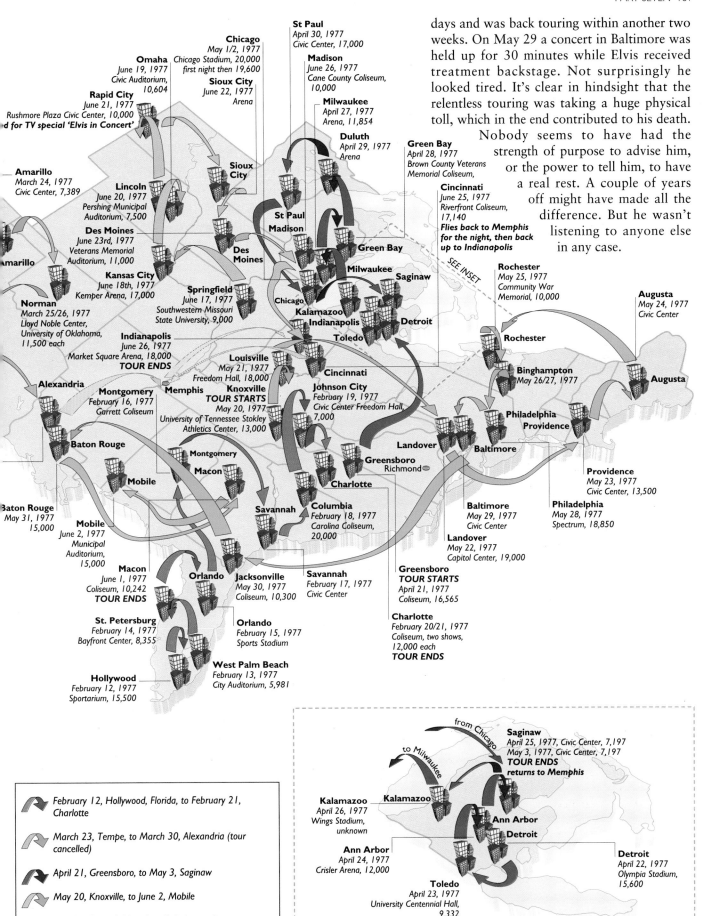

St Paul
April 30, 1977
Civic Center, 17,000

Chicago
May 1/2, 1977
Chicago Stadium, 20,000
first night then 19,600

Omaha
June 19, 1977
Civic Auditorium,
10,604

Sioux City
June 22, 1977
Arena

Madison
June 26, 1977
Cane County Coliseum,
10,000

Milwaukee
April 27, 1977
Arena, 11,854

Rapid City
June 21, 1977
Rushmore Plaza Civic Center, 10,000
d for TV special 'Elvis in Concert'

Duluth
April 29, 1977
Arena

Green Bay
April 28, 1977
Brown County Veterans
Memorial Coliseum,

Amarillo
March 24, 1977
Civic Center, 7,389

Lincoln
June 20, 1977
Pershing Municipal
Auditorium, 7,500

Cincinnati
June 25, 1977
Riverfront Coliseum,
17,140
*Flies back to Memphis
for the night, then back
up to Indianapolis*

Sioux City

St Paul
Madison

Des Moines
June 23rd, 1977
Veterans Memorial
Auditorium, 11,000

Des Moines

Green Bay

Rochester
May 25, 1977
Community War
Memorial, 10,000

Augusta
May 24, 1977
Civic Center

Amarillo

Kansas City
June 18th, 1977
Kemper Arena, 17,000

Springfield
June 17, 1977
Southwestern Missouri
State University, 9,000

Milwaukee
Saginaw

Rochester

Norman
March 25/26, 1977
Lloyd Noble Center,
University of Oklahoma,
11,500 each

Chicago

Kalamazoo
Indianapolis

Detroit

Indianapolis
June 26, 1977
Market Square Arena, 18,000
TOUR ENDS

Toledo

Binghampton
May 26/27, 1977

Augusta

Alexandria

Louisville
May 21, 1977
Freedom Hall, 18,000

Cincinnati

Philadelphia
Providence

Montgomery
February 16, 1977
Garrett Coliseum

Memphis

Knoxville
TOUR STARTS
May 20, 1977
University of Tennessee Stokley
Athletics Center, 13,000

Johnson City
February 19, 1977
Civic Center Freedom Hall,
7,000

Baton Rouge

Montgomery

Macon

Landover

Baltimore

Providence
May 23, 1977
Civic Center, 13,500

Mobile

Savannah

Charlotte

Greensboro
Richmond

Baltimore
May 29, 1977
Civic Center

Philadelphia
May 28, 1977
Spectrum, 18,850

Baton Rouge
May 31, 1977
15,000

Mobile
June 2, 1977
Municipal
Auditorium,
15,000

Columbia
February 18, 1977
Carolina Coliseum,
20,000

Landover
May 22, 1977
Capitol Center, 19,000

Macon
June 1, 1977
Coliseum, 10,242
TOUR ENDS

Orlando

Jacksonville
May 30, 1977
Coliseum, 10,300

Savannah
February 17, 1977
Civic Center

Greensboro
TOUR STARTS
April 21, 1977
Coliseum, 16,565

St. Petersburg
February 14, 1977
Bayfront Center, 8,355

Orlando
February 15, 1977
Sports Stadium

Charlotte
February 20/21, 1977
Coliseum, two shows,
12,000 each
TOUR ENDS

Hollywood
February 12, 1977
Sportarium, 15,500

West Palm Beach
February 13, 1977
City Auditorium, 5,981

February 12, Hollywood, Florida, to February 21, Charlotte

March 23, Tempe, to March 30, Alexandria (tour cancelled)

April 21, Greensboro, to May 3, Saginaw

May 20, Knoxville, to June 2, Mobile

June 17, Springfield, to June 2, Indianapolis

from Chicago

to Milwaukee

Saginaw
April 25, 1977, Civic Center, 7,197
May 3, 1977, Civic Center, 7,197
TOUR ENDS
returns to Memphis

Kalamazoo
April 26, 1977
Wings Stadium,
unknown

Kalamazoo

Ann Arbor
Detroit

Ann Arbor
April 24, 1977
Crisler Arena, 12,000

SEE INSET

Detroit
April 22, 1977
Olympia Stadium,
15,600

Toledo
April 23, 1977
University Centennial Hall,
9,332

Where Did Things Go Wrong?

The unplayed, interrupted and strange concerts

In his last years, Elvis's on-stage behaviour was often markedly bizarre. Here was a man crying for help. Yet sad, embarrassing, and pathetic as this often was, sometimes it re-charged the music. Listen to 'Unchained Melody' on the *Moody Blue* album, recorded live in the final months of Elvis's life. Dark, desperate and churning, the voice shows him pacing the stage like a cornered animal. Without loss of instinct for right and inspired timing, Elvis sings unpredictably, fitfully, in smouldering bursts. You can hear him in the darkness, running ahead of the awful orchestra, trying to shake it off. Hideous and garish, it slurps and rattles behind him like hunting dogs of doom.

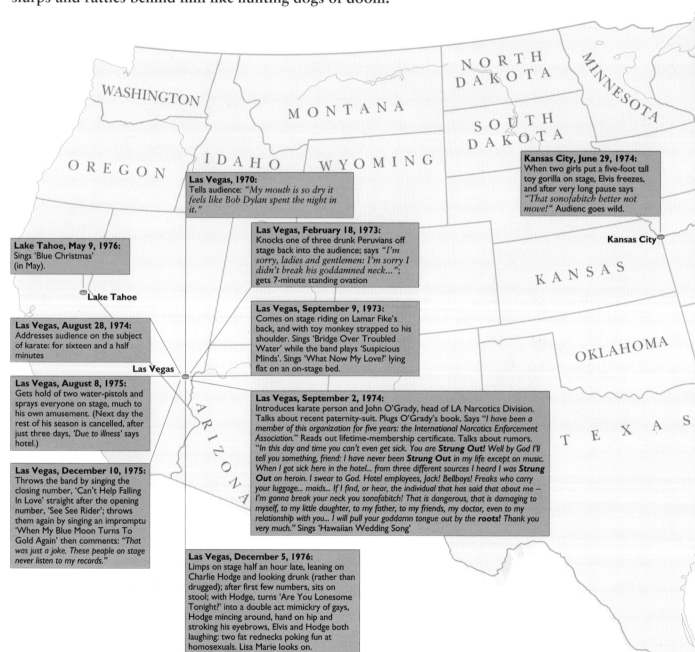

Las Vegas, 1970:
Tells audience: *"My mouth is so dry it feels like Bob Dylan spent the night in it."*

Kansas City, June 29, 1974:
When two girls put a five-foot tall toy gorilla on stage, Elvis freezes, and after very long pause says *"That sonofabitch better not move!"* Audienc goes wild.

Las Vegas, February 18, 1973:
Knocks one of three drunk Peruvians off stage back into the audience; says *"I'm sorry, ladies and gentlemen: I'm sorry I didn't break his goddamned neck..."*; gets 7-minute standing ovation

Lake Tahoe, May 9, 1976:
Sings 'Blue Christmas' (in May).

Las Vegas, September 9, 1973:
Comes on stage riding on Lamar Fike's back, and with toy monkey strapped to his shoulder. Sings 'Bridge Over Troubled Water' while the band plays 'Suspicious Minds'. Sings 'What Now My Love?' lying flat on an on-stage bed.

Las Vegas, August 28, 1974:
Addresses audience on the subject of karate: for sixteen and a half minutes

Las Vegas, August 8, 1975:
Gets hold of two water-pistols and sprays everyone on stage, much to his own amusement. (Next day the rest of his season is cancelled, after just three days, *'Due to illness'* says hotel.)

Las Vegas, September 2, 1974:
Introduces karate person and John O'Grady, head of LA Narcotics Division. Talks about recent paternity-suit. Plugs O'Grady's book. Says *"I have been a member of this organization for five years: the International Narcotics Enforcement Association."* Reads out lifetime-membership certificate. Talks about rumors. *"In this day and time you can't even get sick. You are **Strung Out!** Well by God I'll tell you something, friend: I have never been **Strung Out** in my life except on music. When I got sick here in the hotel... from three different sources I heard I was **Strung Out** on heroin. I swear to God. Hotel employees, Jack! Bellboys! Freaks who carry your luggage... maids... If I find, or hear, the individual that has said that about me — I'm gonna break your neck you sonofabitch! That is dangerous, that is damaging to myself, to my little daughter, to my father, to my friends, my doctor, even to my relationship with you... I will pull your goddamn tongue out by the **roots!** Thank you very much."* Sings 'Hawaiian Wedding Song'

Las Vegas, December 10, 1975:
Throws the band by singing the closing number, 'Can't Help Falling In Love' straight after the opening number, 'See See Rider'; throws them again by singing an impromptu 'When My Blue Moon Turns To Gold Again' then comments: *"That was just a joke. These people on stage never listen to my records."*

Las Vegas, December 5, 1976:
Limps on stage half an hour late, leaning on Charlie Hodge and looking drunk (rather than drugged); after first few numbers, sits on stool; with Hodge, turns 'Are You Lonesome Tonight?' into a double act mimickry of gays, Hodge mincing around, hand on hip and stroking his eyebrows, Elvis and Hodge both laughing: two fat rednecks poking fun at homosexuals. Lisa Marie looks on.

WASHINGTON · OREGON · MONTANA · IDAHO · WYOMING · NORTH DAKOTA · SOUTH DAKOTA · MINNESOTA · KANSAS · OKLAHOMA · ARIZONA · TEXAS

Lake Tahoe · Las Vegas · Kansas City

By the end of his life, touring seemed to be the one thing that kept Elvis going. He'd confided to friends that he wanted to give it up after the 1976 Bicentennial Tour, but he just couldn't stop. He wasn't recording and he wasn't making movies, so he just kept climbing on planes and in and out of limousines.

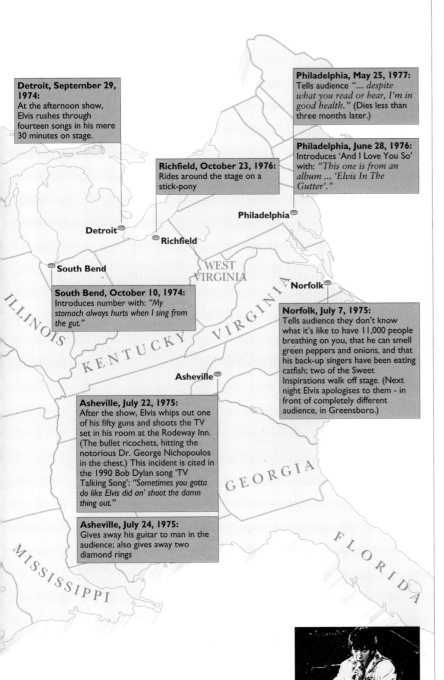

Detroit, September 29, 1974:
At the afternoon show, Elvis rushes through fourteen songs in his mere 30 minutes on stage.

Richfield, October 23, 1976:
Rides around the stage on a stick-pony

Philadelphia, May 25, 1977:
Tells audience *"... despite what you read or hear, I'm in good health."* (Dies less than three months later.)

Philadelphia, June 28, 1976:
Introduces 'And I Love You So' with: *"This one is from an album ... 'Elvis In The Gutter'."*

South Bend, October 10, 1974:
Introduces number with: *"My stomach always hurts when I sing from the gut."*

Norfolk, July 7, 1975:
Tells audience they don't know what it's like to have 11,000 people breathing on you, that he can smell green peppers and onions, and that his back-up singers have been eating catfish; two of the Sweet Inspirations walk off stage. (Next night Elvis apologises to them - in front of completely different audience, in Greensboro.)

Asheville, July 22, 1975:
After the show, Elvis whips out one of his fifty guns and shoots the TV set in his room at the Rodeway Inn. (The bullet ricochets, hitting the notorious Dr. George Nichopoulos in the chest.) This incident is cited in the 1990 Bob Dylan song 'TV Talking Song': *"Sometimes you gotta do like Elvis did an' shoot the damn thing out."*

Asheville, July 24, 1975:
Gives away his guitar to man in the audience; also gives away two diamond rings

Part of the fascination of Elvis's last concerts was their unpredictability. How would he look, what would he sing, how would he behave?

The Cancelled Shows

In 1969 and 1970, no Vegas shows were cancelled; except for one-show opening nights these were month-long seasons of two shows per night. Two days after the 1970 summer Vegas season, Elvis began the first of two short tours. January-February 1971 saw another month-long Vegas season, then some Lake Tahoe shows, the August-September Las Vegas season, a November tour, the January-February 1972 Las Vegas season, an April tour, a June tour incorporating the New York Madison Square Garden shows, the 1972 Las Vegas summer season, a November tour and the 'Elvis Aloha From Hawaii' shows of January 1973 ... All completed without one cancelled show.

After that, the picture changed. Cancelled shows were as follows:

1973
Jan 31	Both shows, Las Vegas (flu).
Feb 1	Midnight show, Las Vegas (flu).
Feb 13	Midnight show, Las Vegas ("an illness").
Feb 14	Midnight show, Las Vegas ("an illness").
May 17-20	All eight shows, Lake Tahoe (flu/chest infection).

1974
May	Two shows out of twenty, Stateline Nevada/Lake Tahoe (flu).
Aug 26	Both shows, Las Vegas (flu).

1975
Jan 26-Feb 9	Las Vegas season postponed till March 18-April 1 ("re-scheduling").
Aug 21-Sep 1	Twenty two shows out of twenty seven, Las Vegas (hospitalized: "fatigue state").

1976 No shows cancelled.

1977
Mar 31	Second half of show, Baton Rouge (hospitalized: flu & fatigue).
April 1	Concert, Mobile Alabama.
April 2	Concert, Macon Georgia.
April 3	Concert, Jacksonville Florida.

The tour scheduled to begin the day after Elvis's death would have comprised:

Aug 17	Portland, Maine.
Aug 18	Portland, Maine.
Aug 19	Utica, New York.
Aug 20	Syracuse, New York.
Aug 21	Hartford, Connecticut.
Aug 22	Uniondale, New York.
Aug 23	Lexington, Kentucky.
Aug 24	Roanoke, Virginia.
Aug 25	Fayetteville, Tennessee.
Aug 26	Asheville, North Carolina.
Aug 27	Memphis.
Aug 28	Memphis.

Solitary Death Of A Public Idol

The events of Tuesday August 16, 1977

In all the controversy and unanswered questions about what killed Elvis Presley, one thing seems clear — the night of August 15 to 16, 1977 at Graceland was not out of the ordinary. There is no doubt Elvis took a large number of pills of one kind and another, but that wasn't unusual. He had been taking pills to get to sleep, to wake up, to calm down, to get hyped up for years. But then it wasn't unusual for him to become unwell as a result of the drugs either. On other occasions the Graceland staff had to revive him or summon his personal physician. It just seems that this time the help came too late. In an attempt to protect Elvis's reputation, the true facts of the cause of his death have never been made public.

In mid August Elvis was preparing for yet another tour. The first concert was to be at Portland, Maine on August 17. It had become normal for Elvis to go on a crash diet before a tour to try to get his weight down to an acceptable level. At this time he was virtually living on fruit, though his weight was still 250 pounds with just three days to go. It was also necessary for Elvis to stock up on prescription drugs to take on tour with him, since it would be impossible to obtain the quantities he needed elsewhere. On Monday his personal physician Dr Nichopoulos ordered a number of drugs from Elvis's usual source, the Prescription House of Irving Jack Kirsch at 1737 Madison Avenue, opposite Nichopoulos's office.

Later that evening, after taking a ride through parts of Memphis with his current girlfriend Ginger Alden and a group of companions, Elvis visited his dentist Dr Lester Hoffman. In line with his normal nocturnal habits, Elvis played a game of racketball back at Graceland from about 4:30a.m. to 6:30a.m. with Billy Smith. After going into his bedroom with Ginger Alden he took some medication to help him sleep. He then went into the adjoining room which doubled as a bathroom and dressing room at around 9a.m. Exactly what medication he took is a matter of dispute. Demerol, Amytal, Codeine, Valmid, Aventyl, Nembutal, Elavil were all available.

Around 2 o'clock on the afternoon of August 16, Ginger Alden found Elvis lying on the floor of the bathroom. She called Al Strada, who then called Joe Esposito. He tried to revive Elvis while a call was put through to the paramedics at the Memphis Fire Engine House 29. They arrived at the same time as Dr Nichopoulos who then went with Elvis in the

ambulance along with Esposito and David Stanley, to the Baptist Hospital. Elvis was declared dead at 3:30p.m. He was just 42 years old.

An autopsy was carried out by Dr Jerry Francisco, before the body was taken to the Memphis Funeral Home. The cause of death was given as cardiac arrhythmia — irregular heart beat. The following day, at a press conference Francisco was not specific about what

Memphis, along with the rest of the world, was shocked at Elvis's death. But the Press-Scimitar's *headline (below) expresses the response of many people. From the outside, Elvis's life seemed to have become tragic in a way which may have made his death less so. Elvis helped to create the idea of a youth culture, and then had to live with the idea of growing out of it. He became the biggest star in the world at the age of 21, and had to live with that legacy for another 21 years.*

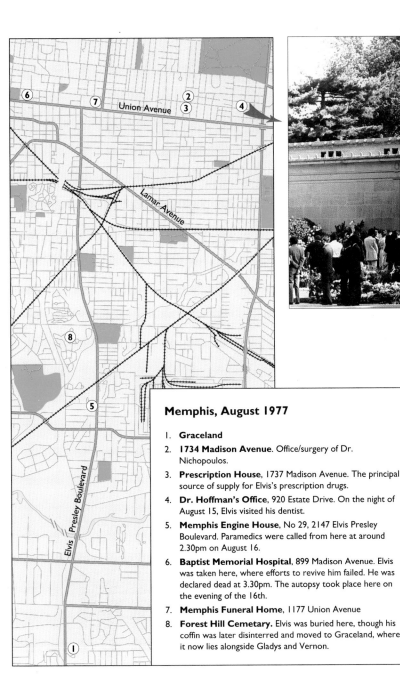

Memphis, August 1977

1. **Graceland**

2. **1734 Madison Avenue.** Office/surgery of Dr. Nichopoulos.

3. **Prescription House**, 1737 Madison Avenue. The principal source of supply for Elvis's prescription drugs.

4. **Dr. Hoffman's Office**, 920 Estate Drive. On the night of August 15, Elvis visited his dentist.

5. **Memphis Engine House**, No 29, 2147 Elvis Presley Boulevard. Paramedics were called from here at around 2.30pm on August 16.

6. **Baptist Memorial Hospital**, 899 Madison Avenue. Elvis was taken here, where efforts to revive him failed. He was declared dead at 3.30pm. The autopsy took place here on the evening of the 16th.

7. **Memphis Funeral Home**, 1177 Union Avenue

8. **Forest Hill Cemetary.** Elvis was buried here, though his coffin was later disinterred and moved to Graceland, where it now lies alongside Gladys and Vernon.

cause Elvis's heart to fail. An enlarged heart, coronary artery obstruction and high blood pressure could all have contributed, he said. In response to questions about drugs, he said that there were no new or old needle marks on Elvis's body.

Other physicians who attended the autopsy later stated their view that Elvis died from a interaction of drugs which caused his heart to fail. They also expressed surprise at the haste with which the cause of death was announced. Francisco denied taking part in a cover–up of the true details of Elvis's death, though there is no explanation of why the stomach contents were disposed of without analysis. On August 24, Dr. George Nichopoulos denied that Elvis had a drug problem, though admitted that he

had taken too many prescription drugs on some occasions. He later also denied that Elvis's death had been caused or induced by drugs.

In the long run, this probably doesn't matter much. Elvis would undoubtedly have gotten the drugs he wanted somehow. By 1977 his personal life was a mess, and in a sense he was already living out the tragedy of the star to whom no one can say no, and therefore to whom no one can be really close. Maybe it had been that way ever since 1958 when his mother died.

Two years later Vernon Presley died at the age of sixty three, and the story of the small family from East Tupelo, was over.

After lying at Graceland from August 17 to 18, Elvis's body was taken to Forest Hill Cemetery, (top) where he was buried next to his mother. Both were later moved to Graceland where, together with Vernon, they lie in the specially created Meditation Garden (above).

Chronology

January 1975–August 1977

1975

Jan. 18	The album *Promised Land* and the single 'My Boy'/'Thinking About You' are released.
Jan. 29	Elvis goes into the hospital for 'a liver problem'. Stays in until February 14.
Mar. 10,11	Recording session at RCA Hollywood studios.
Mar. 18	Opens run at Las Vegas Hilton (to April 1).
Apr. 24	Tour starts in Macon, Georgia.
Apr.	'T-R-O-U-B-L-E'/'Mr Songman' released.
May	*Elvis Today* album released.
May 7	Tour ends at Murfreesboro, Tennessee.
May 30	Tour starts in Huntsville, Alabama.
June 10	Tour ends in Memphis at the Mid-South Coliseum.
June 11	Elvis purchases the airplane which he names the 'Lisa Marie'.
June 16	Enters hospital for treatment for possible glaucoma.
July 8	Tour starts in Oklahoma City.
July 22–24	Plays Asheville, North Carolina. Shoots TV set in hotel room, hitting Dr Nichopoulos in the chest. On stage, gives away guitar and diamond rings.
Aug. 7	Stepbrother and aide Rick Stanley is arrested at Methodist Hospital, Memphis passing a forged prescription for Demerol.
Aug. 16	Elvis's plane forced to land in Dallas, due to his breathing difficulties.

Aug. 18	Opens run at Las Vegas Hilton.
Aug. 21	Ends run early and flies back to Memphis and to the Baptist Memorial Hospital. Stays until September 5.
Oct.	'Pieces Of My Life'/'Bring It Back' released.
Nov. 27	Maiden flight of the refurbished 'Lisa Marie'.
Dec. 2	Opens run at Las Vegas Hilton (to December 15).
Dec. 31	Special concert at Pontiac, Michigan. 62,000 attendance.

1976

Jan.	The album *Elvis–A Legendary Performer, Volume 2* released.
Feb. 2–8	Recording session at Graceland.
Mar.	The album *The Sun Sessions* and the single 'Hurt'/'For The Heart' released.
Mar. 17	Tour starts in Johnson City, Tennessee.
Mar. 22	Tour ends in St Louis, Missouri.
Apr. 21	Tour starts in Kansas City, Missouri.
Apr. 27	Tour ends in Spokane, Washington.
Apr. 30	Starts run at Sahara Tahoe Hotel, Stateline, Nevada (to May 9).
May	The album *From Elvis Presley Boulevard, Memphis, Tennessee* is released.
May 27	Tour starts in Bloomington, Indiana.
June 6	Tour ends in Atlanta.
June 25	Tour starts in Buffalo, New York.
July 5	Tour ends in Memphis.

July 13	Red West, Sonny West and Dave Hebler are sacked from Elvis's entourage and payroll.
July 23	Tour opens in Louisville, Kentucky.
Aug. 5	Tour ends in Fayetteville, North Carolina.
Aug. 27	Tour opens in San Antonio.
Sept. 8	Tour ends in Pine Bluff, Arkansas.
Oct. 15	Tour opens in Chicago.
Oct. 27	Tour ends in Carbondale, Illinois.
Oct. 29, 30	Recording session at Graceland.
Nov. 1	Linda Thompson, Elvis's companion since his separation from Priscilla, leaves him.
Nov. 24	Tour opens in Reno, Nevada.
Nov. 30	Tour ends at Anaheim Convention Center, California.
Dec. 2	Opens run at Las Vegas Hilton (to December 12).
Dec.	'Moody Blue'/'She Thinks I Still Care' released.
Dec. 27	Tour opens in Wichita Falls, Texas.
Dec. 31	Tour ends in Pittsburg.

1977

Jan. 22–24	Goes to Nashville for recording session, but stays in hotel room listening to demo tapes. Flies back to Memphis without going in to studio.
Feb. 12	Tour starts in Hollywood, Florida.
Feb. 21	Tour ends in Charlotte, North Carolina.
Mar.	*Welcome To My World* album released.
Mar. 3	Elvis signs his will.
Mar. 23	Tour opens in Phoenix, Arizona.
Mar. 31	Baton Rouge concert cancelled during intermission.

	Elvis flies back to Memphis, and is admitted to the Baptist Memorial Hospital in the early hours of April 1.
Apr. 21	Tour opens in Greensboro, North Carolina.
May 3	Tour ends in Saginaw, Michigan.
May 20	Tour opens in Knoxville, Tennessee.
May 29	Concert in Baltimore interrupted by Elvis's illness.
June 2	Tour ends in Mobile, Alabama.
June 17	Tour opens in Springfield, Missouri.
June 21	Concert in Rapid City, Dakota filmed for TV special 'Elvis In Concert'.
June	'Way Down'/'Pledging My Love' released.
June 26	Tour ends at the Market Square Arena, Indianapolis, with Elvis's last ever concert.
July	*Moody Blue* album released.
Aug. 8	All-night party at Libertyland Amusement Park.
Aug. 15	Dr Nichopoulos orders large amounts of drugs for forthcoming tour.
Aug. 16	Elvis is found dead in bathroom at Graceland.
Aug. 18	Elvis Aron Presley is buried beside his mother at Forest Hill Cemetery, Memphis.

Part Eight: LIFE AFTER
DEATH – THE MYTHS, THE MONEY
AND THE TRUE LEGACY

"I've been very lucky. I happened to come along at a time in the music business when there was no trend. I was very lucky. The people were looking for something different and I was lucky, I came along just in time."

"I like to think that they remember us with pleasure."

"He had the most intuitive ability to hear songs without having to classify them. It seems like he had a photographic memory for every damned song he heard …He damn sure was intuitive, and he damn sure had an appreciation for the total spirituality of human existence, even if he would never have thought of the term, That's what he cared about."
Sam Phillips

"I wanted to do things that I never cared about until I met him. He was the change that was coming to America."
Jimmie Rodgers Snow on meeting Elvis in 1955

"Nothing really affected me until I heard Elvis."
John Lennon

"There's no way to measure the impact he made on society or the void that he leaves."
Pat Boone

"If anyone deserved to be called a legend and a superstar it would be Elvis."
Hank Snow

"Elvis Presley's death deprives our country of a part of itself. His music and his personality, fusing styles of white country and black rhythm and blues, permanently changed the face of American popular culture. His following was immense and he was a symbol to the people the world over of the vitality, rebelliousness and good humor of his country."
President Jimmy Carter

"His music was the only thing exclusively ours. His wasn't my mom and my dad's music …His voice was a total miracle."
Carl Wilson

Introduction

In his later years Elvis seemed to believe he was different from other people. He was, of course, outrageously gifted. But he also believed that he might have some kind of spiritual mission, for which he was uniquely endowed. At his concerts his costumes revealed him as a great showman, but there was more than a hint of the imperial about his capes, his insignias and his accessories. All of this was reinforced by the reactions of those around him. At his shows people did rush to the front just to be touched, the hundreds of scarves thrown to the crowd were eagerly snapped up. These might have been just the actions of souvenir seekers, but seen from where Elvis was, it looked a lot like adoration. For a man used to being the center of attention for every minute of his adult life, it all added to his sense of apartness.

And now, nearly twenty years after his death, Elvis does stand utterly apart. No other 'entertainer' has a comparable hold on the world's imagination. Paradoxically it was an instinctive decision not to follow the route of most other stars, that has helped to make him such a powerful icon. Elvis should by rights have moved lock, stock and barrel to Hollywood in 1958 and stayed there. He should have left behind his friends and family and moved in the circles of the similarly rich and famous. Instead Elvis remained in Memphis, visiting Hollywood only to make films. He effectively set up court in Graceland and lived the life he wanted to, not one that had been mapped out for him by precedent.

Elvis's long-time residence in Graceland, and its skillful promotion as a tourist attraction since his death, has made it into the second most famous house in America, after the White House. Thanks to tightly controlled franchising deals you can buy Elvis's image reproduced on almost anything from the obvious T-shirts and calendars, to clocks, crockery and keyrings. But most importantly you can buy his records — and people still do. RCA's long overdue decision to issue boxed sets of Elvis's greatest work has helped to reawaken interest in his music, and in his early career in particular. The boxed sets of the Fifties Masters has sold an astonishing 250,000 copies in America, with the Sixties and Seventies sets not far behind. So visit Graceland and buy the T-shirts, and the keyrings. But then go home and listen to the music that Elvis created and hear his true legacy.

The Legend Lives On

Elvis museums, gift shops, fan clubs

When hearing of Elvis's death in 1977, one Hollywood reporter allegedly commented 'Good career move'. He couldn't have known how spectacularly this would come true. After death, Elvis Presley has become a rejuvenated commercial phenomenon. As well as continuing to sell millions of records, Elvis and his old home Graceland have become the center of a worldwide marketing operation. Along with the likes of Coca-Cola and Walt Disney, Elvis has become a trademark, to be used only under license. There is no doubt of the continuing popularity and fascination with all aspects of Elvis's life. But how has his artistic reputation stood up — is Elvis anything more than a logo on T shirt, and Graceland another site on the tourist trail?

The map shows towns with Elvis fan clubs. A good number have two — presumably due to local rivalries. There are also a host of fanzines, one of the best being Elvis, The Man and His Music *published from Newcastle, England.*

Although he was still capable of moments of inspired performance, Elvis's last few years were marked by a declining standard in both his live and recorded output. The sight of his overweight figure going through the motions of a live show without conviction inspired sadness in some, and derision in others. The publication of the book *Elvis — What Happened?* a few weeks before his death revealed an inner world of emptiness and drug–taking. It was difficult to know whether Elvis should be pitied or despised. Then came the first full biography to be written after his death, Albert Goldman's *Elvis*, published in 1980. Though ostensibly a fully researched life of the singer, the book was riddled with inaccuracies. In effect it was an echo of the small town prudes from the fifties, who saw themselves as guarding America's true culture from the savageries of rock and roll. But while they might be forgiven for not seeing the future in front of them, Goldman deliberately set out to humiliate the culture which Elvis had sprung from. The book's sensationalism ensured it a massive sale. The reputation of Elvis Presley in the wider world sank yet lower.

But then, little by little, the music began to fight back, aided by the work of those musicians and writers who understood the real legacy of Elvis Presley. Forget the impersonators, the jumpsuits, the final years of decline, the gift-shops and the guided tours of Graceland. Here is the man who created the music that has dictated the cultural outlook of young people in the second half of the century. In the process he brought hitherto little-known aspects of American music into the full light of day. It is only with the growing interval of years since his death that we are beginning to see Elvis as a serious historical figure,

with as much influence on the cultural life of his country as any other person this century.

With the growing realization of Elvis's long term importance has come a renewed interest in his early music, and by extension, in the music which he himself heard and re-shaped in his own personal style. Blues, country and gospel music are now all regarded as shining examples of a unique cultural synthesis that occurred in America, and in the American South in particular. In mid–century they were regarded with little interest by the music and entertainment industries, who were more interested in Broadway and Hollywood musicals and the increasingly tired products of Tin Pan Alley. Elvis swept all that away and established a new and uniquely American musical culture.

In the last few years, RCA has responded to the intense interest in Elvis's music by issuing three boxed sets of CDs — *The Complete Fifties Masters*, *The Complete Sixties Masters* and *The Complete Seventies Masters*. The care in selecting the material and the supporting discographical information has gone some way towards restoring the reputation of Elvis's record company in the eyes of his followers. The fifties set in particular shows how

Tupelo
The house where Elvis was born has been sympathethically restored and the area is thankfully free of over-commercialization. A museum (right) stands at a discreet distance from the house, together with a memorial church.
The Elvis statue in Memphis (top right) stands near the corner of Beale and Main.

Elvis Museums and Shops

1. *Graceland, Memphis*
2. *Elvis Presley Statue, Beale Street, Memphis*
3. *Sun Studios, Union Avenue, Memphis*
4. *Grand Guitar Museum, Nashville*
5. *Car Collector's Hall of Fame, Nashville*
6. *Country Music Hall of Fame, Nashville*
7. *Country Music Wax Museum, Nashville*
8. *Elvis Museum and Gift Shop, Nashville*
9. *Guiness World Records Exhibition, Gatlinburg*
10. *A Salute to Elvis, Pigeon Forge*
11. *Elvis Presley Museum, Pigeon Forge*
12. *Buford Pusser Museum, Adamsville*
13. *Elvis Presley Birth Place Museum, Tupelo*
14. *Flying Circle G, Walls. Elvis's old ranch*
15. *Boomland, Charleston. Elvis cars and other stuff*
16. *Celebrity Room Restaurant, Richmond*
17. *Church of Elvis, Portland*
18. *Fantastic Museum, Redmond*
19. *Eddie Fadal's, Waco. Mini Museum*
20. *Elvis Presley Museum, Kissimee (nr Disney World)*
21. *Elvis Presley Museum, Ontario (off map)*
22. *Memphis Memories, Levittown*
23. *Murdo Pioneer Auto Museum, Murdo. Has Elvis cars and Harley Davidsons*
24. *Hollywood Wax Museum, Hollywood*
25. *Graceland Wedding Chapel, Las Vegas*
26. *Paradise Gardens Folk Art, Summerville*
27. *Sierra 76 Truck Stop, Sparks*
28. *Elvis, Elvis, Elvis, The All Elvis Shop, Kalakaua (off map)*

Elvis set a musical revolution in motion and then sustained it through an extraordinary succession of electrifying performances on record.

Fan clubs and museums

There are Elvis Presley fan clubs all over the world, and there are Elvis museums of one kind or another spread around the globe. But, despite his hectic touring and his Hollywood years, Elvis always remained a Memphian. His home at Graceland is the second best–known house in America, after the White House. While it has been nicely preserved, the area across the street is home to as many gift shops as you could want. But any visit to Memphis would be incomplete without a call at the Sun Studios on Union Avenue. It is here, rather than at Graceland, that you get closest to the spirit of the time and place and people that helped Elvis to change everything.

All Over America

A summary of Elvis's appearances throughout his life

In an era when records, fuelled by increasingly sophisticated studio techniques, and television, with the possibilities opened up by skillful editing, began to take over the entertainment world, Elvis remained at heart a live performer. Although his initial sound was created in the recording studio, it was taped on a single track machine, with the musicians effectively playing live into microphones. And though Elvis got his big break on the *Louisiana Hayride* radio show, that too was broadcast live with the performers playing in front of an audience. Elvis's break into television came before the days of taping, so that too was broadcast live in the fifties. And in the final years, when his records were no longer topping the charts, Elvis was out on the road, playing to an ever-loyal audience.

"I don't do anything bad when I work. I just move to the music on account of it's the way I feel it."
Elvis Presley, 1956

When Elvis first started recording in the mid–fifties there were no multi–track machines. Every take was recorded and played back to see which one worked best. Musicians essentially played their songs in the studio exactly as they played them on stage — except in Elvis's case he was playing them for the first time in the studio. The genius of men like Sam Phillips was to make the limitations of the equipment work for them. If handled right, the live feel of the studio could be communicated to the audience through the recording. And you could mess around with the sound a little to give it depth — to make it sound like there were twice as many musicians.

So Elvis learned to play 'live' in the studio. But he learned to perform live out on the road. It sounds crazy in retrospect, but it seems that no one had really thought about how Elvis would come over on stage, or how he would appear to his audience. In those days singers got up and stood in front of a microphone, sang their songs, got their applause and then went home. Elvis changed all that. On his second performance he started jigging around while he was singing. The crowd liked it, so he did it some more — and kept on doing it.

But it wasn't just his movements on stage that changed the way that music was presented. Elvis made popular music into a possession of youth. In the fifties his audience became almost exclusively young people, and they regarded him as *their* property – something which had nothing to do with their parents. So, despite his polite charm off–stage, when he hit the boards Elvis became the dream of youth, and the nightmare of respectable America. He was young, beautiful,

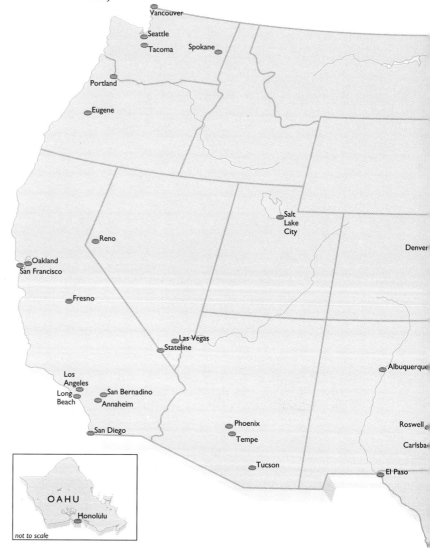

sexual, dangerous and he played at being sullen and surly. Every rock and roll band has tried to come over in the same way ever since. But the man who created the revolution in music was the one who did it best.

The fifties and the seventies.
Elvis's performances in the fifties were an instinctive response to his music, though there's no doubt that he worked hard at his stage act. He often set out to deliberately shock an audience even before he'd started singing, by spitting out gum onto the stage, or belching into the microphone. He was electrifying and he knew it. In the seventies at his best he was still capable of great concerts, but he wasn't turning the world upside down. He'd already done that.

1. Greenville
2. Hawkins
3. Tyler
4. Gladewater
5. Kilgore
6. West Memphis
7. Ripley
8. Muscle Shoals
9. Niagara Falls

Elvis Heaven

A musical heaven in Elvis's gospel songs

Gospel music has been largely ignored compared to jazz, blues and rock. This is not because the devil has the best tunes. Many of God's tunes are so good they've been filched for the devil, like 'How Jesus Died', secularized by Ray Charles into his classic 'Lonely Avenue'. That likeable song from Love Me Tender, 'We're Gonna Move', is a re-write of the spiritual 'You Gotta Move (To A Better Home)'. There has also been a tradition, dating back at least to the medicine-shows, of sacrilegious re-writes. In 1928 Memphis blues singer Jim Jackson recorded a version of the English hymn 'I Heard The Voice Of Jesus Say Come Unto Me And Rest' as 'I Heard The Voice Of A Pork Chop'. Clearly, gospel has been neglected because the devil has the best words — and perhaps because scholars of popular culture tend to be uncomfortable with, and bored by, the pious simplicity of the gospel message. This was never a difficulty for Elvis, who grew up in the simple faith of the First Assembly Church of God, and whose first musical experience was in the Church.

The Presleys' church was Pentecostal. Its faith is fundamentalist, accepting the literal truth of the Bible and disavowing alcohol, tobacco, theater and dancing, though its music was declamatory, and Gladys and Elvis Presley's love of gospel music flowed from their experience within the Tupelo congregation.

Yet the gospel music Elvis inherited was neither timeless nor uncontentious. Two controversies had stirred it in the 1930s–40s. The first was: should syncopation read *sincopation*? Wasn't singing church songs with a beat tantamount to dancing? Black gospel quartets had been recorded since 1902, but the first rhythmic spiritual wasn't made until 1936. This was 'Standing By The Bedside Of A Neighbour' by the Golden Gate Quartet, the most successful outfit of them all. The song was by the reformed blues-singer Georgia Tom, who with Tampa Red made the huge-selling pre-war blues hit 'It's Tight Like That'. He became the Rev. Thomas A. Dorsey, America's pre-eminent gospel composer and music-publisher of the 1940s–50s. But many deplored Dorsey's success in creating a new me-me-me kind of song, replacing the communally-centred spirituals of an earlier era. This went with the drive by preachers to take control of church worship instead of servicing their congregations' participatory democracy.

Dorsey's 'Take My Hand Precious Lord' typified the genre and proved massively popular. When Elvis recorded his first gospel collection, in 1956, it was no surprise that he should include two Dorsey songs, this and

Peace In The Valley
(right) Behind Elvis on this cover, a rural American landscape is used to represent heaven. This follows the example of the Quaker painter Edward Hicks (1780–1849). His famous painting, "The Peaceable Kingdom", is based on the same biblical passage as the Elvis EP's title-song, and uses Pennsylvania for the heavenly valley.

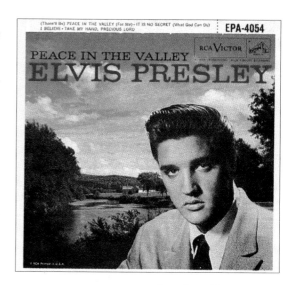

'Peace In The Valley'.

What great recordings they are: real soul-in-torment stuff. There is nothing artificially pious here. 'Peace In The Valley' had been a hit in the early 1950s by white artist Red Foley on Memphis black radio-station WDIA. Elvis brings out its gothic spookiness, in which "the night is as black as the sea". It re-states the biblical vision of the Peaceable Kingdom: "...the lion shall lay down with the lamb / And the beasts from the wild shall be led by a child / And I'll be changed, changed from this creature that I am." The way Elvis sings it is as sexy as hell.

The white groups who had influenced him most were the Statesmen (Jake Hess is Presley's vocal prototype in many ways) and the Blackwoods, his mother's favorites; yet he

How Great Thou Art
(far right) Recorded in May 1966 (apart from 'Crying In The Chapel' from the 1960 gospel session) the album was held for release until Palm Sunday of the following year. RCA promoted it hard, and it went on to sell over a million copies.

loved black gospel groups, including the Harmonizing Four, and must have preferred them. White gospel, rigid and straitlaced, follows notions of Nice Singing, with rhythms of schooled tidiness, like Pat Boone singing 'Tutti Frutti'.

When Elvis was in Germany, Jordanaire Gordon Stoker sent him gospel records, and when he returned in 1960, after *Elvis Is Back* and the first obligatory film soundtrack, *G.I. Blues*, Elvis made a gospel album.

His Hand In Mine is so old it has an inner

His Hand In Mine (below) Released in December 1960, Elvis's first gospel LP was recorded on October 30 and 31 in Nashville. 'Crying In The Chapel' was also recorded at that session, but not released until 1965, when it became a hit single. In February 1966 RCA bizarrely released 'Joshua Fit The Battle' and 'Milky White Way' as *further singles, though neither sold well.*

title summarizing the sort of God that Elvis must have envisaged)?: "The steps that lead to any church / Form a stairway to a star / They're part of God and should be trod / More often than they are." Yet Elvis transcends this risible religiosity, making it a memorable showpiece for his impeccable timing and phrasing, which is alert and humorous, knowing yet devout, sumptuous but strong.

To turn from this pellucid sound to the murk of the multi-tracked *How Great Thou Art* (1967) is to receive a nasty object–lesson in how hi-fi took a dive in the 1960s, as well as to admit that by the time of its creation Elvis was recording in a formulaic, weary way. The arrangements are florid and the music has largely lost a sense of connection to the gospel music Elvis grew up on — indeed the spirit of the enterprise seems no longer religious at all. 'He Touched Me' (1972) is worse.

Elvis was brought up believing in a simple kind of heaven, and must have felt, later, doomed to exclusion from it. His fall from the church's teaching to dissolute self-abuse must have been self-perpetuating pain. In his last years, it seems self-contempt ran so deep that even gospel music seemed to lose its appeal to him — but before that, gospel music, which he loved, gave him a corridor back to the better world of his childhood and his self-respect.

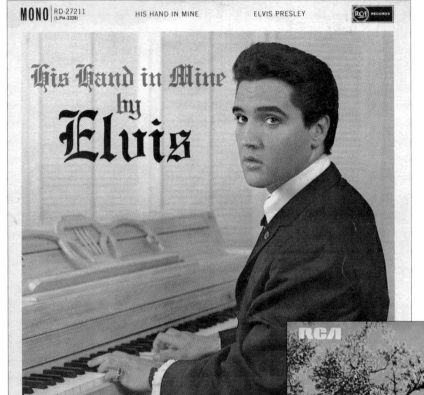

sleep explaining "What Is Stereophonic Sound". Recorded on the two-track Nashville Studio B, it seems to have been made in heaven. It has a liquid clarity, a shimmering mercury perfection, every voice and note clear yet blending into a whole so cohesive that you feel no intrusion by technology. Presley's voice is at its mature best (as opposed to its youthful best, which is of course at least as good but different). The voice on His Hand In Mine is mellow yet expressive, free yet exact. While the Jordanaires' harmonies are, as ever, "too white", the "blackness" of Elvis's vocals rescues and transforms this into one of his best records.

It is a great album. Is there a finer example of unintended bathos anywhere than in the intro to 'I Believe In The Man In The Sky' (a

Live Appearances

We have included only those professional appearances for which there is a written record, or other specific evidence, and for which there is a specific date.

1954		
July 17	Memphis	Bon Air Club
July 30	Memphis	Overton Park Shell
August 1	West Memphis	KWEM Radio
August 7	Memphis	Eagle's Nest
August 16	Memphis	Eagle's Nest
August 18	Memphis	Bellevue Park
August 27	Memphis	Eagle's Nest
August 29	Memphis	Kennedy Hospital, Getwell Road
September 9	Memphis	Lamar–Airways Shopping Center
September 18	Memphis	Eagle's Nest
September 24	Memphis	Eagle's Nest
September 25	Memphis	Eagle's Nest
October 1	Memphis	Eagle's Nest
October 2	Nashville	Grand Ole Opry, Ryman Auditorium
October 6	Memphis	Eagle's Nest
October 8	Atlanta GA	Silver Slipper
October 9	Memphis	Eagle's Nest
October 13		Eagle's Nest
October 16	Shreveport	Louisiana Hayride, Municipal Auditorium
October 20	Memphis	Eagle's Nest
October 23	Shreveport	Louisiana Hayride
October 29	Memphis	Eagle's Nest
October 30		Eagle's Nest
November 6	Shreveport	Louisiana Hayride
November 8	Memphis	Memphis State
November 13	Shreveport	Louisiana Hayride
November 17	Memphis	Eagle's Nest
November 19	Shreveport	Lake Cliff Club
November 20	Shreveport	Louisiana Hayride
November 21	Houston TX	Magnolia Gardens (mat), Cook's Hoedown Club (eve)
November 22	Gladewater TX	KSIJ Radio, Mint Club
November 23	Gladewater TX	Roundup Club
November 24	New Boston TX	
November 25	Houston TX	Paladium Club
November 26	Houston TX	Paladium Club
November 27	Shreveport	Louisiana Hayride
December 2	Helena AR	Catholic Club
December 3	Texarkana AR	Municipal Auditorium
December 4	Shreveport	Louisiana Hayride
December 10	Memphis	Eagle's Nest
December 11	Shreveport	Louisiana Hayride
December 18	Shreveport	Louisiana Hayride
December 22	Shreveport	Lake Cliff Club
December 25	Shreveport	Louisiana Hayride
December 28	Houston TX	Cook's Hoedown Club

1955		
January 1	Houston TX	Eagles Hall
January 4	Odessa TX	High School Auditorium
January 5	San Angelo TX	City Auditorium
January 6	Lubbock TX	Cotton Club
January 7	Midland TX	Midland High School
January 8	Shreveport	Louisiana Hayride
January 12	Clarksdale MS	City Auditorium
January 13	Helena AR	Catholic Club
January 14	Marianna AR	
January 15	Shreveport	Louisiana Hayride

January 17	Booneville MS	Northeast Mississippi Community College
January 18	Corinth MS	Acorn County Courthouse Assembly Hall
January 19	Sheffield AL	Community Centre
January 20	Leachville AR	
January 21	Sikeston MO	National Guard Armory
January 22	Shreveport	Louisiana Hayride
January 24	Hawkins TX	Recreation Hall, Humble Oil Camp
January 25	Tyler TX	Mayfair Building, Fairgrounds
January 26	Gilmer TX	Rural Electrification Administration Building
January 27	Longview TX	Reo Palm Isle Club
January 28	Gaston TX	High School Auditorium
January 29	Shreveport	Louisiana Hayride
February 4	New Orleans LA	Golden Cadillac Club
February 5	Shreveport	Louisiana Hayride
February 6	Memphis	North Hall of Ellis Auditorium
February 7	Ripley MISS	Ripley High Gymnasium
February 10	Alpine TX	High School Audtorium
February 11	Carlsbad NM	Sports Arena
February 12	Carlsbad NM	American Legion Hall
February 13	Lubbock TX	Fair Park Coliseum (mat), plus Cotton Club
February 14	Roswell NM	North Junior High School
February 15	Abilene TX	Fair Park Auditorium
February 16	Odessa TX	Senior High School Field House
February 17	San Angelo TX	City Auditorium
February 18	West Monroe, LA	High School
February 19	Shreveport	Louisiana Hayride
February 20	Little Rock AR	Robinson Auditorium
February 21	Camden AR	City Auditorium
February 22	Hope AR	City Hall
February 23	Pine Bluff AR	Watson Chapel High School
February 24	Bastrop LA	South Side Elementary School
February 25	Texarkana AR	City Auditorium
February 26	Cleveland OH	Circle Theatre
March 2	Newport AR	Armory plus Porky's Rooftop Club
March 4	DeKalb TX	High School
March 5	Shreveport	Louisiana Hayride, televised in Shreveport area
March 8	Helena AR	Catholic Club
March 9	Poplar Bluff MO	Armory
March 10	Clarksdale MS	City Auditorium
March 12	Shreveport	Louisiana Hayride
March 19	College Station TX	G Rolle White Coliseum 8pm
	Houston TX	Eagles Hall 8 to 11pm
March 20	Houston TX	Magnolia Gardens (mat) Cook's Hoedown Club (eve)
March 30	El Dorado ARK	High School Auditorium
March 31	Longview TX	Reo Palm Isle
April 1	Odessa TX	Ector County Auditorium
April 2	Houston TX	City Auditorium
April 7	Corinth MS	Court House Meeting Room
April 8	Gobler MO	B&B Club

April 9	Shreveport	Louisiana Hayride	June 25	Shreveport	Louisiana Hayride
April 10	Houston TX	Magnolia Gardens (mat)	June 26	Biloxi MS	Slavonian Lodge
		Cook's Hoedown Club			Auditorium
		(eve)	June 27, 28	Keesler MS	Air Force Base
April 13	Breckenridge TX	High School Auditorium	June 29, 30	Mobile AL	Radio Ranch Club.
April 14	Gainesville TX	Owl Park Baseball Field	July 1	Plaquemine LA	Casino Club
April 15	Stamford TX	High School (7pm)	July 2	Shreveport	Louisiana Hayride
		Roundup Hall (9pm)	July 3	Corpus Christi TX	Hoedown Club
April 16	Dallas TX	Sportarium	July 4	Stephenville TX	City Recreation Hall
April 20	Grenada MS	American Legion Hut			(10am)
April 22	Texarkana AR	Arkansas Municipal		DeLeon TX	Hodges Park, (afternoon)
		Stadium		Brownwood TX	Soldier's and Sailor's
April 23	Waco TX	Heart O' Texas Coliseum			Memorial Hall (8pm)
April 24	Houston TX	Magnolia Gardens (mat)	July 9	Shreveport	Louisiana Hayride
		Cook's Hoedown Club	July 20	Cape Girardeau MO	Cape Arena
		(eve)	July 21	Newport AR	Silver Moon Club
April 25	Wichita Falls TX	M–B Corral Club	July 23	Shreveport	Louisiana Hayride
	Seymour TX	High School Auditorium	July 25	Fort Myers FL	City Auditorium
April 26	Big Spring TX	City Auditorium	July 26, 27	Orlando FL	Municipal Auditorium
April 29	Lubbock TX	Cotton Club	July 28, 29	Jacksonville FL	Gator Stadium Baseball
April 30	Gladewater TX	High School Gymnasium			Park
May 1	New Orleans LA	Municipal Auditorium	July 30	Daytona Beach FL	Peabody Auditorium
May 2	Baton Rouge LA	High School Auditorium	July 31	Tampa FL	Ft Homer Hesterly Armory
May 4, 5	Mobile AL	Ladd Stadium	August 1	Tupelo MS	Fairgrounds
May 7	Daytona Beach FL	Peabody Auditorium	August 2	Muscle Shoals AL	Sheffield Community
May 8	Tampa FL	Ft Homer Hesterly			Center
		Auditorium	August 3	Little Rock AR	Robinson Auditorium
May 9	Fort Myers, FL	City Auditorium	August 4	Camden AR	Municipal Auditorium
May 10	Ocala FL	Southeastern Pavilion	August 5	Memphis	Overton Park Shell
May 11	Orlando FL	Municipal Auditorium	August 6	Shreveport	Louisiana Hayride
May 12, 13	Jacksonville FL	Gator Bowl Baseball Park	August 7	Houston TX	Magnolia Gardens (mat)
May 14	New Bern, NC	Shrine Auditorium			Cook's Hoedown (eve)
May 15	Norfolk VA	Norfolk City Auditorium	August 8	Tyler TX	Mayfair Building
May 16	Richmond VA	Mosque Theater	August 9	Henderson TX	Rodeo Arena
May 17	Asheville NC	City Auditorium	August 10	Gladewater TX	Bear Stadium
May 18	Roanoke VA	American Legion	August 11	Longview TX	Reo Palm Isle Club
		Auditorium	August 12	Kilgore TX	Driller Park
May 19	Raleigh NC	Memorial Auditorium	August 13	Shreveport	Louisiana Hayride
May 20	Kilgore TX	KOCA Radio. No venue	August 20	Shreveport	Louisiana Hayride
		given.	August 22	Wichita Falls TX	Spudder Park
May 21	Shreveport	Louisiana Hayride	August 23	Bryan TX	Saddle Club
May 22	Houston TX	Magnolia Gardens (mat)	August 24	Conroe TX	High School Football Field
		Cook's Hoedown Club,	August 25	Austin TX	Sportcenter
		(eve)	August 26	Gonzales TX	Baseball Park
May 25	Meridian MS	American Legion Hall	August 27	Shreveport	Louisiana Hayride
May 26	Meridian MS	Junior College Stadium	September 1	New Orleans LA	Pontchartrain Beach
May 28	Dallas TX	Sportarium	September 2	Texarkana AR	Arkansas Municipal
May 29	Fort Worth TX	North Side Coliseum			Stadium
		(4pm)	September 3	Dallas TX	Sportarium then Roundup
	Dallas TX	Sportarium (8pm)			Club
May 31	Midland TX	High School Auditorium	September 5	Forrest City AR	St Francis County Fair and
		(7:30pm)			Livestock Show
	Odessa TX	High School Field House	September 6	Bono AR	High School Gymnasium
		(8:30pm)	September 7	Sikeston AR	National Guard Armory
June 1	Guymon OK	High School Auditorium	September 8	Clarksdale MS	City Auditorium
June 3	Lubbock TX	Johnson-Connelley Pontiac	September 10	Shreveport	Louisiana Hayride
		Showroom (7pm)	September 11, 12	Norfolk VA	City Auditorium
		Fair Park Coliseum (8pm)	September 13	New Bern NC	Shrine Auditorium
June 4	Shreveport LA	Louisiana Hayride	September 14	Wilson NC	Fleming Stadium
June 5	Hope AR	Coliseum in Fair Park	September 15	Roanoke VA	American Legion
June 8	Sweetwater TX	Auditorium			Auditorium
June 10	Breckenridge TX	American Legion Hall	September 16	Asheville NC	City Auditorium
June 11	Shreveport	Louisiana Hayride	September 17	Thomasville NC	High School Auditorium
June 14	Bruce MS	High School Gymnasium	September 18, 19	Richmond VA	WRVA Theater
June 15	Belden MISS	High School Gymnasium	September 20	Danville VA	Fairgrounds
June 17	Stamford TX	Roundup Hall, High	September 21	Raleigh NC	Memorial Auditorium
		School	September 22	Kingsport TN	Civic Auditorium
June 18	Dallas TX	Sportarium	September 24	Shreveport	Louisiana Hayride
June 19	Houston TX	Magnolia Gardens (mat)	September 28	Gobler MO	B&B Club
		Cook's Hoedown Club	October 1	Shreveport	Louisiana Hayride
		(eve)	October 3	College Station TX	G Rolle White Coliseum,
June 20, 21	Beaumont TX	Unknown			A&M University
June 23	Lawton OK	McMahon Memorial	October 4	Paris TX	Boys Club Gymnasium
		Auditorium (8pm)	October 5	Greenville TX	City Auditorium
		Southern Club (11pm)	October 6	San Marcos TX	Southwest Texas State
June 24	Altus OK				University (matinee)

Date	City	Venue
	Austin TX	Skyline Club
October 8	Houston TX	City Auditorium
October 10	Brownwood TX	Soldiers and Sailors Memorial Hall
October 11	Abilene TX	Fair Park Auditorium
October 12	Midland TX	High School Auditorium
October 13	Amarillo TX	City Auditorium
October 14	Odessa TX	Unknown
October 15	Lubbock TX	Fair Park Auditorium later at Cotton Club
October 16	Oklahoma City OK	
October 17	El Dorado AR	Memorial Auditorium
October 19	Cleveland OH	Circle Theatre
October 20	Cleveland OH	Film locations (day) Circle Theatre (eve)
October 21-23	St Louis MO	Missouri Theatre
October 24	Newport AR	Silver Moon Club
October 26	Prichard AL	Greater Gulf States Fair, Blakely Island.
October 29	Shreveport	Louisiana Hayride
November 5	Shreveport	Louisiana Hayride
November 6	Biloxi MS	Community House
November 7, 8	Keesler MS	Airmen's Club, Keesler Air Force Base
November 12	Carthage TX	Carthage Milling Co. (aft)
	Shreveport	Louisiana Hayride (eve)
November 13	Memphis	Ellis Auditorium
November 14	Forrest City AR	High School Auditorium
November 15	Sheffield AL	Community Center
November 16	Camden AR	City Auditorium
November 17	Texarkana	Arkansas Municipal Auditorium, later Hut Club
November 18	Longview TX	Reo Palm Isle Club
November 19	Gladewater TX	High School
November 25	Port Arthur TX	Woodrow Wilson Junior High School
November 26	Shreveport	Louisiana Hayride
December 2	Atlanta GA	Sports Arena
December 3	Montgomery AL	State Coliseum
December 4-7	Indianapolis IN	Lyric Theater
December 8	Louisville KY	Rialto Theater
December 10	Shreveport	Louisiana Hayride
December 17	Shreveport	Louisiana Hayride
December 19	Memphis	Ellis Auditorium
December 31	Shreveport	Louisiana Hayride

1956

Date	City	Venue
January 1	St Louis MO	Kiel Auditorium
January 3	Booneville MS	Von Theatre
January 4	Jonesboro AR	Community Center
January 7	Shreveport	Louisiana Hayride
January 14	Shreveport	Louisiana Hayride
January 15	San Antonio TX	Municipal Auditorium
January 16	Galveston TX	
January 17	Beaumont TX	City Auditorium
January 18	Austin TX	Austin Coliseum
January 19	Wichita Falls TX	Memorial Auditorium
January 20	Fort Worth TX	North Side Coliseum
January 21	Shreveport LA	Louisiana Hayride
January 28	New York NY	TV Broadcast, Stage Show
February 4	New York NY	TV Broadcast, Stage Show
February 5	Richmond VA	Mosque Theater
February 6	Greensboro NC	National Theater
February 7	High Point NC	Center Theater
February 8	Raleigh NC	Amassador Theater
February 9	Spartanburg SC	Carolina Theater
February 10	Charlotte NC	Carolina Theater 4 shows
February 11	New York NY	TV Broadcast, Stage Show
February 12	Norfolk VA	Montecello Auditorium
February 13	Newport News VA	Paramount Theater
February 14	Wilson NC	Charles L Coon High School Auditorium
February 15	Burlington NC	Walt Williams High School
February 16	Winston-Salem NC	Carolina Theater
February 18	New York NY	TV broadcast, Stage Show
February 19	Tampa FL	Ft Homer Hesterly Armory
February 20	West Palm Beach FL	Palms Theater
February 21	Sarasota FL	Florida Theater
February 22	Waycross GA	City Auditorium
February 23, 24	Jacksonville FL	Gator Bowl
February 26	Pensacola FL	Municipal Auditorium
March 3	Shreveport LA	Louisiana Hayride
March 10	Shreveport LA	Louisiana Hayride
March 14, 15	Atlanta GA	Fox Theatre
March 17	New York NY	TV Broadcast, Stage Show
March 18	Charleston NC	County Hall
March 19	Columbia SC	Township Auditorium
March 20	Augusta GA	Bell Auditorium
March 21	Lexington NC	YMCA Gymnasium
March 22	Richmond VA	Mosque Theater
March 23	Washington DC	SS Mt Vernon Riverboat
March 24	New York NY	TV Broadcast, Stage Show
March 31	Shreveport	Louisiana Hayride
April 3	San Diego CA	TV Broadcast from USS Hancock
April 4, 5	San Diego CA	Arena
April 8	Denver CO	Coliseum
April 9	Wichita Falls TX	Municipal Auditorium
April 10	Lubbock TX	Fair Park Auditorium
April 11	El Paso TX	Coliseum
April 12	Albuquerque NM	Armory
April 13	Amarillo TX	Municipal Auditorium
April 15	San Antonio TX	Municipal Auditorium
April 16	Corpus Christi TX	Memorial Coliseum
April 17	Waco TX	Heart O' Texas Coliseum
April 18	Tulsa OK	Fairgrounds Pavilion
April 19	Oklahoma City OK	Municipal Auditorium
April 20	Fort Worth TX	North Side Convention Center
April 21	Houston TX	City Auditorium
April 23–May 6	Las Vegas NV	Frontier Hotel
May 13	St Paul MN	Auditorium (mat)
	Minneapolis MN	City Auditorium (eve)
May 14	La Crosse WI	Mary E Sawyer Auditorium
May 15	Memphis TN	Ellis Auditorium
May 16	Little Rock AR	Robinson Auditorium
May 17	Springfield MO	Shrine Mosque
May 18	Wichita KS	Wichita Forum
May 19	Lincoln NE	University of Nebraska Coliseum
May 20	Omaha NE	Civic Auditorium Arena
May 21	Topeka KS	Municipal Auditorium
May 22	Des Moines IA	Veterans' Memorial Auditorium
May 23	Sioux City IA	Municipal Auditorium
May 24	Kansas City MO	Municipal Auditorium Arena
May 25	Detroit MI	Fox Theater
May 26	Columbus OH	Veteran Memorial Auditorium
May 27	Dayton OH	University of Dayton Fieldhouse
June 3	Oakland CA	Auditorium Arena
June 5	Los Angeles CA	TV Broadcast Milton Berle Show
June 6	San Diego CA	San Diego Arena
June 7	Long Beach CA	Municipal Auditorium
June 8	Los Angeles CA	Shrine Auditorium
June 9	Phoenix AZ	State Fairground
June 10	Tucson AZ	Rodeo Grounds
June 22, 23, 24	Atlanta GA	Paramount Theater
June 25	Savannah GA	Sports Arena
June 26	Charlotte NC	Coliseum
June 27	Augusta GA	Bell Auditorium
June 28	Charleston SC	College Park Baseball Field
June 30	Richmond VA	Mosque Theater
July 1	New York NY	TV Broadcast Steve Allen Show
July 4	Memphis TN	Russwood Park

August 3, 4	Miami FL	Olympia
August 5	Tampa FL	Fort Homer Hesterly Armory
August 6	Lakeland FL	Polk Theater
August 7	St Petersburg FL	Florida Theater
August 8	Orlando FL	Municipal Auditorium
August 9	Daytona Beach FL	Peabody Auditorium
August 10, 11	Jacksonville FL	Florida State Theater
August 12	New Orleans LA	Municipal Auditorium
September 9	Los Angeles CA	TV, *Ed Sullivan Show* CBS TV City
September 26	Tupelo MISS	Mississippi-Arkansas Fairgrounds
October 11	Dallas TX	Cotton Bowl
October 12	Waco TX	Heart O'Texas Coliseum
October 13	Houston TX	Sam Houston Coliseum
October 14	San Antonio TX	Bexar County Coliseum
October 28	New York NY	TV, *Ed Sullivan Show*
November 22	Toledo OH	Sports Arena
November 23	Cleveland OH	
Novembr 24	Troy OH	Hobart Arena
November 25	Louisville KY	Jefferson County Armory
December 15	Shreveport LA	Hirsch Youth Center, Louisiana Fairgrounds

1957

January 6	New York	TV Broadcast, *Ed Sullivan Show*
March 28	Chicago IL	International Amphitheater
March 29	St Louis MO	Kiel Auditorium
March 30	Fort Wayne IN	Memorial Coliseum
March 31	Detroit MICH	Olympia Stadium
April 1	Buffalo NY	Memorial Auditorium
April 2	Toronto CAN	Maple Leaf Gardens
April 3	Ottawa CAN	Auditorium
April 5, 6	Philadelphia PA	Sports Arena
August 30	Spokane WA	Memorial Stadium
August 31	Vancouver CAN	Empire Stadium
September 1	Tacoma WA	Lincoln Bowl (mat)
	Seattle WA	Sick's Stadium (eve)
September 2	Portland OR	Multnomah Stadium
September 27	Tupelo MS	Fairground
October 26	San Francisco	Civic Auditorium
October 27	Oakland CA	Oakland Auditorium
October 28, 29	Los Angeles CA	Pan Pacific Auditorium
November 10	Honolulu HI	Honolulu Stadium
November 11	Schofield Barracks HI	Post Bowl

1961

February 25	Memphis	Ellis Auditorium
March 25	Honolulu HI	Bloch Arena

1969

July 31–Aug. 28	Las Vegas NV	International Hotel

1970

January 26–Feb. 23	Las Vegas NV	International Hotel
February 27–Mar. 1	Houston TX	Astrodome
August 10–Sept. 7	Las Vegas NV	International Hotel
September 9	Phoenix AZ	Veterans Memorial Coliseum
September 10	St Louis MO	Kiel Auditorium
September 11	Detroit MI	Olympia Arena
September 12	Miami FL	Miami Beach Convention Center
September 13	Tampa FL	Curtis Hixon Hall
September 14	Mobile AL	Municipal Auditorium
November 10	Oakland CA	Oakland Coliseum
November 11	Portland OR	Memorial Coliseum
November 12	Seattle WA	Coliseum
November 13	San Francisco CA	Cow Palace
November 14	Los Angeles CA	Forum, Inglewood
November 15	San Diego CA	International Sports Arena
November 16	Oklahoma City OK	State Fair Grounds
November 17	Denver CO	Denver Coliseum

1971

January 26–Feb. 23	Las Vegas NV	International Hotel
July 20–Aug. 2	Stateline NV	Sahara Tahoe Hotel
August 9–Sept. 6	Las Vegas NV	Hilton International Hotel
November 5	Minneapolis MN	Metropolitan Sports Center
November 6	Cleveland OH	Public Hall Auditorium
November 7	Louisville KY	Freedom Hall, Expo Center matinee
November 8	Philadelphia PA	Spectrum Hall
November 9	Baltimore MD	Civic Center
November 10	Boston MA	Boston Garden
November 11	Cincinnati OH	The Gardens
November 12	Houston TX	Hofheinz Pavilion
November 13	Dallas TX	Memorial Auditorium
November 14	Tuscaloosa AL	University of Alabama Field House
November 15	Kansas City	Municipal Auditorium
November 16	Salt Lake City	Salt Palace

1972

January 26–Feb. 23	Las Vegas NV	Hilton International Hotel
April 5	Buffalo NY	Memorial Auditorium
April 6	Detroit MI	Olympia Stadium
April 7	Dayton OH	University of Dayton Arena
April 8	Knoxville TN	University of Tennessee, Stokley Athletics Center
April 9	Hampton Rds VA	Coliseum
April 10	Richmond VA	Coliseum
April 11	Roanoke VA	Civic Center Coliseum
April 12	Indianapolis IN	Fair Ground's Coliseum
April 13	Charlotte NC	Coliseum
April 14	Greensboro NC	Coliseum
April 15	Macon GA	Coliseum
April 16	Jacksonville FL	Veteran's Memorial Coliseum
April 17	Little Rock AR	T H Barton Coliseum
April 18	San Antonio TX	Convention Center Arena
April 19	Albuquerque NM	Tingley Coliseum
June 9, 10, 11	New York NY	Madison Square Garden
June 12	Fort Wayne IN	Memorial Coliseum
June 13	Evansville IN	Robert's Memorial Stadium
June 14, 15	Milwaukee WI	Auditorium Arena
June 16, 17	Chicago IL	Chicago Stadium
June 18	Fort Worth TX	Tarrant County Convention Center Arena
June 19	Wichita KS	Henry Levitt Arena
June 20	Tulsa OK	Civic Assembly Center
August 4–Sept. 4	Las Vegas NV	Hilton Hotel
November 8	Lubbock TX	Municipal Coliseum
November 9	Tuscon AZ	Community Center Arena
November 10	El Paso TX	Coliseum
November 11	Oakland CA	Coliseum
November 12, 13	San Bernadino CA	Swing Auditorium
November 14, 15	Long Beach CA	Arena
November 17, 18	Honolulu HI	International Center

1973

January 14	Honolulu HI	International Center, TV special 'Aloha From Hawaii'
January 26–Feb. 23	Las Vegas NV	Hilton Hotel
April 22	Phoenix AZ	Veterans Memorial Coliseum (matinee)
April 23, 24	Anaheim CA	Convention Center
April 25	Fresno CA	Selland Arena
April 26	San Diego CA	International Sports Arena

April 27	Portland OR	Coliseum
April 28	Spokane WA	Coliseum
April 29	Seattle WA	Seattle Center Arena
April 30	Denver CO	Coliseum
May 4–16	Stateline NV	Sahara Tahoe Hotel
June 20	Mobile AL	Municipal Auditorium
June 21	Atlanta GA	Omni
June 22, 23, 24	Uniondale NY	Veterans Memorial Coliseum
June 25,26	Pittsburgh PA	Civic Arena
June 27	Cincinnati OH	Cincinnati Gardens
June 28	St Louis MO	Kiel Auditorium
June 29	Atlanta GA	Omni
June 30	Atlanta GA	Omni 2 shows
July 1	Nashville TN	Municipal Auditorium 2 shows
July 2	Oklahoma City OK	Myriad Center Arena
July 3	Atlanta GA	Omni
August 6–Sept. 3	Las Vegas NV	Hilton Hotel

1974

January 26–Feb. 9	Las Vegas NV	Hilton Hotel
March 1, 2	Tulsa OK	Oral Roberts University
March 3	Houston TX	Astrodome
March 4	Monroe LA	Civic Center
March 5	Auburn AL	University Memorial Coliseum
March 6	Montgomery AL	Garrett Coliseum
March 7, 8	Monroe LA	Civic Center
March 9	Charlotte NC	Coliseum
March 10	Roanoke VA	Civic Center
March 11	Hampton Roads VA	Coliseum
March 12	Richmond VA	Coliseum
March 13	Greensboro NC	Coliseum
March 14	Murfreesboro TN	Middle Tennessee State University
March 15	Knoxville TN	University of Tennessee Stokley Athletic Center
March 16, 17	Memphis TN	Mid-South Coliseum
March 18	Richmond VA	Coliseum
March 19	Murfreesboro TN	Middle Tennessee State University
March 20	Memphis TN	Mid-South Coliseum
May 10	San Bernadino CA	Swing Auditorium
May 11	Inglewood CA	Forum
May 12	Fresno CA	Selland Arena
May 13	San Bernadino CA	Swing Auditorium
May 16–27	Stateline NV	Sahara Tahoe Hotel
June 15, 16	Fort Worth TX	Tarrant County Convention Center
June 17, 18	Baton Rouge LA	University of Louisiana Assembly Center
June 19	Amarillo TX	Civic Center
June 20	Des Moines IA	Veterans Memorial Auditorium
June 21	Cleveland OH	Convention Center Public Hall
June 22	Providence RI	Civic Center Auditorium
June 23	Philadelphia PA	Spectrum
June 24	Niagara Falls NY	International Convention Center
June 25	Columbus OH	St John's Arena
June 26	Louisville KY	Freedom Hall
June 27	Bloomington IN	Indiana University Assembly Hall
June 28	Milwaukee WI	Milwaukee Arena
June 29	Kansas City MO	Municipal Auditorium
June 30, July 1	Omaha NE	Civic Auditorium Arena
July 2	Salt Lake City UT	Salt Palace
August 19–Sept. 2	Las Vegas NV	Hilton Hotel
September 27, 28	Baltimore MD	Fieldhouse, College Park
September 29	Detroit MI	Olympia Stadium matinee
Sept 30, Oct. 1	South Bend IN	Notre Dame Athletic and Convention Center
October 2, 3	St Paul MN	Civic Center

October 4	Detroit MI	Olympia Stadium
October 5	Indianapolis IN	Expo Center
October 6	Dayton OH	Dayton Arena
October 7	Kansas City MO	Levitt Arena
October 8	San Antonio TX	Convention Center
October 9	Abilene TX	Expo Center
October 11–14	Stateline NV	Sahara Tahoe Hotel

1975

March 18–April 1	Las Vegas NV	Hilton Hotel
April 24	Macon GA	Coliseum
April 25	Jacksonville FL	Veterans Memorial Coliseum
April 26	Tampa FL	Curtis-Hixon Stadium
April 27, 28	Lakeland FL	Civic Center
April 29	Murfreesboro TN	Middle Tennessee State University
April 30–May 2	Atlanta GA	Omni
May 3	Monroe LA	Civic Center
May 4	Lake Charles LA	Civic Center
May 5	Jackson MS	Miss State Fair Coliseum
May 6, 7	Murfreesboro TN	Middle Tennessee State University
May 30–June 1	Huntsville AL	Von Braun Civic Center
June 2	Mobile AL	Municipal Auditorium
June 3	Tuscaloosa AL	University of Alabama Memorial Hall
June 4, 5	Houston TX	Hofheinz Pavilion
June 6	Dallas TX	Convention Center Memorial Auditorium
June 7	Shreveport LA	Hirsch Coliseum
June 8, 9	Jackson MS	State Fair Coliseum
June 10	Memphis TN	Mid-South Coliseum
July 8	Oklahoma City OK	Myriad Convention Center
July 9	Terre Haute IN	Hulman Civic Center
July 10	Richfield OH	Cleveland Coliseum
July 11, 12	Charleston WV	Civic Center
July 13	Niagara Falls NY	International Convention Center
July 14, 15	Springfield MA	Civic Center Hockey Arena
July 16, 17	New Haven CT	Veterans Memorial Coliseum
July 18	Richfield OH	Cleveland Coliseum
July 19	Uniondale NY	Nassau Coliseum
July 20	Norfolk VA	
July 21	Greensboro NC	Coliseum
July 22, 23, 24	Ashville NC	Civic Center
August 18–20	Las Vegas NV	Hilton Hotel
December 2–15	Las Vegas NV	Hilton Hotel
December 31	Pontiac MI	

1976

March 17–19	Johnson City TN	Freedom Hall
March 20	Charlotte NC	Coliseum
March 21	Cincinnati OH	Riverfront Coliseum
March 22	St Louis MO	Kiel Auditorium
April 21	Kansas City MO	Kemper Arena
April 22	Omaha NE	City Auditorium Arena
April 23	Denver CO	McNichols Arena
April 24	San Diego CA	Sports Arena
April 25	Long Beach CA	Arena
April 26	Seattle WA	Coliseum
April 30–May 9	Stateline NV	Sahara Tahoe Hotel
May 27	Bloomington IN	University of Indiana Assembly Hall
May 28	Ames IA	James W Hilton Coliseum
May 29	Oklahoma City OK	Myriad Center Arena
May 30	Odessa TX	Ector County Coliseum
May 31	Lubbock TX	Municipal Coliseum
June 1	Tucson AZ	Community Center Arena
June 2	El Paso TX	Civic Center Grand Hall
June 3	Ft Worth TX	Tarrant County Convention Center

June 4, 5, 6	Atlanta GA	Omni
June 25	Buffalo NY	Memorial Auditorium
June 26	Providence RI	Civic Center
June 27	Largo MD	Capitol Center
June 28	Philadelphia PA	Spectrum
June 29	Richmond VA	Coliseum
June 30	Greensboro NC	Coliseum
July 1	Shreveport LA	Hirsch Coliseum
July 2	Baton Rouge LA	Louisiana State University Assembly Center
July 3	Ft Worth TX	Tarrant County Convention Center
July 4	Tulsa OK	Oral Roberts University Mabee Center
July 5	Memphis TN	Mid-South Coliseum
July 23	Louisville KY	Freedom Hall
July 24	Charleston WV	Civic Center
July 25	Syracuse NY	Onondaga War Memorial Auditorium
July 26	Rochester NY	Community War Memorial Auditorium
July 27	Syracuse NY	Onondaga War Memorial Auditorium
July 28	Hartford CT	Civic Center
July 29	Springfield MA	Civic Center
July 30	New Haven CT	Veterans Memorial Auditorium
July 31–August 1	Hampton Roads VA	Hampton Coliseum
August 2	Roanoke VA	Civic Center
August 3-5	Fayetteville NC	Cumberland County Memorial Auditorium
August 27	San Antonio TX	Convention Center
August 28	Houston TX	Hofheinz Pavilion
August 29	Mobile AL	Municipal Auditorium
August 30	Tuscaloosa AL	University of Alabama Memorial Coliseum
August 31	Macon GA	Coliseum
September 1	Jacksonville FL	Coliseum
September 2	Tampa FL	Curtis Hixon Hall
September 3	St Petersburg FL	Bay Front Center
September 4	Lakeland FL	Civic Center
September 5	Jackson MS	Mississippi State Fair Civic Center
September 6	Huntsville AL	Von Braun Civic Center
September 7, 8	Pine Bluff AR	Convention Center
October 14, 15	Chicago IL	Chicago Stadium
October 16	Duluth MN	Arena
October 17	Minneapolis MN	Metropolitan Sports Center
October 18	Sioux Falls SD	Arena
October 19	Madison WI	Dane County Coliseum
October 20	South Bend IN	Notre Dame University
October 21	Kalamazoo MI	Wings Stadium
October 22	Champaign IL	University of Illinois Assembly Hall
October 23	Richfield OH	Cleveland Coliseum
October 24	Evansville IN	Roberts Stadium
October 25	Ft Wayne IN	Memorial Coliseum
October 26	Dayton OH	University of Ohio
October 27	Carbondale IL	Southern Illinois University Centennial Coliseum
November 24	Reno NV	McArthur Court
November 25	Eugene OR	Memorial Coliseum
November 26	Portland OR	McArthur Court
November 27	Eugene OR	Cow Palace
November 28, 29	San Francisco CA	Convention Center
November 30	Anaheim CA	Hilton Hotel
December 2–12	Las Vegas NV	Texas State University Henry Levitt Arena
December 27	Wichita Falls TX	Memorial Auditorium
December 28	Dallas TX	Civic Center
December 29	Birmingham AL	Omni
December 30	Atlanta GA	Civic Center Arena
December 31	Pittsburgh PA	

1977

February 12	Hollywood FL	Sportarium
February 13	West Palm Beach FL	City Auditorium
February 14	St Petersburg FL	Bayfront Center
February 15	Orlando FL	Sports Stadium
February 16	Montgomery AL	Garrett Coliseum
February 17	Savannah GA	Civic Center
February 18	Columbia SC	Carolina Coliseum
February 19	Johnson City TN	Civic Center Freedom Hall
February 20, 21	Charlotte NC	Coliseum
March 23	Tempe AZ	Arizona State University
March 24	Amarillo TX	Civic Center
March 25, 26	Norman OK	Lloyd Noble Center, University of Ok
March 27	Abilene TX	Taylor County Coliseum
March 28	Austin TX	Municipal Auditorium
March 29, 30	Alexandria LA	Rapides Parish Coliseum
March 31	Baton Rouge LA	Cancelled in intermission
April 21	Greensboro NC	Coliseum
April 22	Detroit MI	Olympia Stadium
April 23	Toledo OH	University Centennial Hall
April 24	Ann Arbor MI	Crisler Arena
April 25	Saginaw MI	Civic Center
April 26	Kalamazoo MI	Wings Stadium
April 27	Milwaukee WI	Arena
April 28	Green Bay WI	Brown County Veterans Memorial Coliseum
April 29	Duluth MN	Arena
April 30	St Paul MN	Civic Center
May 1, 2	Chicago IL	Chicago Stadium
May 3	Saginaw MI	Civic Center
May 20	Knoxville TN	University of Tennessee Stokley Athletics Center
May 21	Louisville KY	Freedom Hall
May 22	Largo MD	Capitol Center
May 23	Providence RI	Civic Center
May 24	Augusta, ME	Civic Center
May 25	Rochester NY	Community War Memorial
May 26, 27	Binghampton NY	
May 28	Philadelphia PA	Spectrum
May 29	Baltimore MD	Civic Center
May 30	Jacksonville FL	Coliseum
May 31	Baton Rouge LA	
June 1	Macon GA	Coliseum
June 2	Mobile AL	Municipal Auditorium
June 17	Springfield MO	Southwestern Missouri State University
June 18	Kansas City MO	Kemper Arena
June 19	Omaha NE	Civic Auditorium
June 20	Lincoln NE	Pershing Municipal Auditorium
June 21	Rapid City SD	Rushmore Plaza Civic Center
June 22	Sioux Falls SD	Arena
June 23	Des Moines IA	Veterans Memorial Auditorium
June 24	Madison WI	Cane County Coliseum
June 25	Cincinnati OH	Riverfront Coliseum
June 26	Indianapolis IN	Market Square Arena

Bibliography

Books detailed here are not always first, or best, editions/printings: they are those that were available to us. nd. = date or other details unknown.

Bane, Michael: *White Boy Singin' The Blues*; London; Penguin Books, 1982

Bartel, Paula: *Reel Elvis! The Ultimate Trivia Guide To The King's Movies*; Dallas, Texas; Taylor Publishing, 1994

Bible, The: King James Version, London; Collins, nd. (placed by the Gideons)

Booth, Stanley: *Rythm Oil*; London; Cape, 1991

Broughton, Viv: *Black Gospel: An Illustrated History Of The Gospel Sound*; London; Blandford Press, 1985

Bryson, Bill: *The Lost Continent: Travels in Small Town America*; London; Abacus Books, 1990

Bryson, Bill: *Made In America*; London; Secker & Warburg, 1994

Burk, Heinrich: *Elvis In Der Wetterau: Der "King" In Deutschland 1958–1960*; Frankfurt; Eichborn Verlag, 1995

Cajiao, Trevor, ed.: *Elvis The Man And His Music (fanzine)*; Tyne & Wear; Now Dig This, 1990 onwards

Cantor, Louis: *Wheelin' On Beale*; New York; Pharos Books, 1992

Carr, Roy & Farren, Mick: *Elvis: The Illustrated Record*; New York; Harmony Books, 1982

Charles, T & Wardman, G, eds.: *Return To Sender: A Collection Of Poems For Elvis Presley*; Somerton; Headlock Press, 1994

Cotten, Lee: *All Shook Up: Elvis Day-By-Day, 1954–1977*; Ann Arbor, Michigan; Popular Culture Ink, Rock & Roll Referemce Series, 1993

Cotten Lee: *Did Elvis Sing In Your Home Town?*; Sacramento; High Sierra Books, 1995

Dawson, Jim & Propes, Steve: *What Was the First Rock'N'Roll Record?*; Winchester, Maryland; Faber & Faber, 1992

Dixon, Robert M.W. & Godrich, John: *Blues & Gospel Records 1902–1942*; Chigwell, Essex; Storyville, 3rd edition 1982

Escott, Colin & Hawkins, Martin: *Sun Records: The Discography*; Vollersrode, Germany; Bear Family Books, 1987

Garon, Paul & Beth: *Woman With Guitar: Memphis Minnie's Blues*; New York; Da Capo Press, 1992

Gillett, Charlie: *The Sound Of The City*: London; Sphere Books, 1971

Goldman, Albert: *Elvis*; New York; McGraw-Hill Book Co., 1981

Guralnick, Peter: *Last Train To Memphis: The Rise Of Elvis Presley*; New York; Little, Brown, 1994

Hardy, Phil & Laing, Dave, eds.: *The Encyclopaedia Of Rock, Volume One: The Age Of Rock'n'Roll*: London: Panther Books, 1976

Hayes, Cedric J. and Laughton, Robert: *Gospel Records 1943–1969: A Black*

Music Discography; 2 Vols (A–K, L–Z); London; Record Information Services, 1992

Hitchcock, H. Wiley and Sadie, Stanley, eds.: *The New Grove Dictionary Of American Music*; 4 Volumes; New York; Grove Dictionaries, 1986

Hopkins, Jerry: *Elvis*; New York; Simon and Schuster, 1971

Krivine, J.: *Juke Box Saturday Night*; London; New English Library, 1977

Leadbitter, Mike & Slaven, Neil: *Blues Records 1943 to 1970*; London; Record Information Services, 1987

Lomax, Alan: *The Penguin Book Of American Folk Songs*; Harmondsworth; Penguin 1964

Lomax, Alan: *The Land Where The Blues Began*; London; Methuen London, 1993

Marcus, Greil: *Mystery Train*; London; Omnibus Press, 1977

Naipaul, V.S.: *A Turn In The South*; New York; Alfred Knopf (and London; Viking), 1989

Oliver, Paul: *The Story of the Blues*; Harmondsworth; Penguin, 1969

Oliver, Paul ed.: *The Blackwell Guide To Blues Records*; Oxford & Cambridge Mass.; Basil Blackwood Ltd. & Basil Blackwood Inc., 1989

Palmer, Tony: *All You Need Is Love; The Story Of Popular Music*; London; Weidenfeld & Nicolson and Chappell & Co., 1976

Road Atlas: *United States, Canada, Mexico*; Chicago; Rand McNally (54th ed.), 1978

Rowe, Mike: *Chicago Breakdown*; London; Eddison Press, 1973

Santelli, Robert: *The Big Book Of Blues: A Biographical Encyclopedia*; London; Pavillion Books, 1994

Schröer A, Knorr M & Hentschel O: *Private Elvis: Elvis In Germany – The Missing Years*; London; Boxtree, 1993

de Silva, Anil & von Simson, Otto: *Man Through His Art Vol. 1: The Human Face*; East Ardsley, Yorkshire; Educational Productions Ltd., 1963

Svedberg, Lennart and Ersson, Roger: *Aren Med Elvis*; Soderhamn, Sweden; AB Sandins Tryck, 1992

Thompson, Hunter S.: *Fear And Loathing In Las Vegas: A Savage Journey To The Heart Of The American Dream*; London; Granada Publishing, 1972

Walker, John, ed.: *Halliwell's Film Guide*; London; Harper Collins, 1995 (11th edn.)

West, West, Hebler & Dunleavy: *Elvis: What Happened?*; New York; Ballantine Books, 1977

Worth, Fred L. and Tamerius, Steve D.: *Elvis: His Life From A to Z*; London; Corgi, 1989

Index

PLACES

Not all placenames on maps are
indexed, only those relevant to text
entries

Acknowledgements

The Authors would like to thank the following photographic agencies:

E.M.I. records (The Gramophone Company Ltd) Hates, Middlesex, England: **24** *(Hollywood box, Dean Martin)*

London Features: **63tl, 74, 75, 76tl, 76cl, 79br, 81tr, 81bl, 85, 88, 89, 92, 97, 107, 109, 115tl, 115tc, 115tr, 117tr, 117cr, 118, 119, 121cr, 121br, 123tr, 123bl, 135c, 137cl, 139, 141, 145, 155t, 155b, 157tl, 160, 163, 165tr, 175tl, 175tr**

William Neill: **113r**

Roger Osborne: **20cr, 30cl, 30cr, 31cl, 31tr, 32, 33r, 33bc, 34br, 34cr, 35, 36c, 36tr, 45t, 45b, 46, 47, 157br, 165cr, 172,**

RCA Records Limited: **176, 177**

Redferns: **143, 159; 173** (Ebert Roberts); **25** *(Nashville box, Hank Snow),* **56c** (GEMS); **25** *(Nashville box, Hank Williams),* **18bl, 18br, 31c, 44, 52, 55r, 57, 59l, 83, 86bl, 137tl** (Glenn A. Baker); **49t, 51, 61tc, 61br, 65tr, 91bl, 106** (Michael Ochs Archive);

Sylvia Pitcher: **19, 20br, 23l, 23r, 25** *(Mississippi and New Orleans box, Arthur 'Big Boy' Crudup),* **73; 25** *(Appalachians box, Bill Monroe)* (The Weston Collection);

Further Acknowledgements

Design and Layout:
Ralph Orme

Editorial:
Rhonda Carrier
Stephen Haddelsey
Roger Osborne

Production:
Andrea Fairbrass
Barry Haslam
Ralph Orme
Charlotte Taylor

Maps Completed and Produced by:
Andrea Fairbrass
Elsa Gibert
Ralph Orme
Kevin Panton
Peter Smith
Julian Baker

Indexing:
Jean Cox
Barry Haslam

Picture Research:
Roger Osborne
Charlotte Taylor

Typesetting:
Charlotte Taylor

Colour Seperations:
Central Systems, Nottingham